THE
FUNCTIONING
TRANSCENDENT

Other books by Ann Belford Ulanov

The Feminine in Jungian Psychology and in Christian Theology
Receiving Woman: Studies in the Psychology and Theology of the Feminine
Picturing God
The Wisdom of the Psyche
The Female Ancestors of Christ
The Wizard's Gate: Picturing Consciousness

with Barry Ulanov

Religion and the Unconscious
Primary Speech: A Psychology of Prayer
Cinderella and Her Sisters: The Envied and the Envying
The Witch and the Clown: Two Archetypes of Human Sexuality
The Healing Imagination: The Meeting of Psyche and Soul
Transforming Sexuality: The Archetypal World of Anima and Animus

THE FUNCTIONING TRANSCENDENT

A STUDY IN ANALYTICAL PSYCHOLOGY

ANN BELFORD ULANOV

CHIRON PUBLICATIONS • WILMETTE, ILLINOIS

Grateful acknowledgment is made for the following reprint permissions:

"Spiritual Aspects of Clinical Work," from *Jungian Analysis*, 2d ed., ed. Murray Stein. © 1995 by Open Court Publishing Company, Chicago, Illinois. Adapted with permission of the publisher.

"Fatness and the Female," from *Psychological Perspectives* 10.1 (1979). © 1979 by the C. G. Jung Institute of Los Angeles. Adapted by permission.

"The Perverse and the Transcendent," from *The Transcendent Function: Individual and Collective Aspects—Proceedings of the Twelfth International Congress for Analytical Psychology, Chicago, 1992*, ed. Mary Ann Mattoon. © 1993 by Daimon Verlag, Einsiedeln, Switzerland. Adapted by permission.

"Birth and Rebirth," from the *Journal of Analytical Psychology* 18.2 (1973). © 1973 by the *Journal of Analytical Psychology*, London, England. Adapted by permission.

"The Search for Paternal Roots," from *Fathering: Fact or Fable?* ed. Edward V. Stein. © 1977 by Abingdon Press, Nashville, Tennessee. Adapted by permission.

"Follow-Up Treatment in Cases of Patient/Therapist Sex," from the *Journal of the American Academy of Psychoanalysis* 7.1 (1979). © 1979 by Guilford Press, New York. Adapted by permission. Originally delivered on 11 December 1977 at the 21st Winter Meeting of the American Academy of Psychoanalysis, Clinical Studies.

"Transference/Countertransference," from *Jungian Analysis*, 1st ed., ed. Murray Stein. © 1982 by Open Court Publishing Company, LaSalle, Illinois. Adapted with permission of the publisher.

"Self Service," from *Cast the First Stone*, ed. Lena B. Ross and Manisha Roy. © 1995 by Chiron Publications, Wilmette, Illinois.

"Disguises of the Anima," from *Gender and Soul in Psychotherapy*, ed. Nathan Schwartz-Salant and Murray Stein. © 1992 by Chiron Publications, Wilmette, Illinois. Originally delivered in June 1990 at the Ghost Ranch Conference on "Anima and Animus in Clinical Practice."

"Vicissitudes of Living in the Self." Originally delivered in July 1993 to the Professional Enrichment Program in Jungian Theory and Practice, Center for Advanced Studies in Depth Psychology, at Shelter Island, New York.

Library of Congress Catalog Card Number: 95–49753

Printed in the United States of America.
Copyedited by Sharron Dorr.
Book design by Kirk Panikis.
Jacket design by D. J. Hyde.

Library of Congress Cataloging-in-Publication Data:

Ulanov, Ann Belford.
    The functioning transcendent : a study in analytical psychology / by Ann Belford Ulanov.
      p.   cm.
Includes bibliographical references and index.
Contents: Spiritual aspects of clinical work — Fatness and the female — The perverse and the Transcendent — Birth and rebirth — The search for paternal roots — Follow-up treatment in patient/therapist sex — Transference/countertransference — Self service — Disguises of the anima — Vicissitudes of living in the Self.
      ISBN 0-933029-99-3 (pbk.)
      I. Title
BF109.U57A25 1996
150.19'54—dc20
                                        95–49753
                                          CIP

For Barry

Contents

Introduction

The Transcendent functions in our lives all the time, whatever we choose to call it—God, or the unknown, or the holy, or the numinous, or the all-in-all. When we take notice of this reality, it responds by showing us how it functions in us, and this response in turn elicits our cooperation. This process quickly changes how we experience the Transcendent, moving from seeing it as something that simply happens to us, whether good or bad, to having an ongoing conversation with a presence that touches us intimately and reveals itself as altogether Other.

If we go on paying attention to the Transcendent, we develop a sense of symbolic life. Here-and-now things point to something beyond themselves. Then, if we keep our eye on Otherness, we begin to unfold in relation to it, discovering a sense of self at the same time that we see more and more of an objective Self in the midst of our subjectivity.[1] Recollecting what keeps unfolding, claiming what we recollect, shows us a spiritual life that passes through our days like a colored thread. Our ego enlarges as the Other becomes more visible. It adopts a provident attitude, looking out for all that is Other. This process of mutual growth and disclosure is the subject of the first chapter in part 1, "Spiritual Aspects of Clinical Work." The spirit is unmistakably, if subtly, present in analysis, as I attempt to show with examples.

Psyche always includes body. The second chapter in part 1, "Fatness and the Female," touches on the troubled area in which a woman must deal with her body and its growing poundage. Anxiety about growing weight discloses a spiritual issue. Who is in charge of this psyche, ego or Self? The struggle over relation to the Transcendent hides in the fight over avoirdupois.

This subject of the functioning Transcendent is not an airy esoteric matter tacked onto clinical work like so much embroidery. Not at all, for our psyche really wants to address its conflicts by presenting first one side of an argument and then the opposite. If we can stand the tension, we may come to see our conscious awareness enlarging to include two opposing viewpoints and then arriving at a third which resolves the conflict by including the essence of each side in its own perspective. This process is what Jung formulated as "the transcendent function," which he discovered in the midst of his own psychic suffering during the years from 1913 to 1919 (Jung

1916). Jung points to an extraordinary fact: our psyche does not just repeat fixed contents but also participates in a continued process of creating the *new*. It is the *new* that transcends the clashing opposites in us, releasing us from the torments of insoluble problems and functioning like the grace it is, streaming into us.

I want to carry this understanding of Jung's somewhat further, to where my own clinical and teaching experience insists it must go. The Transcendent, as I say in these chapters, is something beyond us that functions right here within each of us, intrapsychically. In religious terms, we can speak of the incarnating God, or the hidden Buddha nature, of that scintilla of the divine which we must gather and offer back as our act of redemption. In the midst of dogged clinical work, with mild or severe cases of psychic suffering, analysand and analyst can witness the Transcendent clearly at work and at home in the psyche. The last chapter in part 1, "The Perverse and the Transcendent," illustrates the transcendent function working in masochistic suffering and the Transcendent itself unfolding through this process.

The Transcendent functions in the nitty-gritty of analytical work because it is the stuff of human relationships. That is the focus of part 2. The first chapter, "Birth and Rebirth," concentrates on the effect of an analyst's pregnancy on three woman analysands; the second, "The Search for Paternal Roots," focuses on the effect of the anima function of the analyst on two men who had lost their fathers. In both sets of situations, maternal and paternal, the analyst carries the transcendent function at first, making a bridge to lost parents. Through the analysands' experiences in their own psychic process of linking up to a longed-for parent, Transcendence makes itself felt. What each analysand makes of that presence of the "more," or the "beyond," or the ultimate "purpose" differs as widely as the persons themselves do.

Vexing and important issues arise in the analytical relationship when sexual feeling explodes into transference and countertransference between analysand and analyst. The numinous can manifest itself through sexual energies, making each party in the analytical couple feel in danger of being swept away despite ethical strictures to the contrary. What is to be done if sexual energies literalize into actions? "Follow-Up Treatment in Cases of Patient/Therapist Sex" tries to answer that question. "Transference/Countertransference" addresses the same question in a broader way, focusing on how the archetypal dimension—the anima in particular—makes a bridge for a specific analysand's relation to

Transcendence. "Self Service" explores the real alternatives to acting out transference or countertransference and attempts to show
the positive possibilities of sexual passion in analysis, moving into
service to what the Self is engineering.

The two chapters in part 3 stand at the edge of the unknown,
reaching over into death and then climbing fully back into life. In
"Disguises of the Anima," this archetype of life pulls a man in two
opposite directions until he feels desperate enough to ask, What is
the point of such a struggle? The answer comes just at the edge of
death, where he gathers all of himself to respond to what he now
glimpses of the Transcendent. The second man in this chapter, the
son of the first and one who benefits from his father's psychological
legacy, faces a similar dilemma of splitting into opposing alternatives. His struggle leads him back into a life that now promises full
living instead of lifeless disguises.

Such struggles between life-and-death forces can reach suicidal
proportions. Their successful resolution, happily, will reveal that a
sense of the beyond is critically important for living in the here-
and-now. In "Vicissitudes of Living in the Self," a series of dreams
by a woman bring together her childhood sufferings and her suicidal temptations in an extraordinary order that unrolled a future for
her in terms of quite specific tasks and possibilities. The Self wants
to be lived in the present and in joyful ways; it is not content with
speculative forays into the beyond.

To sum up, what brings these chapters together is the discovery
that if we consciously engage the transcendent function in our psyches, we may experience Transcendence at the source, working in
us and through us. Written and delivered over many years, these
chapters give different examples of the way Transcendence touches
us and of how different analysands respond to this presence. I want
to emphasize that our experience of the Transcendent has a universal reach and breadth and thus shows infinite variety and complexity. I have tried to avoid reductions or determinist classifica-
tions of such sacred moments of communication back and forth.
Attention to these experiences in clinical work should be all but
routine, I believe, and these facts of our experiences, at whatever
end of the clinical exchange, should be placed in relation to a theory of the functioning Transcendent. That is the structuring purpose of this book.

I would like to express my deep thanks to those analysands who
generously gave permission for the use of material which instructs
us all.

Note

1. Self with a capital letter refers to the center of the whole psyche, conscious and unconscious. Ego is the center of our conscious mind. Our sense of self includes both.

Reference

Jung, C. G. 1916. The transcendent function. In *CW* 8: 67–91. New York: Pantheon, 1960.

The Transcendent in Intrapsychic Work

1

Spiritual Aspects of Clinical Work

Looking

When we ask prospective analysands why they seek Jungian analysis, most often they say something like: "Because you take the spiritual seriously," or, "You don't reduce religion to something else," or, "You respect dreams as really speaking about life and not just our conflicts." One young woman arriving from another country sought analysis immediately because, as she said in her first session, her Jungian therapist there had "helped me trust 'It' and now I know I have to go on with 'It.'" These comments recognize a spiritual aspect of clinical work and find it a necessity. Jungian analysis seems to promise serious consideration of this aspect and to avoid premature closure around it by avoiding defining it in denominational religious terms.

Jung recognizes the many meanings of "spirit" but focuses on it specifically as a psychic factor, which is what I will do here (Jung 1926, pars. 601–2). By this I mean that I will concentrate on what actually happens in the consulting room, in contrast to the focus of many fine investigations by Jungians into the theoretical relationship of spirit to religious concepts or to specific symbols (e.g., Allenby 1961; Seligman 1965; Dreifuss 1965; Sanford 1968; Kelsey 1968; von der Heydt 1970; Dreifuss 1971; Dreifuss 1972; Gammon 1973; Lambert 1973; Sanford 1974; Ulanov 1975; von der Heydt 1977; Gordon 1977; Kluger 1978; Coward 1978; Dourley 1981; Clift 1982; Ulanov and Ulanov 1982; Coward 1983; Hoy 1983; Moore 1983; Edinger 1983; Powell 1985; Stein 1985; Stein and Moore 1987; Gibson 1988a; Gibson 1988b; Grosbeck 1989; Downton 1989; Charet 1990; Mogenson 1990; Ross 1992).

Jung looks at spirit in the consulting room and looks hard. He sees spirit as a reality that transcends the whole psyche as well as the ego, as energy that can attach itself to any complex (so that we can speak, for example, of the spiritual aspect of the anima); he sees it as directly related to religion but not necessarily to be named in clinical work as belonging to a specific religious tradition. It is this last point that distinguishes clinical work from spiritual direction, for spiritual direction leads to a distinct end by means of disciplined development within the container of a specific faith tradition. Though we can see that all religions arrive at a place that might be described in similar terms, as the joy of connecting with the heart of what is—a joy so great that it is called a life of praise—Jung recognizes that the Buddhist route differs from the Christian one and that, as an analyst, he must never impose a route on a person but instead look through symptoms, dreams, and life events at what route the person's psyche indicates as its own.

Still, Jung takes with the utmost seriousness the connection of the spiritual with religion and, specifically and most centrally, with God, or with whatever the analysand experiences as ultimate reality (e.g., see Jung 1973, 338–39; Jung 1975, 64–65, 235–38, 383–84; see also Jung 1956, pars. 564–65). So, for example, when an analysand of mine engaged in Zen Buddhist practice reports a dream in which his "Buddhist bowls" sit in front of him, without utensils, the meaning may well have to do with his spiritual state. He feels two kinds of anxieties: one, that the neighbor's bowls are more beautiful than his and two, that someone may have stolen his tools. He sees clearly what his problem is. "I create diversions," he says, "instead of doing my 'practice' (sitting and meditating). I lose myself in envy or in feeling deprived. The Zen Master gives you the bowls as the containers, symbols of mind responding to the universal mind. The utensils are your sitting, breathing, and pushing to the edge and falling into 'not knowing,'" he said. When the man looked seriously at his spiritual state, the dream responded by showing him his self-hatred—he felt that of all the millions of people doing Zen, he alone could not achieve enlightenment. "Somewhere in the Zen texts," he said with humor, "it is written that everybody can obtain enlightenment except me." This dream poked him, he felt; it made him see the right approach to his practice: "Do it!"

For Jung, even though the Buddhist does not name God as God, such a dream speaks of the spiritual dimension and cannot be fully grasped without it. Jung speaks directly about God:

The strange force against or for my conscious tendencies is well known to me. So I say: "I know Him." But why should you call this something "God"? I would ask: "Why not?" It has always been called "God." An excellent and very suitable name indeed. (Jung 1975, 523; see also Jung 1926, pars. 625–27ff.)

Jung goes further. He builds into his picture of the psyche the religious instinct and our experience of the numinous; he sees archetypes as having a spiritual as well as an instinctual pole; he sees a transcendent function working in the psyche with which we can cooperate through engaging in active imagination. He finds the spirit personified in the symbols of specific archetypes, especially the Wise Old Man or Wise Old Woman, Mercurius, and the Holy Spirit. In theory and in practice, then, Jungian analysis deals openly, clearly, and welcomingly with spiritual aspects (Jung 1948a, pars. 396, 398, 401–2).

Other schools of depth psychology have dealt more and more with spiritual aspects of clinical work, especially in recent decades (Ulanov 1986a, 47–61), but they do so with varying degrees of openness and welcome. At best we might describe their approach as the phenomenological reduction that allows a religious "fact" something like its own reality (Dumery 1975). Hans W. Loewald, a Freudian, suggests that we might explain a religiously toned experience as the cooperation and balance of the two principles of mental functioning, the unconscious principle of unity and identification and the conscious principle of multiplicity and differentiation. He gives as an example our sense of eternity, the *nunc stans*, "the abiding now . . . that one experience which then stands for all experience . . ." (Loewald 1978, 65). W. R. D. Fairbairn writes of persons relating to persons as the heart of life's meaning and purpose, of object relations as the basic stuff of the psyche, not the instinctual drives (Fairbairn 1962, chap. 7; Sutherland 1989, chap. 5). Harry Guntrip, who followed Fairbairn, says at the end of his life that only the personal relation heals and matters. He says it so often and with such feeling that, for him, the person clearly has become the locus of numinous mystery (Guntrip 1973, chap. 5). Jacques Lacan, despite his idolization of language and his fear of the feminine as the source of alienation, nonetheless recognizes experience of the ultimate in his notion of *jouissance*, a joy so full and profound that it seems to partake of Being itself (Lacan 1978). W. R. Bion uses the sign "O" to denote ultimate reality and believes that, whether in an analytic session or in life, we must attend to it and seek to be it (Bion 1970). Donald Winnicott points to that "space between," the transitional space where we feel alive and real in shared existence with others, creating the self we find and finding the self we create. In that space symbols are born (as well as madness) that sustain and enliven culture. The paradox that characterizes these symbols applies as well to God:

> In terms of the transitional object it is that although the object was there to be found it was created by the baby . . . in theology the same thing appears in the interminable discussion around the question: is there a God? If God is a projection, even so is there a God who created me in such a way that I have the material in me for such a projection? (Winnicott 1968, 204–5)

M. Masud R. Khan, in his last book, writes of the ethic of care that he learned first from his father and then again from Winnicott, his analyst. In addition, for him, religions, and in particular monotheisms, emphasize a kind of "self-realisation" akin to the goal of "any psychotherapeutic venture," what he calls "awakening" to the deeper forces in our human nature (Khan 1988, 64, vii–viii). Christopher Bollas locates not just the meaning of therapy but the joy of life in the unfolding of our "true self" in space and time through experience of others in the world (Bollas 1991, 12). Heinz Kohut, in holding out the elusive "self" with its structure, cohesiveness, harmony, and health (but not its precise definition) as the cure and goal of analysis, probes our capacity of our being at all (Kohut 1984, 44–45, 70, 98–99). Marion Milner uses a religious vocabulary to describe the risks of relating in a deeply open and perceptive way to what is:

> To recognise the real spiritual identity of other people in everyday contact . . . might seem . . . fraught with dangers. . . . to allow them to be themselves, [they] must be linked up with one's capacity to allow oneself to be oneself. . . . [That includes knowing] the worst about oneself, not in order to wallow in self-punishment and despair, but because in fact something quite surprising happened, like the breaking down of a prison wall. The phrase "resurrection of the body" kept coming into my mind. . . . [Such insights are like those] moments of transfiguration . . . in which apparently the inner and outer become fused in the transfigured object. (Milner 1979, 43, 92–93)

Discovery

Many analysands, in the process of working on their problems, discover what Jung calls the religious instinct (Jung 1946, par. 13;

Jung 1956, par. 512; Jung 1953, pars. 12–13; see also Ulanov 1971, 12, 85–88, 290–91). This is never an abstract concept but an empirical process, and the analyst is not the one who "knows" and "tells," but the one who goes with the analysand to face what the unconscious presents (Jung 1926, par. 604). The discovery that so astonishes both persons is that the unconscious does present things specifically addressed to—we could even say custom-made for—this particular analysand. Whether through symptom, symbol, or dream, the analysand feels summoned—some force or power or someone is communicating. "Look!" it says.

One middle-aged woman who painfully realized that she scorned a helpless child-like dependence in herself, and even imagined herself "hurling it against the wall," discovered that this very dependence was the lost key to her fuller sexual response as a woman. She discovered this through the exercise of what Jung calls the transcendent function when she actively imagined herself facing the scorned little girl inside her. She felt terror—the little girl was so full of longing! Longing overcame her and evoked another image that had appeared in our work months before: an opening pink flower which represented her clitoris to her. Its appearance now led directly to her sexual center and passion. So the dependence she rejected, when faced and felt as longing, proved the key to her muted desire. The stone the builders rejected became the cornerstone. This was a numinous event to the woman and to the analyst, too. The precision and succinctness of the matching of unconscious response to conscious need here is moving, impressive as it often is in analysis. It gives us confidence in our capacity to relate to something beyond our conscious awareness of being, something that feels bigger and as if it knows more. And it feels as if this bigger something does know us intimately and wants to communicate with us.

This is what Jung means by religious instinct: we feel we have "the dignity of an entity endowed with, and conscious of, a relationship to Deity" (Jung 1953, par. 11). But the woman of the pink flower would not have discovered this connection if she had not taken her courage in her hands and faced the dreaded dependence. She engaged it. She looked at the girl-child within, so full of longing, and let herself experience the child's effect on her. The child's helplessness was real to her now; it was not a concept or symbol of dependence, but a real being who needed her. That is precisely Jung's definition of the unconscious with which we must come to terms, which is, he says, "the fundamental question, in practice, of all religions and philosophies. For the unconscious is not this thing or that; but the Unknown as it immediately affects us" (Jung 1958, 68).

We might object and say: But this woman did not mention God or anything spiritual, so how is this the religious instinct? This is just the ego contacting and being contacted by the unconscious which exceeds the ego's finite domain. True enough, but aren't we forgetting the feeling of actual clinical experience? For any of us to connect with what transcends our egos feels numinous. It may feel negative, as this woman's terror certainly did. Or it may feel positive, like some dreams that seem to come as blessings (see for examples Clift 1985; Ulanov 1986a, 76 ff., 164). We feel touched by the beyond, by something big, by a power that we had better pay close attention to and that we come to trust. This attitude is what Jung calls the core of the religious experience (Jung 1940, pars. 2, 6, 8–9, 71; Ulanov 1975).

Transcendent, then, means two things in the workings of Jung's idea of the transcendent function. It means specifically the spontaneous psychic process where our ego confronts and converses with a counter position in the unconscious, represented by a symbol, or better, a personification, such as the dependent child in the above example (Jung 1971, pars. 825–28; Jung 1963, pars. 257, 261; Jung 1966, pars. 184–89). This conversation leads to a third thing arising from the conflict of the two, something that both expresses and transcends the two opposing viewpoints. The arrival of this "third" always impresses us as marvelous, a gift, even though the strenuous work that went before readies us to receive it. In this way, the transcendent function also builds up our ego strength while it simultaneously negotiates the conflict between our egos and the unconscious (Moore 1975), for we must hold to our conscious position in the imaginative dialogue with the opposing position in the unconscious. Thus, we clarify our position to ourselves as we learn to look beyond it.

The second meaning of transcendent implied in Jung's concept of the transcendent function is the Transcendent itself—that which exists beyond our whole psyche, conscious and unconscious, and is not just our egos (Ulanov 1992b)—for the symbol or insight or new attitude that arrives through the workings of the transcendent function exerts a numinous effect upon us. Through it, we feel that we glimpse something of the heart of being, or of life itself. In this area lies Jung's work on the God-image and its relation to God.

Another clinical example helps here. In this case, a woman not

only succeeded in reconnecting with split-off bits of her unconscious, but also reached something holy that named itself as such.
She entered analysis, in her early twenties, because of a feeling of
inner necessity that felt like a search and a threat of insanity. The
hard work she put in for years can be summed up in the following
progression. A dead space existed in her because of an early and
deep wound—a feeling that her mother did not love her. "She loved
me in a collective way," this woman would say, "as one of her children, but she did not love me; when we could have a quiet lunch together, she would always suggest we have a reading lunch, which
meant that mother could read her mystery." The dead space in this
young woman felt like a yawning abyss, a void that would swallow
her up or into which she would fall forever and disintegrate. It was
this feeling that threatened her with madness. With much stress,
she learned to turn and face that abyss and engage it in active
imagination. Slowly it changed to limitless pain, to sorrow so great
that the image expressing it when it came seemed the only fitting
one: the *Mater Dolorosa* weeping tears of blood (see also Ulanov
1979, 25). This was the Transcendent reaching to her by indicating
that through her personal pain she was touching everyone's pain,
the pain of the world.

When this image appeared, she remembered her very first dream
of analysis so many years before:

> *She circles a pool and thinks of escaping the scene through a back
> door, but decides against it. When she returns to the pool area, she is
> drawn to her knees before a red, gold, and blue statue of the Virgin.*

This dream had greatly moved her. The later appearance of the
Mater Dolorosa image seemed another version of her worship in the
early dream, as if she, or some part of her, had been in conversation
with this archetypal figure all along. But the present work went
further. She knew the tears of blood and the womanly presence that
wept them was a larger-than-life image, not a role model for her ordinary ego. Falling into identification with this archetype would
have resulted in a perilous inflation, something that Jung constantly warns against, especially when one is in contact with spiritual contents. Accordingly, she continued crossing back and forth
from her conscious position to that of the *Mater Dolorosa* archetype
—the work of the transcendent function persisted. Gradually, the
archetypal presence fed and enlarged her personal ego, which kept
within its own bounds and simultaneously deepened. The limitless
tears of blood expressing the pain of this dead space in her turned

into limitless human tears and finally found their limits. They stopped. The dead space now filled with personal human feeling. She felt in immediate contact with the Suffering Mother, the Theotokos Virgin of her earlier dream, but she felt her own small human identity too which had digested and integrated her portion of the world's sorrows. A dream summed it up:

> *I dream I have found the place of truth, far away from civilization, in the mountains. This is what matters. Everyone sees the mountain from their own perspective.*

To have such an experience acquaints us with a presence in the unconscious, what Jung calls the Self (Jung 1971, pars. 789–91). This archetypal presence is not God or Spirit, but it acts within us as if it knew about God and knew about how the Spirit moves in us. It centers us in a realm between ego and the unconscious, including them both. It connects us to others—all others, not just those in our own time and vicinity—and to our deepest, ownmost identity as well. It impresses us. We are moved to put ourselves under its authority. Or, we may be moved to fight against its presence tooth and nail. One woman, who consulted a great number of analysts, one after the other, found herself compelled at each first session to attack the analyst viciously, demanding to know what the analyst could do to help her, then violently chewing up and spitting back whatever the analyst offered. I could only speculate that the cumulative trauma she had sustained over the years was such that her entrance to the precincts of the Self must be through her rage at persons and events that seemed to have conspired to rupture any relationship she had to a caring source. Whether experienced positively or negatively, contact with the Self is momentous.

What such contact engenders in us is what Jung calls a sense of vocation (Jung 1934). We feel called out to become our very own self, whatever that is. This call addresses each one of us. There we are equal. What we do with the call, how we develop, varies according to our constitutional endowment, the extent to which our environment (including persons) helps our unfolding, and what blows of fate or moments of grace come our way. This sense of vocation, I believe, is what Winnicott is getting at with his idea of the true self and what Bollas means by discovering our own unique idiom (Winnicott 1960; Bollas 1991, 9–10, 71–75, 109–13). Discovering our vocation feels to us as if fate had been transformed into destiny (Bollas 1991, 44). We can take on the events of our lives, even those outside our control, because now we can discern a thread

of continuity running through all our years that underlines a precious sense of being given our ownmost self, to make a whole of it.

This sense of vocation feels paradoxical. It summons the uniqueness of our personality into being, but that uniqueness is not our
property to dispose of as we choose. Rather, our freedom lies in our
ability to respond to this call to come into being or to refuse to do
so. We feel then the independent power of spirit behind this vocation. Spirit exists in its own right; it is not under our control (Jung
1926, pars. 643, 645; Jung 1948a, par. 392).

If we identify our ego with spirit, we reduce spirit to a much more
limited concept. Then our ego seems, because weakened, to become
paranoid; the power of spirit, excluded by our diminished understanding of it, appears to threaten us from the outside (Abenheimer
1956). And the left-out spiritual aspects keep turning up behind
and through other complexes or contents to increase their urgency
and power over us. For example, a woman in group therapy told
this dream:

> She sees a white horse under her door. It is a dutch door that can be
> opened either at the bottom or the top half. She opens the bottom half
> and sees a horse's legs stamping there. "The horse pulled at me," she
> said. "It needed me to ride it."

When the woman told this dream, she simply reported it; she
could not really experience it. Yet she said the figure of the horse
was so strong that she "obsessed about it all morning." Other group
members felt the horse's power, too. When one woman said the
dream seemed like a real fairy tale carried right into life, the
dreamer said she felt she was about to swoon, as she often did if a
remark really hit home. It was as if the dreamer's conception of
what she could handle, and of the spirit available to her, was just
too small. She could only open to the conscious half of things, and
then only through thinking about them. So the left-out spirit had to
reach her by burgeoning through her thinking, making it obsessive.

In her dream, she finds a more direct route to the left-out spirit,
through opening the bottom half of the door to find that the spirit
has taken up residence in the image of the horse that bids her to
ride it. Another woman in the group confirmed the dreamer's sense
that this fairy-tale image was right on the mark by describing how
crazy she had felt before being able to continue a writing project. At
that time, she had felt pulled into a mythical world and could begin
to write only when she had harnessed the energy of its magnetism.
A man added that all this talk about the horse made him feel a rush

of energy that gave him confidence to stand up against his sadistic judging father who kept attacking him from inside himself, a cruelty that he frequently projected onto the group as a whole. Still another woman said she suddenly felt full of a joyous feeling. It was as if some fund of energy was present, and they could all partake of it, according to each of their needs. In the group, both halves of the dutch door opened. Not only the dreamer, but all the others could experience the possibility of riding the horse-energy where the spirit had alighted for the moment. This example shows clearly how looking for, finding, and receiving spiritual aspects in clinical work happen in groups as well as to individuals (Zinkin 1989)—but only if we have eyes to see and ears to hear.

If our concept of spirit is too small, we will fail to see the spirit as itself. Instead, its unnoticed energy will inflame our use of familiar analytical concepts or play havoc with transference-countertransference reactions and responses. We can mistakenly deify our notions of the intersubjective field or the soul and make gods and goddesses out of unconscious complexes. It is vitally important to clinical work, we can see, that we explicitly acknowledge its objectively spiritual dimension.

Re-collection

Paying attention to the spiritual aspects of our clinical work is not simply a spiritual exercise; it is a fundamental way of extending and deepening our analytical skills. In confronting the shadow and anima-animus aspects of the personality, for example, we see now how important it is at the same time to re-collect or gather into consciousness what belongs to the ego. At this late date in our century, we have learned, finally, that it is not enough to see and withdraw projections to bring about resolution of conflict, whether between parts of our psyche, persons, groups, or nations. Evil still exists and often enough must be faced head on in combat. We need to know, then, who and what we are, what we have, and what we believe in, to do the best we can against destructive forces. Re-collection—that central resource of psyche and soul—must go on simultaneously with shadow confrontation and integration. We gather into consciousness the good that belongs to us, has come to us, and stirs our gratitude—and thus we strengthen its holding of us. Otherwise, we fall into the shadow and allow it to overwhelm us. While we are facing what is evil in us and toward us—shadow contents and impulses—we must also be gathering into awareness all we have been given to be. We do this re-collecting, this gathering of resources, from a point of view of looking toward the good. Kohut says, for example, an analyst should not mirror a person's pathology but rather should mirror the growing self structure that deals with the illness (Kohut 1971, 29–30).

The process of re-collection means looking for and discovering the point of view of the Self. Re-collection is a process of selecting. If the ego needs to be made stronger to house the Self, then we work on the ego; if we find that we are denying the shadow, then we work to loosen those defenses; if the threshold to Self is opened by an anima or animus interaction of erotic intensity, then we face that fire, hoping to see through it the attraction of the Self. We can see, from this vantage point, how transference-countertransference dynamics reproduce a field of interaction that forecloses the path of individuation (Schwartz-Salant and Stein 1991). Then we work to repair the analysand-analyst relation so that the analysand can begin to focus on the interaction of his own ego and Self (Ulanov 1982; Stein 1982). Re-collecting what belongs to us, what we have lived and integrated, what good has come to us, and even what has persisted of our own unmistakable identity through trauma and madness, puts living in the Self as the goal, not the uncovering of complexes. Our complexes can be uncovered and we can deal with them, but that is not the goal. In fact, we cannot always be sure what the goal is; we must wait on the Self to show us; we must wait to be surprised.

For example, one woman, after her re-collecting work, was able to face and successfully use shadow parts of herself to combat her destructive inner fragmentation. If she had stopped after simply withdrawing her shadow projection, without the later levels of re-collection, she would have fallen once again into pieces, as was her affliction and her great defense. She had this dream:

> *There is a feral woman full of savage sexuality, with steel teeth, who is going to bite the rest of us women to death. She is a killing machine of indomitable savage energy. I steal her teeth and take off.*

The dreamer recognized this woman in herself. She represented her "dangerous energy," both sexual and aggressive, untamed and often put on to other people, which left the dreamer feeling defenseless before them. In this dream, she felt cheered that the energy appeared in a female, even if grim, form. In previous dreams, the energy had been pictured as a brown car out of control, or a psychotic man who had to be put to death. She was also cheered that in the dream she had stolen the lady's teeth and made her escape. How would she use this steel?

Months later, steel came up again, but in a very different context. She was saying in a session that trying to make order in her complicated business life frightened her, made her feel helpless, because there was so much she did not know. She also felt mad because she could not understand all the forms and systems of order she might be able to put to good use, if only she could "get" them. Suddenly she wept and said, "It is as if blind walls are looking at me, stainless steel walls, and my eyes are looking out; the walls see; there are eyes on them." Then the image reversed: "I was thinking I was blind, but the walls, which are high, are blind back to me. They do not see me or recognize me. They do not even acknowledge me." Then she remembered a dream of her early twenties (she was then in her forties):

> It was an antebellum dream. I am in junior high school and fighting in face-to-face killing. Hurt and maimed, I claw my way out of a pit, my fingers raw to the bone. I have to reach home, which is through a wooden door. There, on the other side, people dance a quadrille in hoop skirts and a woman's hoop skirt goes across my face. They do not even see me.

Wiping her tears, she then said, "Boy, that's missing mother love!" I said, "You were too little to keep yourself alive all by yourself." She said, "I feel safer now." As she was leaving, she said, "I bet I can order things and run this whole business."

The steel teeth had sprung from the steel walls, even though the teeth image had come first in our sessions, before the walls revealed themselves as we worked our way down to the early and deep deprivation the woman had suffered. The teeth expressed her rage at being unseen and unsheltered, as well as her aggressive biting into life to get the toe-hold which enabled her to become adult and create a thriving career for herself. The teeth represented her sexual passions, which at one point, she said, had run wild, quite out of control, making her feel in retrospect as if she had been wanton and had seriously endangered her feminine center. The teeth were in her mother who nearly bit her to death both in fantasy and in reality, when the mother suffered psychotic fits and beat her little daughter. The teeth had all these meanings, which the woman now saw, gathered, and re-collected into herself, knowing now in her grief that she also possessed strength of the caliber and toughness of steel. Thus her spontaneous burst of confidence that she could, after all, order her affairs and had in fact been doing so. She gathered again in re-collection the strength that had been there all along.

In subsequent sessions, she explored the way her loss of order protected her from recognizing that her mother did not really see her. In her scattering of duties, chores, phone messages, contracts, schedules, etc., she could hide her pain from herself. Only in re-collecting all the strong ways she had dealt with this wound, as well as the hurt, rage, and passion the wound aroused, could she gather its deeper meanings—spiritual strengths, we might say. Instead of seeing her early childhood deprivation only as dire fate—the luck of the draw, the cards that chance had dealt—she began to gather that difficult past into a sense of destiny, as part of her own special way. She began to see it as a major part of her contribution to the collective human response to the suffering of innocents. What is more, she needed those steel teeth in her business career, which constantly turned up cutthroat edges. She was better able to use the teeth now; she herself had stolen them back into consciousness from the feral woman in her dream who had just used them to kill the feminine. Now she saw behind their defensive function to the inner reality whence these symbolic representations arose. From this perspective of always looking toward that originating reality behind our symbols, we can dare to ask the question that should arise in even the most wounding and degrading circumstance: What is the Self engineering?

The re-collecting process balances the intimacy of the analytical relationship with a growing intimacy with the Self, and does so for both analysand and analyst. If an analysand can deal symbolically with an intransigent transference—say, of the anima or amimus kind, one of intense erotic or hateful feelings—and can muddle through to some degree of success, then he or she will be faced with a reality problem that inevitably opens in two apparently opposed directions. It is as if the intense passion pulls us to the issues of life and death (Ulanov 1982; Kalsched 1992; Ulanov 1992a, 1992b). If we can stand the heat and keep looking through the flames of desire, they will lead us to discover not only an actual difficulty that we must solve, but also a great influx of energy—the Self energy rising to be lived in us—that will necessitate a rearrangement of our sense of reality. That Self energy will be lived, one way or another. The urge to individuation is the strongest of all human urges and will manifest itself in a negative form if we refuse to attune to it consciously (Jung 1939, par. 490; Jung 1950, par. 551). Marie-Louise von Franz says it succinctly:

> [I]nstead of finding the philosopher's stone within oneself, one becomes petrified. . . . Instead of being dissolved in the bath of the unconscious for renewal, one is dissolved in the unconscious in the form of a dissociation. (von Franz 1977, 115)

The role of the re-collecting process in a transference-countertransference situation locates the anima as a bridge to the Self and makes it possible to deal with a pressure moving to rearrange one's life at the center. The spiritual aspects of these clinical events reside not just in their numinous quality, but also in the deep reorientation of personality that comes about when one undertakes things with a view toward the Self, not toward problem-solving or merely utilitarian ends. Von Franz puts it dramatically:

> Making contact with one's inner great personality means a double fate for both; it is like making friends with an inner figure, for from now on you die or go on together, your fate is absolutely intertwined. (von Franz 1977, 105)

Even failure may be useful here, as it uncovers in us something that feels like our devotion to a higher power:

> [We] concentrate entirely on keeping . . . loyalty to God, and accepting . . . [our] fate of even missing [the target], if God has planned this for [us]. (ibid., 112)

What happens to the analysand also deeply affects the analyst. A dramatic shift toward living in relation to the Self may occasion the same in the analyst, or at least raise its possibility, or confirm its value if the shift has already occurred, which is most often the case given the intense psychological work the analyst has done *en route* to becoming an analyst. At the very least, the change that occurs in the transference-countertransference relationship opens the analyst wide to the influx of his or her own life problems and the energies of the Self that he or she must house.

Here is a trenchant example. A man in his forties worked hard to free himself from a life-long orientation of revolving around a woman's orbit, instead of finding his own. This pattern brought him much success with women, but also much hatred for them. All this was mirrored in the transference. He could use his considerable charm and kindness to build easy, friendly, sexually satisfying connections with women in which he often gave them much support to augment their lives. But he could not give himself to a lasting commitment to the woman herself and felt rage and outrage when a woman responded to their good relationship by wanting to make it permanent. He thought she might eat him or bleed him white, in order to feed her needs and wishes. He would be trapped!

The built-in restraints of the analytical relationship against any living out of sexual or aggressive dynamics brought this man's ambivalence toward women quickly into bold relief, for here he had no life experience that soothed and softened its edges. He had only our sessions and our mutual trust not to trespass, either into action or by verbal evasion, but to sit with the intense feeling and see what would come through from the Self. This meant re-collecting into consciousness, gathering what we knew, so to speak, from the accumulated work of the analysis. It meant being alert to what lies behind ego needs and desires that instigates the ego's growth and keeps it going (von Franz 1980, 15).

In the following small fragment of a long analysis, the man experienced a dramatic sequence. In association to a short dream of a woman he had once loved lavishly, he spoke passionately about her ecstatic quality. "She has real glamour," he said, "which is spiritual, sexual, joyous! She makes me feel more alive, breathing the air of angels, hearing the highest note of heaven. It was the end to which all our work pointed (they had worked together professionally at one time). This was the pay-off; it was electrifying."

At the same time, he felt she was nervous, incomplete, and in some basic way not grounded. In any case, the affair ended for all sorts of reasons, and they remained good friends. In his mind, she retained her powerful symbolic valence, summed up by his exclamation when she appeared in his dream: "She is the goddess!"

A second dream about her came a month or so later. We had in the meantime been toiling away in the direction of locating the generative feminine within himself, instead of in its projected forms in other people outside himself, including the analyst. This dream stunned him—and me too. In it, the woman's real-life husband appears, the husband whom the dreamer hated as the epitome of all the shadow qualities he detested: ruthlessness, aggressiveness, arrogance, a bullying coarseness, a basely commercial approach to things, and a complete lacking of gentility. This bully negotiates for the transfer of his wife to the dreamer! The only sticking points are practical: can the dreamer arrange to provide for all the things she needs, which are many—involving schedules, transportation, helpers, maids, etc. What was going on here was no less than the breakup of the anima-shadow duo that had always left the man and his ego out in the cold, able to give to women, but never to receive, able to fuse his boundaries with another's in an ecstatic moment, but not to live his passion in an ongoing permanent relationship. The dream said that now he faced a different problem. He no longer had to find the woman and then defend himself against her. She was now to be his. His problem now was how to house this air of the angel, this ecstatic high heavenly note where sex and spirit were joyfully mingled. Could he make provision for her in his everyday ego life? In the dream, the ruthless energy of the shadow collaborates with the dream-ego to just that end, which suggests that some of the aggressive energy the dreamer despised he could now accept and use in this precious task. The shadow figure thus displayed some of its function as guide and guardian.

The appearance of the realistic problem of housing anima energy and living it in daily life is one result of this man's hard work, both in facing the unconscious figures and in re-collecting who he was and where he was going, with an eye always cocked to the Self. The other result, one that always faces any of us in such an encounter, is that the deep unconscious then opens even further. It was as if, in having received the anima content into his conscious life, the man was now faced with the archetypal realities that lie behind the anima, with those even more archaic contents of Self to which the anima provides the bridge (Ulanov and Ulanov 1994, chap. 1).

An ensuing dream confirmed this surmise by removing another obstacle. In this dream, the sovereign power of the man's judging father was dethroned. The dream featured his father as a bit demented, laughing with him about women as sexual beings. The dreamer was needed to care for his father, who at last was expressing his feeling (which before had only been jammed into emotional judgments of his son). Here was a man-to-man camaraderie, and a son tenderly looking out for his slightly deranged father.

What came next (now through the mail, because of our summer recess) was a courageous act. The man faced and wrote out his deepest sexual fantasies, which held in their imagery the key to his fierce attraction to women and the deep repugnance he felt for them. I say "faced," not because he did not know his fantasies, but because he had never risked sharing them with anyone. To reveal our imagery to another requires a great act of trust and intimacy. As was to be expected, anger at the analyst and self-revulsion followed. He transferred his non-acceptance of his chthonic drama to the analyst, whom he now experienced as a condemning, contemp-

tuous, rejecting woman. The raw power of the fantasy, unmodu-
lated by ego values, showed its source in the archaic unconscious.
As Esther Harding says, "This is the work of the *mana* aspect of the
archetypal figure. When one such figure is brought up and assimilated to consciousness, its mana retreats farther into the unconscious depths and . . . devolves upon the archetypal figure that
stands next behind it" (Harding 1977, 314).

Here is his next dream:

> *He is captured by four Muslim figures in a square, in a capital city the*
> *dreamer knew well. He protests that by this action they are denying*
> *the love of Allah for all men and sinning against the Koran. One of the*
> *Muslims, greatly distressed at the dreamer's words, is comforted by*
> *the other three. This man takes the sin of their action on himself so*
> *that the others will be spared of blame. The dreamer knows an ordeal*
> *lies before him as well; he thinks of Jesus and his nearness to those*
> *who are despised and puts his hand in the Christ's: "My heart is full*
> *of joy, even as I am frightened."*

Behind the anima fascination of this dreamer, then, lies his meeting with the Self, this time expressed in the frank religious terms
of a God-image. This image of what he cares enough about to ask
its support in time of fear, and even to die for it, is what stands behind his fascination with the anima and accounts for some of its extraordinary power.

The God-image, for Jung, is a major manifestation of the Self and
one of its most important symbols. Whether or not correspondence
exists between our God-image and the transcendent deity, Jung de-
clines to answer clearly. Most often, he says, he just does not know
(Jung 1952a, par. 757; Jung 1956, pars. 565–66; Jung 1975, 384;
Jaffé 1989, 59–66, 80; Ulanov and Ulanov 1991, 27, 30–33). He de-
nies that a complete identity exists between the two, thus leaving a
lot of room for persons' differing God-images. He asserts that
through our God-image we catch the only glimpses we can achieve
of the Holy itself (Jung 1926, par. 625; Jung 1952b, par. 1508).

We can see how powerful the recognition of the spiritual aspects
of clinical work is in Jungian analysis and why Jung says half the
people who come to him have fallen ill because they have lost any
sense of meaning in their lives (Jung 1932, par. 497; Jung 1931). Direct connection exists between the spirit (lighting on one or another
of our complexes, as in the man's anima complex), the Self symbol
(here actualized in a God-image, as Jesus, and the shadow as
Allah), and the Transcendent that the Self knows about (Ulanov
1992a, 160).

Sometimes the Self is manifested through animal symbols, which underlines Jung's observation that archetypes possess an instinctive, body-based pole as well as a spiritual one (Jung 1954, pars. 414, 416–17). For example, one woman dreamt that she was dressed in black, about to take initiatory orders as symbolized by the headdress consisting of a little chair and of reindeer horns. The dream struck her hard; she felt something coming to her. Sure enough, her next dream brought up her central negative mother complex and images of the excruciating physical disorder she suffered in childhood that expressed her severe pain. To the chair, she associated sitting unaided by its back, as if in meditation, right on her "sit-bones." She also thought of the mysterious mercy seat inside the Ark of the Covenant in Judaism, a symbol that had long fascinated her as a place where Yahweh sat, or hovered. She discovered the chair was associated with the Egyptian goddess Isis, who is often depicted with the hierglyph of the throne on her head, designating that she is both Queen of Heaven and the Great Mother, earth. The reindeer horns led her to do research. She was amazed to discover that for many they symbolized a powerful feminine spirit, both delicate and sturdy, that roamed free, and also symbolized renewal and the tree of life (Cooper 1982, 50, 171). Another woman found numinous the image of a giant sloth that appeared in her dreams, a creature she had seen in reality on one of her journeys to a wild country. To her, it was a spiritual animal, fooling everyone by hanging upside down as if asleep. In fact, she mused, it was engaged in intense mystical experience, communing with the spirit world, and was probably the first shaman.

If the spiritual impulse falls to the body level where it does not belong, then it is cursed or bewitched and wreaks harm, as if poisoning the instincts (von Franz 1977, 121, 168; see also Moore 1983). If we sacrifice everything to the spirit and forget our body life, then "this passion turns spirit into a malignant growth" (Jung 1926, pars. 646–47). If the spiritual impulse drags us away from life, in the body and in the world, then almost invariably it proves a false spirit and can exert lethal effects. This particular danger threatens spiritually gifted people; their bodies may have to pay the price for an unbalanced enthusiasm for the enormous creative power of spirit. In some cases I have seen, only cancer offers relief. The person finds rest from a kind of spiritual excitement and performance, a space to enjoy simple happiness in being, while paradoxically being threatened by lethal disease. Jung stresses the ambiguity and ambivalence of the spiritual element. It may be good or bad (Jung 1948a, par. 455). Without it, if we live only from the ego, life is dull, for us and for others. As Jung puts it, "Only a life lived in a certain spirit is worth living," but the spirit also needs "completing and perfecting through life" (Jung 1926, par. 645; Jung 1948a, pars. 398, 454). What then makes the difference? What helps us live the spiritual aspects of our being without being overcome by them?

Becoming Provident

What makes the difference in our relation to spirit is the ego. Paradoxically, the ego is both dethroned and pivotal. The ego no longer acts as the center of our identity. It sees the Self in the center. But we need the ego to look for and discover the Self, and to recollect that it has been there all along. We could sum up the goal of Jungian analysis by saying it aims to facilitate conversation between ego and Self. The analyst acts as translator for these dynamics, but as the analysand comes to learn the idiom, the analyst becomes increasingly unnecessary. The living is what counts. As Jung puts it, "Everything essential happens in the Self and the ego functions as a receiver, a spectator, and transmitter" (Jung 1973, 325–26). Analysis, in the long range, then, gets the ego ready—tough enough and alert enough—to devote itself to the service of the Self (see, for example, Ulanov 1994).

One of the explicit examples of spirit in clinical work is its manifestation through archetypes of the spirit—personified figures such as the Wise Old Man or Woman, or Mercury (Jung 1948a, pars. 396, 398, 401–2; Jung 1948b, 230–35; Jung 1954). We need a lot of ego strength to encounter and survive symbols of such extraordinary power. A woman dreamt, for instance, of visiting her female analyst in a foreign country to play a game with her in which the dreamer spins a primitive feminine house into being. The analyst throughout is naked and comprises in herself all the opposites. She shows soft young shoulders and youthful breasts, yet she is in fact an old woman. She possesses both kinds of sexual organs, her usual female one and a penis almost like an elephant's trunk but not as long, and as if with a mouth on its end. The dreamer felt this image as fearsome and arresting. The figure of her analyst was transmogrified into a kind of human monster. The more deeply we go into the unconscious, the farther away from human representation we go, to where symbols can be so alien as to be repellent. Sometimes people dream of the Wise One archetype as a combination of animals—one man saw a beast both rooster-like and turtle-like with a wasp bottom. We can appreciate Jung's statement that we will do anything rather than look into ourselves! Such figures can make us feel unbalanced, as if in a territory altogether detached from the human. In the woman's dream mentioned above, the analyst is presented as being wise with the wisdom of the ages and yet young, naked of defense, totally open and revealed. To the dreamer, she seemed both her familiar trusted guide and yet archaic, strangely other. Both animal and human, female and male, she possessed the trunk of a wisdom animal, yet a penis with a mouth, so that it was both an organ of penetration and of reception, of spurting and of taking in. The dreamer needed all her grounded-ness in ordinary reality to engage and respond to this archetypal presence of spirit. It may have been that the dreamer, with a sense of play, was spinning a primitive feminine house in order to make a new container for this chthonic feminine energy. Similarly, at points of great crossings in our lives—from childhood into puberty, or at the crises of midlife, or at the crossroads into death—the archetype of Hermes may suddenly appear in one of his many tricky guises to act as psychopomp (Stein 1983, 5, 8–9, 13, 22; Kerényi 1976; Schwartz-Salant and Stein 1991; von Franz 1986, 70, 72). This sort of imagery makes the hair stand up. We must hold still. We need to feel the ground under our feet. Then we can go forward.

To get and to keep that ground is the primary ego work. It is all the work we do in analysis—uncovering repressions, recalling split-off parts, withdrawing projection, mending dissociation, working on transference-countertransference conflict, and in everything opening to the Self, which is always there, operating on us and in us. It is our ego work to look at what is there to be lived and at what Jung calls our religious instinct, that open-ended connection to something beyond us that really knows about us. It is our ego work to discover our threads of vocation and, in our sense of calling, to find our path, recognizing in our response to a prior summons our answer to the great antecedent questions: What can we make of our lives? How can we give them back to life itself? It is our ego work to re-collect all that was ever ours, the good as well as the bad, to claim and own and sense in our body that this is who we are and where we stand. All these exercises in analysis touch on spirit and convey spiritual aspects. In fact, they give us a new imagining of spirit's location: Spirit is downward. Because so much that moves us in analysis moves us to uncover what is buried, to haul up what has been acting like a leaden anchor impeding our growth forward, we are now driven to lift the top off what has been shut up. Spirit, for us in the late twentieth century, at the end of a millennium, is depth.

The goal of all this ego labor is reached through the accrual of an attitude accumulated through all these analytical experiences. The ego becomes provident. We become thrifty in a new alertness, discovering a new foresight about the where and when of the Self-reality. We care about it and prepare to encounter, greet, meet, and house the Self. We are on the lookout to provide for its welfare. We are now willing to take on those troublesome ego problems that confront us when we see through a hot transference issue to the originating reality behind it. One woman, after many years in analysis, put onto me the trauma of her original rupture from the Self and then revenged herself through repeated angry accusations. She left treatment and then returned to work through the block. This effort met with only partial success. We could not go further because the woman needed to carry more of the conflict of opposites within herself, rather than insisting that I, as the analyst, continue to bear half of it. That was the reality problem facing the woman just as a result of her insight. But she said no to it; she wanted to go on having the analyst carrying her half and give it back to her in each weekly session. This is a negative example of the point I am trying to make—that the reality problem facing us is a large one, requiring a major reorientation. Willingness is demanded of us. We now see the issue; we must know that we are now capable of acting. Whether we do so depends on our willingness to move directly and consciously into the Self. We can well ask, as this woman did, Why should I? For what purpose should I take on what feels like more suffering and the turmoil of a major overhaul in the way I go about my daily business? The answer is an odd one, but true in its bluntness: Do so for the sake of the Self—to take care of it, to look out and provide for its welfare.

Becoming provident is to make crucial judgments using all our resources, knowing our precise limits, and willingly receiving our interdependence with others. To do so, we need to have been looking, discovering, and re-collecting, because only then can we be alive to actual situations and not just to those we simply wish for or that someone tells us ought to be ours—no, we can handle the real ones now. We are alive to "is" and "are," to what feels like being open and open-ended, free. We feel able to be surprised by new things coming into being—new internal objects, images, feelings, attitudes, and ideas that were not in us before because they were crowded out by our defenses, repetitive wishes, and prescriptive oughts. What now comes may come from outside us—a new connection with an old person, a new person suddenly there drawing us toward relationship, or a startling synchronicity of events that lead to a new job or new money or new faith. We are alive to see the new and to see the old put in a new light. We can deal with either because we are looking from a different place—a Self place—which for some of us feels like a higher place, for others a deeper one.

In this new place the actual work in analysis changes drastically. We analyze less and behold more. We evoke, receive, greet what arrives, enable it, facilitate its existence more and worry about understanding it less (see also Bollas 1991, 19, 49, 202). By moving into experience from this Self center, we come to meet more suffering as well as more joy, because this center is so much bigger than our accustomed one in the ego. We are stretched to the limit to let it all be. We may be attacked by others, or buffeted by their lack of solicitude, as perhaps they see our wider view as eclipsing their own focus, or as our choosing a quiet, contemplative response instead of the action they are urging upon us. Such a contemplative look at things generates and originates action, but will seem passive to those who feel pressed to urge a certain agenda (see Milner 1960 and 1967).

Becoming provident means looking all the time to house the Self and receive its bulletins. Though the Self is not the spirit per se, it conveys a sense of the enlargement of the spirit, of the autonomous Other, of the bigger center that exists both within and beyond us. All archetypes convey this sense, but the Self does it most of all, because of its power to center the unconscious and the whole psyche. Our ego is toughened and loosened from its moorings to do this housing of the Self. Feeling certain and at ease in its capacity to receive, translate, and transmit the Self, the ego also sees that its own workings are manifestations of the Self, not ultimate in themselves. Even more loosening is the perception that the Self which feels like this big center is neither spirit nor God per se but that within us which knows about God or the spirit. It is this knowing unknowing that gives us the sense, I believe, of that center living in us which is not us, so near to St. Paul's description of it, "Not I, but Christ lives in me."

A man's dreams illustrate the awe evoked by such coming upon this Self center and the ego work that must follow upon it. Two dreams came the same night. Here is the first:

He finds himself in a high mountain range under a clear blue sky
with a bright shining sun. He looks at a huge crater deep in the earth.
The bottom is not visible, "but amazingly deep, with colored layers on
the sides. As the layers go deeper the colors grow more intense, with
blues and purples and finally a blinding white color where my eye can
see no more."

The dreamer is lying on his stomach looking over an entire
canyon. About this dream, he said:

I lay on my stomach because I was terribly afraid of the enormity and
grandeur of the scene, and overwhelmed to the point of being afraid
that somehow I would lose my balance and fall in. It was like coming
face to face with heaven, and therefore with the "Land of God," and
needing to fall immediately on one's face.

He had done a great deal of analytical work, stretching over
years. At the time of these dreams, he had been working for months
on rescuing his creativity into daily living so that he could feel alive
and real in his daily tasks and also make time for his writing.

The man's second dream followed on the same night; it features
him in conversation with an attractive woman to whom he was ex-
plaining how the word processor of his computer (with which he
types his dreams and does his creative writing) connected with the
film they were watching in order to write about it. The film turned
out to be about the previous canyon dream. Here we can hazard the
idea that the dream woman (a type the dreamer instantly recognizes as his own woman-part, his anima) needs the ego to translate
into language the vision of the Land of God; that is, to communicate
the sight of something so awesome in its spirituality. The anima is
somehow connected to the film—the stream of images—as the ego
is to the word processor by which the writing is to be accomplished.
Helping each other, anima and ego can bring into daily living the
news of where God or spirit dwells. This is the Self content the ego
must now house, with help from the anima. The dream also shows
the dreamer where his habitual tendency to arrange himself in a
helping role to any woman he engages romantically really belongs.
Positioning himself as helper does not enhance the attempt at a romantic relationship; it usually sabotages the attempt because the
woman invariably complains that he does not share enough of himself with her, and he quickly comes to resent the criticism, feeling
that he gives but never receives. Here his helping the woman part
of himself finds its true role, which is to help bring to the surface of

consciousness his particular vision of the Land of God, not just for himself but through writing and film for other people, too.

An odd phrase in one of Jung's letters describes the change that happens in analysis when the ego is bent on serving the Self:

> [Y]ou can not only analyse your unconscious but you also give your unconscious a chance to analyse yourself, and therewith you gradually create the unity of conscious and unconscious without which there is no individuation at all. (Jung 1973, 460)

The ego becomes tough enough to see through the two-way mirroring process. The ego becomes provident, which is to say, it goes on the lookout to mirror the Self—its promptings, its chastenings, its hints of direction to proceed or to shun, and above all, its being, its being right there, flowing without cease into the world. At the same time, the ego senses the Self mirroring *it*. We know that we are *known*. An Other exists in us, right at the center of us, making a center out of us. This Other seems to be looking at us, and does not so much discover as uncover us. It collects all the bits of us which we can then re-collect and knows about our connection to the Transcendent. Could the Self then act in us like a bridge to this God, just as the other archetypes act as bridges to the Self?

When our ego becomes provident, the Self becomes our great resource for preparing for the future. The transformation of our sense of fate into a sense of destiny, which always occurs when we discover our religious instinct and our vocation, now is transformed still another time: Our sense of destiny changes to a sense of Providence. Beneath and beyond our anxieties, compulsions, complexes, guilts, power schemes, and splittings, dwells another presence that seems to be looking out at us, looking into us, present and constant. Here the frankly religious person and the analysand are very close. Both want to take account of this presence. The religious person is apt to concentrate more on who this presence is, the analysand to concentrate more on how to house this presence (Ulanov 1986a). In any case, the sense of being known is stunning. It stops our words and our usual processes of knowing. It works on us; it may even analyze us, in the words of Jung's letter. It searches us out to show us to ourselves. In Christian tradition, this transformation is so momentous it must be likened to the resurrection and the receiving of our *name* from God (Revelations 2:17; see also Dupré 1984, 27, 67). This is the name known only to God and to the person receiving it. It symbolizes the true personality, our person at the core, the absolute identity that exists in God throughout time. And it is particu-

lar, not general; it is not our being human, or women, or men; it is
our being Robin, or Cathy, or Jan, or Missy, or Don, or Nathan, or
Peter, or George, or Joe. We come into this consciousness as a gift.
It is like the lapis in the philosopher's stone of alchemy (see von
Franz 1977, 157). It is secret and unutterable, held between the
spirit as it dwells in us and the Spirit as it dwells in God.

This knowing that we are known reveals to us that we have been
known all along. Another man's dream gave him some sense of this
astonishing ongoing process by reminding him of earlier dream images that circle round the same reality. After some dramatic action,
the dreamer sees what he calls

> *a wall of water and it is going over the edge of a railing. How did the
> water get there? I go look and see water going around and down into
> a hole that has no bottom. I feel it can draw me into it. I have seen
> God.*

Narrating the dream in his analytic session he remembers other,
similar images. One, from years ago, at a time of great upheaval in
his life, was of a "whirlwind coming straight at me which also felt
of God." Another was "a dream of a flaming tree, most beautiful and
of God." The recent image stands out in the dreamer's mind as quite
different, however. Here the whirling wave is contained. A railing
marks the water's descent and guards the dreamer from falling in.
This vision of the powerful spirit is contained not only within the
dream image but also within the dream. Hence, the dreamer is doubly protected and thus doubly afforded his view of the Holy without
"falling in."

This experience in analysis communicates a spiritual presence
that has been in conversation with us all along. The change that occurs is in our becoming conscious of this presence—one that seems
to have been conscious of us forever. We become alert to a continuing communication, one that is clear but not necessarily verbal.
Just as earlier we saw how analysis can reveal a thread of vocation
that marks a path to our life, now we see a line of continuing
speech, reaching us through image, gesture, body-feeling, coincid-
ing events. They mark out for us a path from the other side that is
breaking through to us with the shock of revelation. Jung knew
that analyzing the psyche, if we can withstand the impact, must
sooner or later bring us to this spiritual encounter. He writes:

> Only in this spiritual centre is there any possibility of salvation. The
> concept of the centre was called by the Chinese Tao, which the Je-
> suits in their day translated as Deus. This centre is everywhere, i.e.,

in everybody, and when the individual does not possess this centre he
infects all the others with this sickness. Then they lose the centre too.
*Deus est circulus cuius centrum est ubique circumferentia vero
nusquam!* (Jung 1973, 470–71)

References

Abenheimer, K. M. 1956. Notes on the spirit as conceived by dynamic psy-
chology. *Journal of Analytical Psychology* 1(2): 113–133.
Allenby, A. I. 1961. The church and the analyst. *Journal of Analytical Psy-
chology* 6(2): 137–157.
Bion, W. R. 1970. *Attention and Interpretation*. London: Tavistock.
Bollas, C. 1991. *The Forces of Destiny: Psychoanalysis and the Human
Idiom*. London: Free Association Books.
Charet, F. X. 1990. A dialogue between psychology and theology: the corre-
spondence of C. G. Jung and Victor White. *Journal of Analytical Psy-
chology* 35(4): 421–443.
Clift, W. 1982. *Jung and Christianity: The Challenge of Reconciliation*.
New York: Crossroads.
Clift, W. and J. 1985. *Symbols of Transformation in Dreams*. New York:
Crossroads.
Cooper, J. C. 1982. *An Illustrated Encyclopedia of Traditional Symbols*.
London: Thames and Hudson.
Coward, H. G. 1978. Jung's encounter with Yoga. *Journal of Analytical Psy-
chology* 23(4): 339–358.
———. 1983. Jung and karma. *Journal of Analytical Psychology* 28(4):
367–377.
———. 1985. Jung and kundalini. *Journal of Analytical Psychology* 30(4):
379–393.
De Gruchy, J. W. 1984. Jung and religion: a theological statement. *Jung in
Modern Perspective*. Ed. R. K. Papadopoulos and G. S. Saayman. Dorset:
Prism Press, 1984.
Doty, W. G. 1978. Hermes: guide of soul. *Journal of Analytical Psychology*
23(4): 358–365.
Dourley, J. P. 1981. *C. G. Jung and Paul Tillich*. Toronto: Inner City Books.
Downton, J. V. 1989. Individuation and shamanism. *Journal of Analytical
Psychology* 34(1): 73–89.
Dreifuss, G. 1965. A psychological study of circumcision in Judaism. *Jour-
nal of Analytical Psychology* 10(1): 23–33.
———. 1971. Isaac: the sacrificial lamb (a study of some Jewish legends).
Journal of Analytical Psychology 16(1): 69–79.
———. 1972. The figures of Satan and Abraham. *Journal of Analytical Psy-
chology* 17(2): 166–179.
Dumery, H. 1975. *Phenomenology and Religion*. Berkeley: University of
California Press.
Dupré, L. 1984. *The Common Life*. New York: Crossroads.

Edinger, E. F. 1983. The transformation of God. *Quadrant.* 16(2): 23–37.

———. 1986. *Individuation and the Old Testament.* Toronto: Inner City Books.

———. 1987. *The Christian Archetype: A Jungian Commentary on the Life of Christ.* Toronto: Inner City Books.

Fairbairn, W. R. D. 1962. *An Object-Relations Theory of the Personality.* New York: Basic Books.

Gammon, M. 1973. Window into eternity. *Journal of Analytical Psychology* 18(1): 11–25.

Gibson, T. L. 1988a. Secrets and soul: a Jungian fable about pastoral care. *Journal of Pastoral Care* 42(1): 3–14.

———. 1988b. Recovering masculine spirituality: a Jungian reflection. *Journal of Religion and Mental Health* 27(3): 195–205.

Gordon, R. 1977. The symbolic experience as bridge between the personal and the collective. *Journal of Analytical Psychology* 22(4): 331–343.

Grossbeck, C. 1989. C. G. Jung and the shaman's vision. *Journal of Analytical Psychology* 34(3): 255–277.

Guntrip, H. 1973. *Psychoanalytic Theory, Therapy, and the Self.* New York: Basic Books.

Harding, M. E. 1977. *Psychic Energy: Its Source and Its Transformation.* Princeton: Princeton University Press.

Hoy, D. J. 1983. The numinous: frequent or rare. *Journal of Analytical Psychology* 28(1): 17–33.

Jaffé, A. 1989. *Was C. G. Jung a Mystic?* Einsiedeln: Daimon Verlag.

Jung, C. G. 1926. Spirit and life. In *CW* 8: 319–338. New York: Pantheon, 1960.

———. 1931. The spiritual problem of modern man. In *CW* 10: 74–97. New York: Pantheon, 1964.

———. 1932. Psychotherapists or the clergy. In *CW* 11: 327–348. New York: Pantheon, 1958.

———. 1934. The development of the personality. In *CW* 17: 165–187. New York: Pantheon, 1954.

———. 1940. Psychology and religion. In *CW* 11: 3–107. New York: Pantheon, 1958.

———. 1939. Conscious, unconscious, and individuation. In *CW* 9i: 275–290. New York: Pantheon, 1959.

———. 1946. Analytical psychology and education. In *CW* 17: 63–133. New York: Pantheon, 1954.

———. 1948a. The phenomenology of spirit in fairy tales. In *CW* 9i: 207–255. New York: Pantheon, 1959.

———. 1948b. The spirit mercurius. In *CW* 13: 191–250. Princeton: Princeton University Press, 1967.

———. 1950. A study in the process of individuation. In *CW* 9i: 290–355. New York: Pantheon, 1959.

———. 1952a. Answer to Job. In *CW* 11: 355–475. New York: Pantheon, 1958.

———. 1952b. Religion and psychology: a reply to Martin Buber. In *CW* 18: 663–671. Princeton: Princeton University Press, 1976.

———. 1953. *Psychology and Alchemy. CW* 12. New York: Pantheon.

———. 1954. On the psychology of the trickster figure. In *CW* 9i: 255–275. New York: Pantheon, 1954.

———. 1956. The undiscovered self. In *CW* 10: 245–307. New York: Pantheon, 1964.

———. 1958. The transcendent function. In *CW* 8: 67–92. New York: Pantheon, 1960.

———. 1963. *Mysterium Coniunctionis. CW* 14. New York: Pantheon.

———. 1966. *Two Essays on Analytical Psychology. CW* 7. New York: Pantheon.

———. 1971. *Psychological Types. CW* 6. Princeton: Princeton University Press.

———. 1973. *Letters.* Vol. 1. Ed. G. Adler and A. Jaffé. Princeton: Princeton University Press.

———. 1975. *Letters.* Vol 2. Ed. G. Adler and A. Jaffé. Princeton: Princeton University Press.

Kalsched, D. E. 1992. The limits of desire and the desire for limits. *The Fires of Desire: Erotic Energies and the Spiritual Quest.* Ed. F. R. Halligan and J. J. Shea. New York: Crossroads.

Kelsey, M. T. 1968. *Dreams: The Dark Speech of the Spirit.* Garden City, N.Y.: Doubleday.

———. 1984. Jung as philosopher and theologian. *Jung in Modern Perspective.* Ed. R. K. Papadopoulos and G. S. Saayman. Dorset: Prism Press.

Kerényi, K. 1976. *Hermes: Guide of Souls.* Zurich: Spring Publications.

Khan, M. M. R. 1988. *When Spring Comes: Awakenings in Clinical Psychoanalysis.* London: Chatto and Windus.

Kluger, R. S. 1978. Old Testament roots of women's spiritual problem. *Journal of Analytical Psychology* 23(2): 135–149.

Kohut, H. 1971. *The Analysis of the Self.* New York: International Universities Press.

———. 1984. *How Does Analysis Cure?* Chicago: Chicago University Press.

Lacan, J. 1978. *The Four Fundamental Concepts of Psychoanalysis.* New York: International Universities Press.

Lambert, K. 1973. Agape as a therapeutic factor in analysis. *Journal of Analytical Psychology* 18(1): 25–47.

Loewald, H. W. 1978. *Psychoanalysis and the History of the Individual.* New Haven: Yale University Press.

Milner, M. 1960. The concentration of the body. *The Suppressed Madness of Sane Men.* New York: Tavistock, 1987.

———. 1967. The hidden order of art. *The Suppressed Madness of Sane Men.* New York: Tavistock, 1987.

———. 1979. *On Not Being Able To Paint.* New York: International Universities Press.

Moacanin, R. 1986. *Jung's Psychology and Tibetan Buddhism: Western and Eastern Paths to the Heart.* London: Wisdom Publications.

Mogenson, G. 1990. The resurrection of the dead: a Jungian approach to the mourning process. *Journal of Analytical Psychology* 35(3): 317–335.

Moore, N. 1975. The transcendent function and the evolving ego. *Journal of Analytical Psychology* 20(2): 164–183.

————. 1983. The archetypes of the way. *Journal of Analytical Psychology* 28(2): 119–141 and 28(3): 227–253.

Powell, S. 1985. A bridge to understanding: the transcendent function in the analyst. *Journal of Analytical Psychology* 30(1): 29–47.

Ross, C. F. J. 1992. The intuitive function and religious orientation. *Journal of Analytical Psychology* 37(1): 83–105.

Sanford, J. A. 1968. *Dreams: God's Forgotten Language*. Philadelphia: J. B. Lippincott.

————. 1974. *The Man Who Wrestled with God*. New York: Paulist Press.

Schwartz-Salant, N. and M. Stein, eds. 1991. *Liminality and Transitional Phenomena*. Wilmette, Ill.: Chiron Publications.

Seligman, P. 1965. Some notes on the collective significance of circumcision and allied practices. *Journal of Analytical Psychology* 10(1): 5–23.

Spiegelman, J. M. and M. Mikyuki, eds. 1985. *Buddhism and Jungian Psychology*. Phoenix: Falcon Press.

Stein, M., ed. 1982. *Jungian Analysis*. 1st ed. LaSalle, Ill.: Open Court.

————. 1983. *In Mid-Life*. Dallas: Spring Publications.

————. 1985. *Jung's Treatment of Christianity*. Wilmette, Ill.: Chiron Publications.

———— and R. L. Moore, eds. 1987. *Jung's Challenge to Contemporary Religion*. Wilmette, Ill.: Chiron Publications.

Sutherland, J. D. 1989. *Fairbairn's Journey Into The Interior*. London: Free Association Books.

Ulanov, A. B. 1971. *The Feminine in Christian Theology and in Jungian Psychology*. Evanston, Ill.: Northwestern University Press.

————. 1975. Jung and religion. *The International Encyclopedia of Neurology, Psychiatry, Psychoanalysis and Psychology*. Ed. B. J. Wolman.

————. 1979. Fatness and the female. *Psychological Perspectives* 10: 18–36. Adapted and republished as chap. 2 of this book.

————. 1982. Transference/countertransference: A Jungian perspective. *Jungian Analysis*. 1st ed. Ed. M. Stein. LaSalle, Ill.: Open Court. Adapted and republished as chap. 7 of this book.

————. 1986a. *Picturing God*. Cambridge: Cowley Press.

————. 1986b. The God you touch. *Christ and The Bodhisattva*. Ed. D. Lopez and S. Rockefeller. Albany: Suny Press.

————. 1992a. The holding self: Jung and the search for being. *The Fires of Desire: Erotic Energies and the Spiritual Quest*. Ed. F. R. Halligan and J. J. Shea. New York: Crossroads.

————. 1992b. The perverse and the transcendent. *The Transcendent Function: Individual and Collective Aspects*. Ed. M. A. Mattoon. Einsiedeln: Daimon Verlag, 1993. Adapted and republished as chap. 3 of this book.

————. 1994. *The Wizard's Gate: Picturing Consciousness*. Einsiedeln: Daimon Verlag.

Ulanov, A. and ∵lanov. 1975. *Religion and the Unconscious*. Louisville: Westminster Press.

————. 1982. *Primary Speech: A Psychology of Prayer*. Louisville: John Knox/Westminster.

————. 1991. *The Healing Imagination*. Mahwah, N. J.: Paulist Press.

————. 1994. *Transforming Sexuality: The Archetypal World of Anima and Animus*. Boston: Shambhala.

von der Heydt, V. 1970. The treatment of Catholic patients. *Journal of Analytical Psychology* 15(1): 72–81.

———. 1977. Jung and religion. *Journal of Analytical Psychology* 22(2): 175–184.

von Franz, M.-L. 1977. *Individuation in Fairy Tales*. Zurich: Spring Publications.

———. 1980. *The Psychological Meaning of Redemption Motifs in Fairy Tales*. Dallas: Spring Publications.

———. 1986. *On Dreams and Death*. Boston: Shambhala.

Wheelwright, J. H. 1983. Old age and death. *Quadrant* 16(1): 5–29.

Winnicott, D. W. 1960. Ego distortions in terms of true and false self. *The Maturational Processes and the Facilitating Environment*. New York: International Universities Press, 1965.

———. 1968. Playing and culture. *Psychoanalytic Explorations*. Ed. C. Winnicott, R. Shepherd, and M. Davis. London: Karnac, 1989.

Zinkin, L. 1989. The grail and the group. *Journal of Analytical Psychology* 34(4): 371–387.

2

Fatness and the Female

Many women today feel haunted by an obsession with weight. Though in no way psychotic or afflicted with such gross disturbances as obesity or anorexia, these women know the full force of a neurotic preoccupation with food. What to eat, how many calories, when to eat, how much to eat, and what must not be eaten dominate all thoughts. Mealtimes become the focal points of the day. Radical vows to restrict food intake can be demolished by an unexpected dinner invitation. Taking in forbidden food leads to an orgy of abandoned stuffing. Then fateful Monday returns, the great day when dieting begins again, only to inflict some new sabotage.

Many of the women who endure the irrational invasion of their thoughts, feelings, and daily eating habits with the obsession to be thin would never strike the average observer as having any serious weight problem whatsoever. Usually such women are slim, or at most only slightly plump. Sometimes their frenzy gathers around a mere two or three pounds, ten at the outside.

The woman herself may know her behavior is disproportionate, even bizarre. But awareness of the discrepancy between her intense concern and the facts about her weight only makes her feel humiliated. She is caught in something crazy. She knows her obsession with food symbolizes a deeper spiritual hunger as well as an elaborate defense against it. She knows she is entangled in a classical neurotic conflict: the means of dieting she employs to control her obsession with food only tie her more securely to a compulsive preoccupation with it.

Collective cultural images reinforce this obsession. Fashion magazines advertise a single female appearance—long and slender, pencil-thin. Popular magazine articles in almost every language abound with diet suggestions, exercise regimens, and health food programs. The obsession pervades Western culture, affecting huge numbers of women across classes, defining a certain fixed standard of civilization in terms of fashion. An additional source of vexation to many of these hypersensitive women is the fact that while they are concerned with their weight, so many people in the world are starving. On top of feeling caught in a crazy symptom, these women feel shame and guilt, caught in something morally wrong.

In exploring the female fear of fatness, we can expect to find at least hints of collective significance about our disordered relation to the archetypal feminine, and our attempts to reorder it in new ways. Hidden in what many women feel is a shameful weight problem can be found insights about our new understanding of the feminine principle and its place in our community life.

Symptomatology

Obsession with dieting to achieve thinness affects many different kinds of women. Ardent feminists, professional women, housewives, fashion-conscious females, new mothers—all can be numbered among its victims. Though different in occupation, these women usually have in common a better-than-average education and a strong consciousness of themselves. The kind of woman suffering from this problem usually is keenly aware of a need to define her own identity. Who she is and wants to become and how she will contribute to her world are of central concern to her.

This woman is often not significantly fat and her overweight symptoms have not necessarily been long-standing problems, as for example in the eating disorders examined by Hilda Bruch (Bruch 1961, 1978). Her weight problem arises only after she has achieved a certain level of consciousness, not infrequently with the benefit of psychoanalysis or some procedure of consciousness raising offered in women's liberation groups. The problem is less a physical than a psychological one, coming about in the process of enlarging her self-image to make room for new parts of an identity heretofore excluded from consciousness. This psychological enlargement process gets displaced onto the body.

The symptoms of this obsession arrange themselves in a classic clash of opposites. Unconscious instincts (including everything from natural hunger for food to symbolic hunger for whatever food represents) are pitted against the willpower and reason of the ego.

The woman is pulled back and forth between urges to gorge or deny herself, to expand grossly or to contract outlandishly, to indulge her appetite in order to take in substances or to renounce her appetite in order to exclude any invading substance at all, and to gratify or sacrifice herself for the sake of looking thin.

In this war of opposites, a woman's ego and the unconscious matrix of the psyche from which it grows split apart (Jung 1954). Her carefully considered resolutions about how to diet come up against what one woman called her "blank moments," when she would find herself compulsively stuffing all the wrong kinds of food into her mouth. Afterwards, in this case, an equally intense orgy of self-reproach would demolish what little was left of the woman's self-esteem. She would then resort to her "hiding" clothes, a species of camouflage many women know. These clothes disguise body shape in tent-like folds or floppy jeans, men's shirts, and the like. The self-indulgent woman gets stuck in a ceaseless alternation of instinct and will. She can only wait now for a reconciling symbol to emerge. But she is convinced she can do nothing to bring the necessary reconciliation about and hence feels helpless, at the mercy of a dreadful conflict between her mind and body.

The level of conflict of such a woman is similar to that described in Maria Palozzoli's discussion of anorexia, though it is not as crippling (Palozzoli 1971, 197–218). In anorexia, Palozzoli argues, a woman displaces the struggle for self-definition and self-assertion vis-à-vis the world onto the struggle of her ego's will over her body's natural instincts of hunger. Self-definition contracts into a small circle of instincts which dominate the ego. The anorexic woman feels entirely "herself" only when her will tyrannizes over her body. The more weight she loses and the thinner she gets, the more "self" she feels she has acquired. Her rigid control of her body's hunger proves her power to assert herself. Meanwhile, however, her body deteriorates. "Selfhood" turns out to be merely a mental concept, an artificial product without organic roots, sustained only by nerve and willpower, purchased at the price of health, sometimes even of life itself.

In less anguished situations, the battle lines are not so severely drawn. Here again, the struggle occurs between ego and instinct. But now the woman obsessed by diet can transform instinctive archetypal energies to some level of psychic adaptation. Many of these women, unlike the anorexic, have achieved clear definition of their egos in the world—in jobs, in relationships, in marriage, in motherhood. What they are struggling with is how to live in those places they have achieved for themselves, how to integrate their several capacities into a working, harmonious life-giving whole: They are struggling with how to relate their already secured identities to the larger world around them. Within their own psyches, they are attempting to find a way to affiliate their egos to the wider boundaries of the Self.

The Self, as we know, often makes its presence felt to our egos by imposing on it certain necessities that the ego must accept. Body weight and shape serve as good vehicles with which to experience this necessity. Despite what our cultural stereotypes dictate, we are not all built in the same shape to achieve the same weight. We must come to terms with the body contours given us through heredity and environmental conditioning. Our margin of freedom to change that shape is limited. Finally, we must accept what in fact we are, or to put it even more rigorously, we must submit our ego ambitions to the realities of the Self. Failure to do so engages the ego and Self in deadly warfare.

For many women this ego-Self conflict is displaced onto food obsessions, and is fought out in terms of diet and body-image versus instinctive food needs. We are landed then in one of those insoluble conflicts the aim of which seems to be not its own resolution, but rather seems to lead us to what the conflict disguises: whether the psyche centers around the ego or the Self. These two terms—ego and Self—suggest the guidelines for looking more closely at the meaning of the symptomatology of this conflict over fatness.

Regressive and Prospective Analysis

To be landed in such dire conflict that one's own body image is daily sabotaged suggests that something serious has gone wrong or that something important has been left out in the formation of a woman's identity. As I mentioned above, women caught in this way usually present an appearance and a level of accomplished functioning that would never lead others to suspect the shame they feel over their "fatness," the horror they endure at their helplessness to change it, or the energy they consume in obsessive fixation on diet plans.

For such a woman, the ego functions in spite of an unconscious pocket of madness. This accounts for the fact that it is often only after a women has attained a certain degree of self-awareness that this obsession appears. Heretofore, the lacuna in the formation of her ego has been repressed. Only as her consciousness expands, often as a result of analysis, does this repressed area come to light. Only now has she enough strength to cut through the repression that has covered the gap in her development.

This is an important point, for many women patients are shocked by the sudden appearance of this weight obsession. In panic, they see the symptom as a severe reversal in their mental health. On the contrary, the symptom may signal the attainment of an ego sufficiently strong for a woman to look now at what she has been fighting. The symptom heralds the first appearance of a dissociated part of the psyche. Like all debuts of unconscious contents, its form seems primitive or "crazy" to conscious perspective.

A regressive interpretation proves helpful here, for it points the way back to the origin of this weak place in such a woman's ego. It is through this hole in her identity that the food obsession breaks in. The woman who found herself lost in "blank moments" when she went on food binges, for example, said she felt "taken over by something unknown."

In most women's cases this gap reaches all the way back to the earliest feeding rituals of mother and daughter. Something in the daughter was not fed, was not held, was not seen by her mother. Some experience of central rejection occurred, or some "environmental failure" took place in which the parent let the baby down and the baby suffered "an acute confusional state" characterized by "intolerable anxiety" (Winnicott 1971, 70, 138, 143, 216, 229, 236).

In some way the mother turned away from the infant, communicating a feeling of rejection and absence which aroused unmanageable panic in the infant. The infant came to turn away from that part of herself she held responsible for the mother's rejection of her. The infant rejected utterly that part of herself that laid her open to such anxiety. She introjected rejection and turned it against the offending part of herself.

Usually, the offending part is somehow associated with hunger, with demands for food and for emotional nourishment. The infant needed to be seen and attended to, to be held and looked upon lovingly as a source of pleasure and satisfaction. Instead of being knitted into the rest of the personality, this offending part has been left out. It accounts for the gap or missing piece in the woman's later identity.

The daughter's emerging ego suffers a painful wound in this rejection. Her ego's connection to a larger encompassing Self, projected onto the mother and experienced as the containing matrix of a still undefined and undifferentiated body-identity, sustains a break, a rupture, a gap (Neumann 1973, chapters 1, 2, 5; see also Jung 1907). Her ego grows up around the wound, often covering it over, and the break in the ego-Self relation becomes dissociated from her consciousness. She shuts it away from consciousness, as she was shut away from communication and relation to her parent. She is not really aware that a gap exists, and that below the surface of her self-image a wound has been covered over. She manages to develop a reasonably functioning ego in spite of it.

A woman's first discovery of the extent of this wound often occurs in the symptom of her obsession with fatness. The woman herself feels only the suffering of her drive to become thin and her inability to control her preoccupation with food. She knows she is hungry in a strange way. No matter what she eats the hunger is not satisfied. Even if she manages to restrict her weight to a very low figure, she knows she is doing so under great stress, as if waiting for an axe to fall, a horse to break loose, or an uncontrollable "eating attack" to overpower her. Her insatiable hunger leads her regressively to uncover the unfed, empty place in her ego. For *it* is hungry. *It* is starving, in fact! She discovers the displacement onto food in her urge to fill up that hole in her personality. Her symptom takes on symbolic significances.

Because of early rejection, her ego has coalesced prematurely to secure her identity. What is missing is a nourishing connection between her ego and the Self experienced in and though her body; what is missing is a line to the archetypal feminine in the unconscious.

Analyzed prospectively, the symbolic significance of the symptom of her obsession with fatness is found in her efforts to reestablish a feeding connection between ego and Self. Although acted out in displacement onto food, her obsession with eating is an effort to reach back over that gap in her development to see and hold in awareness, and thereby emotionally feed, that part of her ego that was originally rejected. She both wants an ego-Self connection and fears it. Her obsession with fatness symbolizes her fear that the Self will overpower her ego and enlarge it beyond her control. To defend against this threat, she holds tightly to her ego's goal of thinness that symbolizes keeping her life under ego management. But her relentless hunger forces her to go where her symptom may lead her, surrendering to the Self the ego's claim as center of the psyche. Her ego is too thin to conduct non-ego energies into her life, but her symptom can lead to a permanent healing of the wound.

The Ego Wound: The Threat of Madness

A wounded ego affects a woman in basic aspects of her feminine identity. In different women different intensities obtain, but generally the security she takes in her sanity has sustained injury. She feels there is something not quite reliable about her own consciousness, as if it might break down at any moment. And she is right. She experiences random fits of anxiety and attacks of inadequacy. Her self-concept is not reliable because it has been built around a gap that she long ago covered over. Hence at any time she may fall into the hole which unconsciously, like a baby falling out of her mother's arms, she fears as an endless depth below her. When her obsession with fatness appears, all her uneasiness about her fragile consciousness coalesces into one symptom which overruns her, destroying her confidence in her ability to cope.

A very hard thing for any of us to learn is to accept symptoms that plague us, especially those that make us ashamed. For the woman beset by the equal and opposite pulls of wanting to be thin—which means holding her body, instincts, and identity tightly under control while wanting at the same time to give way to an insistent urge to stuff herself (symbolizing her desire to yield to the Self as the psyche's center)—it is a blow to her confidence to accept the conflict and see where it may lead.

It will take her directly to the gap, to the wound in her ego. It will lead back to that intolerable anxiety where she was neither seen nor fed. The fear of falling again into that formless anxiety, so disintegrating in its effects on her identity, underlies the compulsive aspect of her symptom. Her dieting rituals serve as protective devices to keep the empty, hungry place in her own make-up at a safe distance. One woman quipped: "Have wall [of fat]; will travel." Sooner or later a woman must look directly into the gap that threatens her sanity and see what will happen.

The young analysand discussed in chapter 1 (see pp. 8–10) did this work through the use of active imagination. The trustworthiness of the relationship with her analyst made this possible, providing a container of relationship in which to hold these painful fears and anxieties in open awareness. The woman did not have to sustain herself all alone, by a sheer effort of will. She could rely on the surrounding strength of the analyst and the reliable living connection between them. The analytical relationship supplied what had been missing in the original environmental failure that had traumatized the patient. Now, the infant was not "dropped" or "turned away." No matter what happened, the connection between analyst and analysand stayed firm.

Looking beyond her defensive preoccupation with getting fat to what menaced her consciousness, this woman reported feeling "stark terror." Working in active imagination, she displayed signs of terror. She grew deathly pale, and began to sweat and tremble. She felt she had fallen into a void, an abyss that threatened never to end. There, she feared, she would disintegrate into tiny bits and pieces and cease to exist altogether.

Over many months she faced this void again and again. Slowly, and always in the context of her relation with the analyst, her panic subsided—as she reached out into the void to find that the seemingly infinite abyss took on finite boundaries. Her terror knew limits. Within these limits, her terror slowly changed into an emotion of pain. It too felt unbearable to her, because it was unending. She re-lived the rejection that had engulfed her when still a small child. Her pain immersed her. As discussed earlier, her work with active imagi-nation produced an image of a *Mater Dolorosa* weeping tears of blood for all human suffering.

Over a period of time this archetypal image of a figure suffering pain took on more human dimensions. Her ego, heretofore too thin, was enlarged by assimilating this archetypal image of pain into her own personal feeling of sadness for the small child she had been who suffered so much hurt. At the same time, she felt her personal suffering was redeemed from neurotic isolation in its affective link to the collective image of the *Mater Dolorosa*. The tears of blood changed into ordinary human tears which knew human limits. Eventually they stopped.

The abysmal gap that threatened the stability of her ego as long as it lay hidden and dissociated from her consciousness could be filled now that she faced it. Bit by bit, she filled the void with her own human feeling. This feeling could be integrated with her grow-ing consciousness. Her need to be compulsively in control of her "thin ego" lessened significantly as she faced what she feared. She saw her eating compulsion as both a defensive effort to control this void and as an attempt to heal it by reaching back over its gaping presence to establish a feeding connection with the Self.

The Ego Wound: Body Functions

A woman with this type of wounded ego knows her body-image is also injured. Such a woman feels there is something wrong with her body, often centering her anxiety on a rejection of her genitals and bathroom functions. Her obsession with fatness concentrates this unease with her body, projecting it onto worry about her digestive and eliminative processes. Not only can she not reliably take in the right amounts of food, but she also cannot properly get rid of left-over waste products. These bodily dysfunctions serve as vehicles for her experience of the psychic dissociation of her identity as a woman from its roots in the collective feminine elements in her unconscious. In addition to body-image, the collective elements are frequently projected by her onto women as a group. As a result, a woman plagued with a fatness obsession frequently experiences great and continuing trouble in relating to members of her own sex in any numbers larger than a one-to-one relationship.

Because of her experience of maternal rejection, a gap has occurred in the formation of such a woman's ego. Hence her sense of her own female body does not rest on sure ground. Intrapsychically, her self-image as a female does not grow up naturally from an unconscious collective feminine base as mediated by a mother. Such a woman forms her feminine identity over against her mother, in contrast to her mother's identity, sometimes even in spite of it. She thus rescues her feminine ego but at the expense of supportive identification and cooperation with a wider feminine perspective. For such a woman, the personal and collective aspects of the feminine fall into a hostile disjunction, two sides at war with and mutually rejecting and hurting each other.

This wound to a woman's ego often expresses itself in her feeling threatened by other women and failing to find a nurturing sense of solidarity with them. This wound shows up in her unconscious material in the form of an aggravated shadow problem, where she may dream herself pitted against collective feminine elements rather than against a more personal shadow enemy.

One woman, for example, reported many dreams of the following type:

> *Hundreds of girls invade my house and want to use my bathroom. I feel invaded, used, caught. My toilet cannot flush that many times, but clearly they will hate me if I say no.*

The hundreds of girls represented to the dreamer "the feminine, *en masse,*" a collective feminine element in her psychology that had been excluded from her ego. This collective feminine was stuffed up with waste material that needed to be flushed out. To this image, the dreamer associated emotions of angry resentment and hurt that she could not get rid of, and that had come from being misunderstood and rejected by other women. But the dreamer's assimilative mechanism (and toilet) was too small to accept all these girls' pent-up feelings. In other words, she had no suitable way to deposit these feelings. She felt caught in a double bind: if she let the girls use her toilet it would overrun and mess up her house; if she protected herself from this invasion, the girls would dump anger and hate on her.

Significantly, a third alternative never occurred to the dreamer in her associations until the analyst pointed it out. She might permit some of the girls to use her toilet and let the others go on to find a public bathroom, not because she forbids them her toilet but because of the actual limits of the plumbing. Neither she nor her toilet was omnipotent. Accepting her limits, she could say yes to some girls and no to others without feeling overrun or guilty.

This kind of "all or nothing" clash, depicted in the dream as a large group of girls pitted against the single dream-ego, plagued the dreamer in terms of her weight obsession. Either she would stuff herself or starve. Both her symptom and her dream depict how she was cut off from the wider roots of her feminine identity. Holding tightly to her own identity, she could ward off feelings that threatened to overrun her, but also would thereby deprive herself of nourishing connection to the feminine in its impersonal, collective form. As a result, her dependency continued unanswered and unsupported. Moreover, she experienced her dependency needs with shame, as if they would soil a relationship by overflowing its capacity to assimilate them, much like the dream image of overflowing toilet bowls. As a result, she denied her needs. But both her conscious symptom (of compulsively wanting to eat) and the unconscious symbolism of her dreams (the invading females) showed her she could not continue denying her need to connect to the collective feminine for which she was hungry. Her symptoms and her dreams held her to the task of reaching back to mend her connection with the feminine in its collective form.

Much later in this woman's treatment her dreams reflected her increased ability to identify with these rejected collective elements. Now in dreams she became one of those women who needed to rid herself of accumulated resentment and anxiety:

> *I am in my mother's house and have to go to the bathroom. I produce an enormous bowel movement that fills the bowl completely and threatens to overflow it. It is an odd bowel movement: it consists of fat sausages neatly arranged in rows.*

This dream reflects the dreamer's need to empty herself both of her compulsive fat obsession (the fattening sausages lined up in rows) and of the anxiety associated with original maternal rejection. Moreover, she now feels openly—and therefore has assimilated to herself—what used to be symbolized by the invading girls: the anger at being rejected, and the shame at having a need she cannot get rid of. She has a place within her mother's house to put this overflow. She no longer need appease her rejecting mother by holding in all her hurt and rage. Her ego-Self connection is getting unclogged.

Still later in this woman's treatment, her dreams reflected more healing of the wound. She dreamt she was with "some of those many girls" who were feeding her "sweets." Gradually she was building a personal connection to the collective feminine and experiencing it as giving her something pleasurable that heretofore she had displaced onto actual food, like desserts, and denied herself.

To come to this point, however, she had to recognize her constipated feelings of anger and hurt and eventually pass them on—the toilet symbolism. She had to accept not only the feelings, but also the real limits of her actual capacities. She could not assimilate all the girls' hurt, only her own small portion of it. She was not omnipotent. If she fell into the temptation of omnipotence her capacity to assimilate would have broken down as surely as the dream toilet. But accepting and working through the feelings that really belonged to her, she could flush them out eventually, and enable herself to sympathize with the girls' feelings without guilt that somehow she herself had caused all that hurt.

Thus her ego established an affiliation with the collective feminine, but was not swamped by it. Being finite, each of us can have only one identity as a woman, but we derive support from contact with other types of women. We find nourishment for our individuality in a shared feminine perspective. Much of the success of the women's movement depends on this sense of solidarity among females drawn from many walks of life.

The Ego Wound: Dissociated Sexuality

Another kind of wound to the body-identity that often occurs to a woman beset with obsessions about fatness is a deep doubt about her sexual attractiveness. Frequently she experiences her sexual organs as a cause of shame. She may have difficulty reaching orgasm which she takes as proof of her sexual inadequacy, thereby making orgasm even harder to attain. She fears to open herself to her own desire as well as to her partner, for both such yieldings threaten tight ego-control.

Intrapsychically, her ego dissociates from the animus, which then fails to function in its own capacity to mediate the contents of the objective psyche to her ego. Instead, the animus stands apart, outside the ego's orbit, threatening to invade it and yet also tantalizingly out of reach. A woman may experience this intrapsychic split in ambivalent sexual terms—both longing to be reunited with this animus and resisting it strongly. Such opposite pulls clearly symbolize the conflict between her desire for union with something beyond her control and her fear of surrender.

Here we touch on the symbolic role sexuality plays in psychic development. Sexual conflict may in fact portray the psychic splits and spontaneous efforts of the psyche to mend them. To take the sexual symbolism literally is to miss the chance to reunite disparate parts of the personality. One woman, for example, who was deeply involved in her analysis for some years, and who was beset by the fatness problem, found that her dreams presented her with a recurrent motif. In them, she was persistently attracted sexually to unknown and unsuitable men. Her dream ego resisted these attractions because they conflicted with her awareness in the dream of the actual relationship she had to a man whom she valued highly. In the dreams, too, she thought her world and that of the male dream figures were hopelessly far apart and incapable of authentic connection. The sexual motif of the dream symbolized, therefore, what soon clearly became the real issue—the problem of joining opposing parts of the personality. Mixed in with the sexual symbolism here, therefore, is a struggle of the ego against the Self. The Self's pull is carried by the animus figure. The dreamer is confronted with a stalemate, an "insoluble conflict" which by its stubborn persistence forces her to become aware of the basic ego-Self struggle symbolized by the sexual conflict in her dreams. She feels caught in a double bind in the dream: if she abandons herself to the attraction of the animus figure she betrays precious personal values; if she holds fast to her personal values, she rejects the compelling life giving force of her sexuality. How, in the dream, can she enlarge herself to include both her unlived unconscious energies symbolized by sexual desire and her own values?

The woman's repression of this whole conflict had led her to displace it onto an obsession with fatness. In her compulsive eating she was acting out a primitive level of the feminine sexual instinct;

she was letting herself give in to a deep-seated urge to be entered and filled, and connected to a nurturing source of being. She was living her fear of her instinctive desires in her disgust at becoming fat and her panic in the face of this weight obsession. The fatness problem hid her ego-animus conflict, itself symbolic of a tug of war between ego and Self at the center of her psyche. Her sexuality had been dammed up because of early maternal rejection (in the same way as the other woman's bowels were stuffed up). Not being accepted by her mother, she knew no mother-ground which could have fostered the confidence that she could house all that belonged to her—that is, her sexual attractions and her personal values, her pull toward the Self *and* her ego standpoint. The situations of both women are beset by plumbing problems: unconscious material that needs to flow into life just sits there unclaimed, clogging the whole psyche. In an attempt to appease her rejecting mother, each woman blocked essential parts of herself, parts that the woman felt her mother had rejected.

Because of such early maternal rejection, a gap occurs in a woman's development, leaving out part of her feminine identity and its connection to collective feminine elements. When a woman's ego develops into a strong functioning unit, these gaps press for closure, toward conscious assimilation, almost as if a natural process of individuation were seeking to unify her personality and bring to light what has been missing and must now be supplied. The urgency of the dreams' sexual motif could almost be said to be engineered by the unconscious to bridge this gap. Her instinctive desire could propel her over it. What is represented in the dreams, however, is not desire for sexual gratification *per se*. The dream sexuality functions symbolically to express her instinctive need to reach over the gap to bind up her wounds and grow toward wholeness. For that gap means death to the dreamer. Her original rejection by her parent had spelled a degree of psychic death for her nascent personality and a lethal dependency that she felt as bondage rather than as a life-giving connection. She linked the sexual arousal in the dream with a similar psychic danger. To be attracted to an unsuitable man was to be held in a kind of bondage, too. Her linking of sexuality and danger was amplified on a collective level by the analyst with reference to the archetypal theme of the marriage of death, symbolizing the radical change from which there is no turning back, once we really put ourselves into the hands of another person.

Intrapsychically, this theme pictures how the person feels when opened to the Self. The person is never the same again, never again a tight little fortress under conscious management. Instead, there is now an open door between ego and Self. This woman's repeated dream motif, of both desiring and fearing to link up with a dream man, well conveys her intrapsychic struggle to connect with an animus that could open her to the depths of her feminine instincts and satisfy her longing for the Self.

Analyzing step by step the fatness level, the ego-animus level, and finally the ego-Self level of conflict portrayed symbolically in the recurrent dream plot, the woman became able to hold simultaneously, in open awareness, the equal and opposite impulses of longing and resistance depicted in her dreams. Locating her problem at its source, she grew fatter in a psychic way and slowly found her way to the energies of the Self. By recognizing the gap in her femininity, which she experienced as lack of full acceptance of herself sexually, she traced the original hurt of not being fully accepted by her mother to its source. She began to see how this initial maternal rejection had kept her from feeling fully grounded in the matrix of the unconscious for which the mother stood on a symbolic level. Clearly, then, behind the sexual urges in her dreams stood not only the unacceptable part of her own sexuality that she needed to integrate, but also the missing experience of feeling a sure connection between her personal identity and the center of her unconscious, the Self. Transpersonal archetypal energies, we see, become accessible only through a personal portal.

The Ego Wound: Girl Ego versus Wise Woman

A woman beset by obsession with fatness usually has sustained a wound to her aggression as well as to her sanity, her body-image, and her sexuality. The woman who dreamt of invading girls wanting to use her bathroom, for example, initially felt rage toward these females and feared their hatred of her, but she could not use this rage to assert limits about who could use the bathroom and who could not. The woman who imagined the *Mater Dolorosa* realized that her food obsession enacted a hunger displaced from an unfed part of herself, for example, had savagely attacked her body-image as too fat, but could not use this attacking energy to affirm her actual bodily contours. She dreamt that her overweight sister cut huge slabs off her buttocks and breasts in her effort to make herself thinner. This woman often fell victim to a persecuting inner animus voice that criticized her every bite of food, mocked her lack of will power, and held up fashion stereotypes of the thin female body she sought to achieve. That her actual body type conformed to different proportions and contours did not matter at all. Hence, this woman lived under constant pressure, hounded by persistent failure and feelings of inadequacy.

In general, much of this weight-obsessed woman's aggression remained unlived and unconsciously projected onto the people around her, people to whom she did not assert herself fully lest she be attacked. She felt rejected by others because her need for acceptance was so great that she tended to sacrifice her own way to comply with others' expectations. The familiar double bind situation we have seen in previous examples obtained here too: conform to the approval of others at the cost of one's own individuality, or assert one's own individuality at the cost of relation to others. For women suffering from an obsession with fatness, this conflict takes a fascinating form.

Many modern women scorn the traditional feminine stereotypes. Clichés such as "the little wife," "the fashion plate," or "the sex object" threaten to entrap a woman in a prefabricated identity. She wants to fashion her own personal identity and wants that opportunity extended to other women as well. This is the power of the woman's cause in our times, the power to be who and what one is as a woman, in appearance, in life-style, and direction. The problem for a woman beset with an obsession with fatness arises because she has been wounded and thus does not enjoy her full strength. She can throw off one traditional stereotype, but may unwittingly fall victim to another—the thin woman with a boyish figure, without any curves, folds, or openings. She has had enough aggression at her disposal to fight against clearly defined inherited cultural images, but not enough aggression to improvise a positive image of her own identity.

Because of the original maternal rejection, part of such a woman's ego has never "fattened," never been given its proper weight. She is still looking for nourishment for the ego but from the psychological perspective of a girl. The part of her ego that needs to be fed is that of a girl, even when she has become a grown woman, and hence remains replete with the manners of childhood, pubescence, and adolescence. The result is that she is cut off from a mature relationship to the unconscious. What relationship does take place has all the marks of the vicissitudes of youthful modalities: the woman's ego is identified with the unconscious or invaded by the unconscious, or she is immersed in the unconscious; and all of this is compensated for by self-conscious assertions of her "place" in the world. In a world that increasingly welcomes individual styles of female being, an immature little-girl ego is at a distinct disadvantage in trying to do the womanly task of using her energies creatively to fashion her own identity.

At precisely that weakest place in her personality, the animus steps in to make up the deficit by supplying abstract formulas in place of a feeling sense of who she is: the sense of being organically rooted in her body, relating with others, with her unconscious, and with her time in history. The animus steps into this gap precisely at the point where a woman's ego is insecure and unconnected to her deeper Self. Instead of performing the function of connecting her ego to the deeper unconscious layers of her femininity, out of which she might fashion her identity as a woman, her animus latches onto ready-made cultural stereotypes and barrages her with formulas for her appearance, her ideas, her behavior. A dictatory animus steps in, in place of carefully built cooperative affiliation between ego and Self. As a result, her ego becomes encased in an animus shell of abstract prescriptions, unrelated to the concrete person she is. Her ego is stranded, removed from its source in the unconscious, endangered, brittle—a tough little girl, not pliant with a woman's strength and amplitude.

Different women experience different versions of this animus domination. Some focus on their appearance as women, in terms of implicit ideas and values as well as explicit physical qualities. For instance, some become slaves to current fashion images and literally must keep changing their wardrobes to keep in tempo with fashion dictates. Others regress to a tomboy model, renouncing all interest in clothes and, as one thirty-year-old woman described herself: "Schlepping around in blue jeans as if I were an adolescent." Still other women feel constrained by unwritten codes of dress they experience in the women's movement; they dare not deviate for fear of being ostracized. In all these examples, it is the inner animus domination over a woman that compels her to dress or not to dress in a certain way, and the compulsion gets projected onto outer cultural situations.

To work out of this corner where aggressive energies attack the woman herself in demoralizing ways, and where she consumes energy in being angry with herself, she must come to own her aggression; that is, she must come to have it at her disposal instead of the other way around. Here, a woman must claim her anger and accept it openly. This can be unpleasant both for her and the people around her, for her anger is often not free and not in easy relation to immediate events or nearby persons. Her strong anger stems from her experience of early maternal rejection that has been repressed. Coming to terms with it now, she must consciously feel the rage she has so long denied. But her initial way of getting in touch with the dissociated anger is through present events, involving family and coworkers, political issues and social problems. It is these that will touch off sparks and become vehicles for her experience of her repressed rage.

It is essential to distinguish current events from repressed trauma. Otherwise, a woman's anger over present-day issues will be so out of proportion that she will provoke others to reject her once more, which will only reinforce the original trauma and build more rage. To stay put in groups where other people are equally angry—an opportunity too easily afforded by our present society— is no solution either, for to be caught in anger by identification is no better than to be dissociated from rage by repression. Either way, anger acts as a central unconscious motivation in one's personality, limiting what one can do and severely restricting the satisfactions one can enjoy. The task focuses on feeling the anger, integrating its cause, and getting over all negative manifestation or aggression. The hope is ultimately for a woman to have her aggression at her own disposal for living in true relationships in her world.

For a woman to integrate her repressed aggression has meaning on both a personal and collective level. On a personal level she learns that aggression no longer equates with anger and that anger no longer equates with destruction. She can show her anger and accept it as true feeling, even if negative, without expecting that the person she is angry at will necessarily reject her or her feeling. She can also receive anger without being plunged into an abyss of despair where all relatedness seems impossible. She can come instead to experience anger as a human feeling, able to be held—no matter how volatile—within the warm boundaries of human relationship. She accepts her anger in response to her early rejection by her mother, thus filling in a gap that had left her arrested at a young girl's level of psychological development.

Such acceptance frees aggression from manifesting itself simply as anger. It moves instead to take on the wider ranges of self-assertion. One woman reported a dream that expressed her new capacity to accept her psychic hunger, her own style of taking care of it, her newly acquired ability to express anger, and her ability to stand up for herself:

Some women are criticizing how I eat. I stand up and tell them, "I'll eat the way I want to and need to!"

Another woman dreamt of a new resolve at the time her obsession with fatness began to dissolve and she actually had begun to lose weight: "I know my own shape now, so I lose weight." A third example depicts a woman taking personal responsibility for her hungry aggressive side: "I dreamt I was feeding a tigerish aggressive baby I had given birth to. I knew in the dream this was the hungry part of me. I was not hungry; *it* was."

On a collective level, a woman's integration of her rejected aggression expresses a significance greater than that of a personal story, even though it is only through a personal transformation that this collective meaning becomes accessible. None of us lives in a vacuum. What we each do affects what is generally possible for all of us. Moreover, so many women seem to be beset by this fatness obsession and to be struggling individually and together to bring into the world new ways of living their feminine identity that we can speculate that archaic elements from the unconscious life of the collective feminine are positively demanding to be dealt with consciously. Rather than just imitating the collective masculine images of autonomous identity that produce in women the virile-girl personality that is under the sway of the animus, women are finding ways of bringing the resources of the feminine principle into our culture.

Using consciously accepted aggression, a woman can let go of the thin-girl character encased in animus formulas to give way to a wider and wiser identity as a woman possessed of chthonic feminine power. She learns that all is not up to her to control; she can now rely on the Self. Women are looking for and finding their own personal style of relating their ego to the Self, not a style that comes through "authorities," however one defines them. Women are looking for their own personal images, grounded in their own concrete experiences of the Self in a feminine way. Through a woman's personal attunement of ego to Self in her own feminine way, emphasizing concrete personal experience, the transpersonal quality of the feminine principle comes into the world.

One woman will serve as an example. She kept thinking in her analysis that her ego "should move over," "should abdicate" to the Self. She had a mental picture of Jung as an "authority," seeing his schema of the psyche with the Self comprising the center of a series of concentric circles. She felt her ego kept "getting in the way," "hogging center stage." This struggle occupied her for many months in her treatment. Much of her earlier self-criticism and her obsession with fatness shifted to attacks on her ego for not finding a ritual of psychic feeding whereby room could be made for the Self. From the analyst's perspective, it was remarkable to note how gradually and imperceptibly this ego-Self conflict was replacing the conflict over eating and fatness.

What eventually emerged from her painstaking work surprised her—rather than the prescribed "Jungian mandala" image of the Self, it was instead her own original image of the way her ego found connection to the Self as she herself had experienced it. The ego did not move over or get out of the way; it did not break down or disappear; it became "porous." Her ego stayed in the same place and attained transparency to a wider containing Self which "breathed through it." Instead of a little-girl ego, standing like a sentinel to defend her sanity and manage her repressions, there grew a woman's ego—supported, surrounded, and permeated by the greater Self.

In conclusion, we can see that the obsession with fatness symbolically represents the driving search for the right kind of weight—a groundedness in the unconscious rather than mere avoirdupois. This sort of weight does not show on the scale but is measured in one's identity, where a woman gives full gravity to her feminine roots and can face being "fat" with equanimity.

References

Bruch, H. 1961. Transformation of oral impulses in eating disorders. *Psychiatric Quarterly* 35: 458–481.

———. 1978. *The Golden Cage: The Enigma of Anorexia Nervosa*. New York: Random House.

Jung, C. G. 1907. The psychology of dementia praecox. In *CW* 3: 1–152. New York: Pantheon, 1960.

———. 1954. On the nature of the psyche. In *CW* 8: 159–237. New York: Pantheon, 1960.

Neumann, E. 1973. *The Child*. New York: Putnam.

Palozzoli, M. S. 1971. Anorexia nervosa. *The World Biennial of Psychiatry and Psychotherapy*. Ed. S. Arieti. New York: Basic Books.

Winnicott, D. W. 1971. *Therapeutic Consultations in Child Psychiatry*. New York: Basic Books.

3

The Perverse and the Transcendent

The Analysand

Helmut, a man of seventy-six sought analysis. "What brings you?" I asked. "I have suffered from a perversion for seventy years," he answers. "Are you sure you want to be rid of it?" I asked. "Consciously, yes very much," he said, but whether he did unconsciously he did not know. Had he sought treatment before? Yes, once briefly, years ago, with a Freudian who reduced his perversion to a congenital foot injury corrected after birth. That made no deep sense to him so he stopped. Later, he had conversations with a Jungian, conversations which introduced him to Jung, whom he had read ever since, but the discussion of archetypes was too general and had never reached to the core of his complex. "Why me?" I asked. "Because of your dual profession in religion and analysis," he said. "The religious part is essential."

This opening conversation told me that a purely reductionistic approach would not work, that an archetypal approach which omitted the guts and gore of addictive compulsions would not work, and that whatever Helmut meant by religion, it was going to be central. I hope to show with this case that the transcendent function works to loosen the grip of well-entrenched perversion, that it builds up the ego at the same time it constructs the Self, and that, working within the psyche, it connects us to the Transcendent itself in whatever ways we experience the Transcendent. Active imagination and working with the psyche's transcendent function are Jung's techniques for activating our interiority to bring us from ego to Self. When such activation happens, we experience the Transcendent pushing and pulling in us, asserting that the Self is that in us which knows about God.

I discovered this dynamic in working with this man's complicated perversion, which turned out to be a many-faceted complex. A gripping fantasy (no longer acted out with prostitutes) of domination and degradation by an all-powerful female dressed in black, often with whip or boots, compelled Helmut's prostration in complete self-abnegation: "I want to become nothing, to disappear," he said. In one version he saw himself tightly encased in black leather, including his face, and nailed to a cross with silver nails, unable to move an inch, like a parody of a crucifixion. A compulsive fascination with wide, shiny, black patent leather belts—their smell, taste, and touch, their tightness around a woman's waist or his own— lured him to purchase them and to spend hours fingering them when they became part of his collection. Donning a woman's dress, while standing before a mirror, he would cruelly torture his own nipples and climax in orgasm through masturbation.

Maps of Masochism

Various schools of depth psychology map the territory of masochism, fetishism, and transvestism in ways that proved helpful in unravelling this man's vast suffering. Jung's idea of the transcendent function and my own view of it as a link to the Transcendent turned out to be the container in which his suffering could be transformed into new relation to his past and future, redeeming his present from meaninglessness and self-reproach.

For Freud and his followers, the erotogenic transformation of pain into pleasure springs from reversal of the Oedipal drama (Freud 1905, 1919, 1924, 1927; Gillespie 1967; Stewart 1972). The parent we desire becomes the dispenser of punishment instead of caresses. We disavow our genital inadequacy to satisfy our parent sexually—by exalting pre-Oedipal parts, procedures, and body zones—thus obliterating at one stroke the differences between the sexes and the generations (Chasseguet-Smirgel 1985, 154; 1986, 77). The aggression of the death instinct manifests itself in our making ourselves the pleased victim of another's power and authority (Klein 1948, 28). By fetishistic devices we avoid the Oedipal conflict and threat of castration, insisting that we alone are the object of our mother's desire, and thus disqualifying the father (Greenacre 1969, 332; 1970, 341; Limentani 1989, 230). A man in woman's dress simultaneously displays and defeats his identification with the phallic female because his penis under the dress is real, and he achieves orgastic climax (Stoller 1975, 80–81). In perversion we employ dramatic ways to preserve our fragile identity and to ward off disintegration and death. By eroticizing a frightening sense of deadness, we seek control in theatrics of being controlled (McDougall 1980, 50; Bakan 1968, 83).

B. Berliner, Karen Horney, and Esther Menaker map masochism not in relation to instinctual conflict but as a defensive ego-strategy to survive overwhelming anxiety of being annihilated (Berliner 1940; Horney 1939; Menaker 1979, 61–66). Relinquishing ego-autonomy in order to avoid such anxiety, we stay at a pre-ambivalent early stage of development and cling helplessly and dependently to the person who makes us suffer. We introject the other's disparaging attitude towards us and feel unlovable. Neglecting to build other relationships that reflect our worth, we know only experiences of self-depreciation to which we add self-condemnation. Terror of being abandoned stirs our aggression toward our love object, and then we feel guilty for the aggression and deserving of punishment. Yet, we seek secret control of others by relentlessly positioning them in a superior role, thereby limiting them to a pre-determined place in relation to us.

Object-relations theorists see masochism as an expression of psychic pain experienced before our self clearly emerges from the other. Winnicott finds the fetish a transitional object that gets stuck in a delusion of an impinging maternal phallus (Winnicott 1951, 241). Instead of the creative living found in the illusory transitional space, our fetish confines us to addictive literalizing of what should be symbolic (Winnicott 1971, 27, 33). Masochism allows us "in one stroke" to express aggression, get punished for it, and indulge sexual excitement (Winnicott 1984, 90). Khan says we sexualize events as our way of remembering them before we have a fully formed ego with which to recall them. This is particularly true when we experience the event as painful and when an aspect of our parents' psyche intrudes into our own. We build up a collated internal object out of archaic body experience undifferentiated from bits of mother and father, but primarily to cope with a dissociated unconscious element in our parent. We idealize this created object, surround it with intensified phantasy, and substitute it for the more ordinary initiation of experience with a caring parent into an imaginative play space and a developing symbolic life. Hiding in our compulsive routines is psychic pain we have lived and lost in dissociation. We dread total collapse and hold ourselves together against the threat of annihilation by fetish rituals, cross dressing, and libidinized pain that remains under our ego control (Khan 1979, 131, 134, 146, 212, 217).

The self-psychologist theorists see masochism arising from desperate attempts to foster the rudimentary and self-delimiting self in a desert of isolation. Kohut sees such fantasies and activities as feeble attempts to provide a "feeling of aliveness" and to separate in a healthy way from engulfment in the mother (Kohut 1979, 427). We thus maintain psychic structural cohesion (Stolorow and Lachman 1980).

Jung and Jungians

For Jung, neurosis is "a defense against the objective inner activity of the psyche . . . to escape from the inner voice and hence from the vocation. . . . Behind the neurotic perversion is concealed [our] vocation, [our] destiny: the growth of personality, the full realization of the life-will that is born with the individual" (Jung 1954b, par. 313). To reconnect with our lost vocation takes a double move: reduction and synthesis. The first move is a reduction to instinct which leads us back to reality for gratification, but this gratification becomes overvalued as an end in itself. For the personality to grow beyond instinctual gratification, we must sacrifice our overvaluation of it. Such renunciation stimulates fantasies, and we must then move to synthesize them. "This produces a new attitude toward the world . . . a new potential." Jung says, "I have called this transition to a new attitude the transcendent function" (Jung 1971, par. 427). We engage in a continual process of "getting to know the counter position in the unconscious" (Jung 1963, par. 257). We admit the other and engage our differences with it, and it in turn engages us with its views, expressed in image, emotion, or behavior pattern. Out of this conversation—which is often a struggle— emerges a symbol, a third point of view that formulates a uniting of the conscious and unconscious (Jung 1971, par. 171). It is "a creative solution . . . not unjustly characterized as the voice of God. The nature of the solution is in accord with the deepest foundation of the personality as well as with its wholeness. It embraces conscious and unconscious and therefore transcends the ego" (Jung 1964, par. 856). But the "transcendent function is not something one does oneself; it comes rather from experiencing the conflict of opposites. . . . the symbol has a life of its own which guides the subject and eases his task; but it cannot be invented . . . because the experience of it does not depend on our will" (Jung 1973, 269). Jung finds the transcendent function "equivalent to a renewal of life . . . the soul is born again in God." But this involves a perilous "descent to the *deus absconditus*" (Jung 1971, par. 427). We discover this hidden god right in the midst of the opposites inside us and experience it as Transcendent, outside and beyond us, yet apparently guiding what happens to us.

It is this theme I want to emphasize: connecting to the transcendent function working within our psyche opens us to the hidden god transcendent to our whole psyche. We listen through the perversions to receive a bulletin from the Self to our self (Ulanov and Ulanov 1975, 189–90; Strunk 1982). Only thus do we find our vocation, what Jung calls living according to the will of God. When caught in perversion, we treat that inner way with disrespect instead of loyalty, getting caught in the shadow substitute for our psychic need to venerate something beyond ourselves (Wisdom 1988; Proner 1988; Cowan 1982; Gordon 1987).

We need to see in our masochism its symbols for our religious instinct struggling to break down false organizations of self and other. In this way, we can break through to the joyous knowledge that we are known (Ulanov 1971, 87–88). Masochistic submission both masks our efforts to surrender and symbolizes the psyche's efforts to compensate for a deep woundedness by reaching to the meeting between opposing realities of the known and the archetypal worlds (Storr 1957; Williams 1983; Lederman 1986; Wyly 1989).

History

As was clear from our very first conversation, work with Helmut had simultaneously to go backwards to the origins of his long standing masochism and forwards to the purpose it was trying to accomplish (Fordham 1988). Helmut had three histories: his life, his perversion, and the unfolding narrative of his analysis which—intertwined with the other two and the transference—produced symbols that brought him home deep down inside himself and into relation to the Transcendent far outside himself.

Born and raised in Germany into an upper-middle class family, Helmut arrived as the unexpected twin of a sister who was eagerly awaited and planned for. He was "found" in the womb after her birth and became the favorite of both his parents. His left foot, originally turned backwards, making his left leg weaker and slightly shorter, was corrected after birth by a cast. He remembers no teasing or fuss made about his leg, and it did not come up in unconscious material. Of eight children, his twin sister was the third, and he was the fourth.

Helmut remembers having been fascinated with shiny belts at the age of five, and at seven having wanted to be beaten. He remembers wanting to be his sister and wanting to dress in female clothes. At six, he nearly died from attacks of influenza and meningitis, and his next oldest brother—his mother's original favorite and Helmut's own favorite—did die; but Helmut was so ill his parents did not tell him for some weeks.

At the end of our first year of work, many years after the events, he learned crucial facts from his nephew, his sister's child, who had been raised by Helmut's mother after that sister died. Helmut's mother, the nephew revealed, had felt very guilty about Helmut's brother's death. She felt she had not given him enough food even though, because of rationing at the end of World War I, there was simply not enough to go around. The nephew also described Helmut's mother as so overwhelming in her display of motherly affection that she ruined life for her son-in-law, the nephew's father. After the death of Helmut's sister, the boy's father never dared marry again for fear of adding to the maternal grief of his mother-in-law, Helmut's mother.

At puberty Helmut remained utterly naive sexually until he saw dogs copulating and a friend enlightened him. Then masturbatory fantasies of submitting to a dominatrix came to possess him. At the same time, he had an ardent crush on a girl his age which he did not live out. In his twenties he had two long affairs with older women, one with a golf professional in Germany, and one with a woman in Asia. These he described as normal in feeling and sexuality. He remembers his childhood as happy, his mother as beautiful and loving, and his father as wanting him to succeed him in business, which he longed to do to emulate his parent. His twin sister, who like his younger sister died in her thirties from stomach cancer, was the aggressive one; he was a gentle, dreamy, boy. When his twin grew up, she too became another powerful mother. His religion by comparison was calm enough—conventional Protestant. Though interested in spiritual things, he felt no connection to God or Christ.

Helmut felt that he had missed his vocation, that business was the wrong occupation, and that he had wrecked many opportunities because so much energy had been detoured into fetishes, and activities with prostitutes that at times proved dangerous. He felt inferior to other men and though he had some male friends, never felt himself one of the boys. He was often cheated by partners because he lacked ruthless force. In analysis he came to mourn what his perversion had cost him in money, in business failure, and in wasted life: "I used so much of my life in pursuit of my complexes which produce nothing."

An immensely happy, steady part of his life had been meeting and marrying his beloved wife, and living with her for over fifty years. He spoke simply and ardently about her and their life together, and of their daughter and granddaughter. He said that loving his wife had been the most important event of his life. Equal to it he now rated the investigation and healing of his perversion.

His wife knew of his obsessions but not of their extent or power. With her common-sense attitude, she saw them as nonsense he should conquer, and was upset when he entered analysis. She objected to the expense of energy, time, and money. The conflict with his wife over analysis, however, did give Helmut the chance to tell his wife more clearly how important it was to him to understand these complexes, and to stand his ground for the sake of his soul, even in the face of her disapproval.

When as a young man Helmut had fallen in love with the woman who was to become his wife, he had stood up for her in a courageous way. This behavior had created one of the first bridges, I believe, between his dissociated life, filled with his complexes, and his ordinary life in business and with his family. We could say it was the transcendent function unconsciously working a link between opposites and building up his ego at the same time (Moore 1975). He was a gentle man, having enjoyed a dreamy, protected childhood, yet he was internally dominated by fantasies of humiliation and compulsive masturbatory rituals. Just as the Nazis had begun to rise to power, he had fallen in love with his future wife—a beautiful, talented painter from a prominent Jewish family. His parents had not been overly pleased and had sent him on business to Asia to get over her. When he returned to Germany, Hitler was in power. Helmut was twenty-six; the year was 1937. He had seen clearly that the Nazi movement would destroy his country and he violently opposed it, putting him in opposition to both his parents. His father had said, "Oh, it will pass; we must learn to live with it." He even suggested that Helmut join the Brown Shirts. Stunned, Helmut had exclaimed, "I would not dream of it!" The new racial laws which banned marriage with Jews intensified Helmut's struggle with his parents. His father had said, "Oh, forget about her. You've had affairs before. Don't let her determine your life." Helmut had replied firmly: "It exactly does determine my life and to deny that it does is the greatest injustice to me and to her. It insults her family, which is a great family, not to care what happens to them."

Helmut had felt he was rescuing his beloved, and told his mother he would marry right away. His mother said, "You are no longer my son," and left the room. "I wept strongly," he said, "like a primal scream for five minutes. Then I had finished with it and went downstairs to join the ongoing dinner party. I never had a warm feeling toward my mother and father after that. I left the country." After the war he had returned to see his parents, who were "extremely nice," but cool when he spoke of Hitler and the terrible camps. Helmut said he felt he went wrong there: "I was righteous and not forgiving."

He told this tale in a matter-of-fact way, as if it revealed nothing unusual about his behavior. Yet I remembered the theologian Paul Tillich saying in a personal conversation that he had had to get out of Germany because, although consciously he knew the Nazi movement was wrong, he was not sure that unconsciously he could resist the tremendous pressure and danger of the Nazi environment. Yet, here was Helmut, wracked by psychic illness and chronic inferiority feelings, simply standing up to everyone he loved, to his government and to his culture, saying, "No, it's wrong and I won't do it!" His capacity for love and his wife's connecting with his true self opened a deep channel for much energy to back him up. The energy usually locked up in his perversion flowed together here with his love for his wife and enabled him to begin life anew in another land, another language, another culture.

The Work

Helmut's history makes clear that a whole quadrant of his sexual life occupied itself with libidinizing pain. Analyzed reductively, we found he reversed his Oedipal desire for his mother into being punished for his Oedipal strivings and his pre-Oedipal incestuous wishes. He was conscious of wanting to disappear into the womb and to become female. On an unconscious level, he could thus avoid Oedipal conflict. Helmut received scant environmental support for using his aggression to separate and individuate; instead he detoured it into a fantasy loop enacted in submissive rituals with belts, projecting his aggression onto a dominating female.

In persisting in this retrospective analysis for months, we came upon a live bit of Helmut's true self, a small boy hiding and surviving in the perverse fantasies. This discovery initiated his conscious exercise of the transcendent function. The masochistic rituals and fetishistic routines told the story of this lost boy in the only way possible, pre-verbally and pre-conceptually (Miller 1981, 68, 77). It was a story that could only be told, not in words, but in symbolic facts. Helmut and I listened again to his perverse fantasies. We knew we had found something crucial in this little boy, not only because he felt deeply touched, but also because his obsession with belts loosened its power and he responded to the boy whom he could now see. Energy formerly detoured into the loop of masochistic fancy Helmut now used to receive this part of himself. He claimed his ego.

Helmut was a dreamy little boy, unlike the conventional masculine figures of his family and culture. Imaginative, sweet, speculative, feeling-centered, and preoccupied with meaning, he was not a rough-and-ready boy. His introversion was surely heightened as a result of confinement in a cast to correct his foot. Full of feminine sensibilities and passion, loving his mother and father, loved by them as their favorite, he was captured by love. How could he disappoint them? How could he hurt them by being different from what they wanted? How could he abandon their plans for him in business by pursuing the arts instead? Part of his self-punishment grew from this wish to go another way and thus hurt his parents. This boy of imagination degenerated into a boy of compulsive fantasy centered on punishment. Helmut wept for this boy and felt finally that he could love him. Second to meeting his wife, he said, the greatest event of his life was to enter into relationship with this lost part of himself. Indeed, it was this boy that his wife, with her artistic sensibilities, had touched in the grown-up man, that had enabled him to stand against the pressures of family, society, and government in repudiating Nazism.

With his claiming of this boy, a new impetus entered our investigation of Helmut's repetitive fantasies that featured two archetypal females—a white and a black fairy. Lilith, the black fairy, claimed him at birth as her plaything, mixing a dreadful brew of incestuous love for his mother, transvestite desires for his sister's dresses, and jealousy of his father. Prostrate at her feet, he would lust to be her slave (Koltuv 1986). In thrall to Thanatos he wished to destroy himself. Then the white fairy, Sophia-like, banished her sister by changing her into a snake. But the black fairy avenged herself with this curse: that he would see in every shiny black patent leather belt a symbol of her serpentine power over him, the fetish he would come to adore. In turn, the white fairy counters with a promise to aid him by bringing a wife whose deep love would help him overcome the temptations against which he must strive with all his might.

With the boy in mind, Helmut now entered into active dialogues with the black and white fairies. Thus, he engaged the transcendent function, for instead of just submitting to the fantasies, Helmut, with a stronger ego, now took on the fantasy figures in conversation, making his will felt. He no longer wished just to banish the black one and dismiss all his complexes. He looked to see the fairies' views of things, perhaps because he saw they had functioned as the hiding place of the boy. A rapprochement grew between the two fairies, and one day the resultant fantasy surprised him. The two fairy women decided to exchange belts, so that the one all in black now wore the white belt and the one all in white now wore the black. This lessened his wish simply to kill off Lilith and live happily forever after with Sophia. I stressed the integration of the split between the two images of the feminine and this led us to the awe-inspiring mother figure behind the split (Powell 1985).

Helmut called his mother Gaia. She was lovely and loving and huge in power. She never displayed aggression openly; none of her children did either. The violent aggressivity of Helmut's fantasies, we came to see, reflected his mother's dissociated, undifferentiated aggression, aggression that lay all about him in the atmosphere. Her genuine lovingness frightened anyone who loved and depended on her into stifling any aggression they felt toward her for fear of hurting her. We concluded that the undifferentiated quality of the mother's aggression had hindered Helmut in differentiating his own. She remained in his unconscious the original phallic mother. In wearing women's clothes but clearly remaining a functioning male with erection and ejaculation underneath, he was displaying in action something he experienced before words came to him: his mother's power there under her soft dresses, her phallic aggression under her lovely femininity. He thus showed clearly that his masculinity survived there under his feminine identification with her.

It was as if his mother were only the good breast and he lacked a personification of the bad breast (Klein 1948, 34). Helmut felt a phobic dislike of rubber nipples and pacifiers. We speculated that his twin sister, as the first daughter, had more often got the real breast and he, the third son, the bottle; and that he had coped with his rage by detouring his aggression into a loop of punishment fantasies. The little boy had taken on the task of differentiating mother, not just for himself, but, we suspected, for her undifferentiated aggression, too, because it obtruded into his unconscious. Both her daughters channeled their lively childish aggression into being proper, powerful mothers in their own right, and both, sadly, died young from stomach cancer. Could this cancer have symbolized something psychologically indigestible? Could it be that Helmut as a sensitive boy had developed his perversion in place of his sisters' somatization, in which case the perversion might have actually served to save his life? Could it be that his identification with the feminine boy in his crude fantasies was the means by which he began the vitally important differentiation of the mother into black and white, Lilith and Sophia, into the mother you love and hate, the mother who both loves you and rules you?

But Helmut was stuck there. No environmental provision helped encourage his differentiation from his family into his own self. His aggression stayed primordial, archetypal. It held him fast. I risked the interpretation that when his brother died and his mother felt swamped with guilt, Helmut, identified with her, loving her, took on her suffering as his own (Searles 1965, 226). His mother was, I believe, identified with the earth-mother archetype: to lose a child was the worst possible sin. Helmut's punishment rituals were in part to expiate his mother's guilt. Still more darkly, the way she blamed herself for his brother's death, he may have felt her as a female who felt herself in charge of life and death itself. Helmut may have been struck with terror at her power, thus reenforcing the ban against any show of his own aggression to challenge it. He too might be killed!

The Unfolding

Our retrospective analysis opened into prospective work: we uncovered purposes toward which Helmut's complexes were striving. The transference figured centrally. Three months into the work Helmut felt he had fallen in love with me, in his writings calling me Athena as a pseudonym for anonymity and as a symbol of an intelligence that allowed him to reflect on the Gorgon-like power of his complexes. His love sprang from his catharsis of confiding in detail secrets he had kept for seventy years (Jung 1954a, pars. 132–34); from what he found to be my warm interest and my taking his problem seriously without judging him; and from our discovery and care of the little boy together. In addition, I came to link the opposing archetypal white and black fairies for him by refusing to let him spiritualize his problem as a way of getting rid of the perversions. I insisted instead that we engage them and penetrate their meaning (Powell 1985). He also felt power in me; when we had to work out our appointment schedule, he hid his aggression by submissively apologizing for pushing me to give him just the times he wanted. He was astonished when I told him not to worry, that I would push back. That remark broke up any incipient masochism in the transference, and brought the dark feminine into the room for Helmut. He could make use of me to carry some of the Lilith power. For the first time, Helmut felt himself in relation to a woman whom he was experiencing as holding both the black and white powers. It was at this time in active imagination that the "exchange of the belts" occurred. During the next month his obsessions decreased so markedly he declared himself cured. I kept to myself the fact that this was a transference cure, though I was touched by his relief.

From my side I respected Helmut, recognizing how much he had suffered and how much effort he was putting into his analysis now. I found it hard work to figure so centrally in the transference—to find how to confront without hurting and to analyze the hot passion without insulting him. At one point I said, "To be obsessed with me is not much better than to be obsessed with the old rituals." He said, "Oh, but it is, because it is more normal." "You have a point," I agreed. He said, "I see what you mean: it is not the goal." "Exactly," I replied, "the goal is to live that energy, to see what it brings you and wants from you when it is no longer dissociated but part of you."

The belt fetish had gobbled up a lot of energy. It expressed the intrusion into his psyche of his mother's unconscious dissociated aggression. Helmut pulled the belt tight to create a woman's waist, as if to hold himself together against the disintegration of his fledgling masculinity. The belt had also linked him to the mother he loved and his feeling of being in thrall to her power which he could now control through this fetishistic object. Further, the belt had joined him to the feminine side of himself, which did not accord with any conventional masculine role and had had little chance to be mirrored and grow. Altogether, the belt functioned as a link to the boy who was the lost true self and to the unintegrated aggression belonging to him.

In July, after the April exchange of belts between the black and white fairies, Helmut prayed to Sophia, offering her the patent leather belt and all it stood for. In August, he dreamt he tried to give me the belt but found half of it grown into his skin. In December he did something dramatic that followed on our fall work. He bought a belt, brought it to the session, and asked me to put it on, saying, "This is a sacrifice. I give the whole thing up to you, with a prayer to God to be freed and to give it all to God." I stood up and put on the belt, saying, "I receive and accept it." After a few minutes I took it off, to Helmut's distress, and said, "This belt is symbolic, an important part of our analytic work. I cannot wear it as a personal gift." Helmut said, "You take the belt and the perversions. I get the link to Sophia, who loves the boy as he is." In April of the following year, Helmut threw away his entire belt collection, accumulated over sixty years.

During that previous fall Helmut had been dreaming the sadistic side of the masochistic adaptation of his aggression. He was shocked, but I was encouraged. First, and harmlessly, he dreamt I was teaching him to play tennis. To this he associated his tennis coach telling him his game was too defensive—he ought to go on the attack. But then a series of dream images alarmed him: he was looking behind a curtain for murdered children; he was strangling a mouse that would not stay dead; he saw across a gulf between Palestine and Israel a man mercilessly beating a horse; he was being chased by storm troopers. What stood out in all these images was the horrific pain he felt: it was no longer libidinized into pleasure.

During this time his unconscious also punctured his idealization of me, first in an October dream:

> *He and his wife are lying on the ground watching the rise of a giant moon. It suddenly falls and he sees that it is a paper moon, a lamp on a pole which sticks in the ground as if to light the way. He sees it is part of a movie being made by a man who uses Helmut's own pseudonym in his writing.*

He said of the dream, "It shows my love for you is illusion, lighting the way, but not real, not grounded as is my love for my wife." The second dream came the day after he gave me the belt:

> *We have a session in a hospital, but therapy with a young woman goes on in the same room. Helmut protests, but I say nothing can be done. I look sweaty, grubby from the hard work. He wants to stop analysis, feeling his resistance to it when devoid of romanticizing.*

Of my bedraggled appearance in the dream, Helmut said that I had fallen, like Sophia, into matter, where he had found how hard it was to attain the treasure, namely, his whole self. In addition to his resistance, the dream also showed a new feminine part quite outside his perversions, one fully occupied with her own treatment.

In the winter his wife's objections to his analysis intensified and Helmut felt caught. I stood firm against the description of that struggle as being between wife and analyst. That interpretation would only preserve the split Helmut suffered, creating once again a struggle between two powerful women outside himself. He had to decide his course and stand for what he believed. So he entered into another dialogue of opposites—love for his wife and love for the self he was finding in analysis. This opposition was a striking replay of his early conflict between either following his soul and hurting the woman he loved whether mother or wife, or pleasing her at the cost of his soul. The aggression once detoured into perversion was now much more available to Helmut, and he used it to differentiate his mother projection from his wife and consciously to relate to her distress. With conscious psychic suffering, as opposed to sexualized pain, he decided to give up his analysis at the end of June. "This is real suffering," he said, "not masochism." This was a sacrifice, born of his love for his wife (Jung 1956, par. 398).

I watched my countertransference closely for I felt vulnerable, not in sexual but in analytic passion. I had added hours to my schedule to work with Helmut because his problem fascinated me psychically and because I felt he really wanted to settle this lifelong complex to live more freely before he died. I was afraid he was once more sacrificing his soul to please the woman he loved, but I remained firm that he must decide and follow his own way. In my way I too felt the pain of sacrifice, because our work was being stopped in the middle.

The next fall Helmut contacted me but I had no free hours and I felt I had to wait on the Self, so to speak, to open up hours if we were to continue. Early winter that happened and we worked again through June. He returned, saying his transference had quieted down but was still there. He had read Jung's work on transference and apologized for breaking off treatment. He saw now how much the analyst was involved (Jung 1954a, par. 358; Lambert 1973). He also had persisted in telling his wife what understanding his perversions meant to him, in terms of being able to be himself and not just a persona. She grasped his meaning, yet also criticized his tendency to give too much power over to the other: that is, in this case, the analyst.

In the previous year's work, Helmut had told me of praying to an unknown god for forgiveness for wasting so much of his life. In one prayer he felt no audible answer but knew "the slate was wiped clean." In our last spring's work, he said he had felt a conscious longing to worship something bigger than himself rather than to submit and be punished. He felt the erotic longing concealed veneration. Reading Willa Cather, these words struck him: "where there is great love, there are always miracles" (Cather 1927). "Feeling great love for Athena [me]," he said, "I prayed for a miracle and the love turned into a blue flower which grew in my heart, a symbol of God's love."

This image shifted the transference in a major way. Helmut thought of me now as a messenger, a link, not as an end in myself. A theological change also occurred. Before, he had asked God to take care of him—to wipe the slate clean, forgive him, free him from his complexes. Now, he felt he must take care of God—he must tend to this blue flower within.

Helmut researched the symbol of the blue flower, and at the Zurich Jung Institute found a thesis on its symbolism by a man also suffering perversions. Jung's remarks on the symbol of the blue flower addressed Helmut's estrangement from any established religion, his longing for connection to the Transcendent, and his idiosyncratic sexuality that so strongly mixed feminine and masculine. Jung writes, "the 'blue flower' of the Romantics . . . looks back . . . to the medievalism of ruined cloisters, yet . . . modestly proclaims something new in earthly loveliness" (Jung 1953, par. 99). Further, the blue flower, "a friendly sign, a numinous emanation from the unconscious," shows the "modern man . . . robbed of security . . . where he can find the seed that wants to sprout in him too. . . . For the 'golden flower of alchemy' . . . can sometimes be a blue flower: 'the sapphire blue flower of the hermaphrodite'" (Jung 1953, par. 101).

This sprouting happened in mid-March when Helmut dreamt of visiting a hospital nursery:

> *A baby girl lies critically ill. Small and starving, she might die at any minute. He asks a doctor if she will survive. "Maybe," is the reply, "but only if the child is very well cared for."*

Helmut said about this dream: "The dying baby is my newly born faith in God, that precious little thing I had felt inside me that I did not take care of." He felt that I, like the doctor, was stern with him for neglecting what had been given him.

He imagined feeding the baby regularly, but in the fantasy it was clearly not enough. Then a series of synchronistic events strengthened his confidence. He remembered suddenly all the paintings of Mary feeding the Christ child and prayed she would help him. Then a librarian returned to him a postcard from his daughter, found in a book he had returned. On it was a reproduction of the angel of the Annunciation foretelling to Mary her coming motherhood. He went home to a nap. When he awoke, a vision of the heavens opened to show Mary nursing his baby. Then a blinding light came toward him. When it vanished, he found his baby lying in a cradle, now strong and healthy. Full of gratitude, Helmut also noticed that this baby got the breast, not a rubber nipple.

A dream two weeks later carried the theme further: here a blue hyacinth in full bloom stands before Helmut and a small pinkish hyacinth grows next to it in the soil, like a daughter of the blue flower. Helmut felt the dream symbolized that his new life was now grounded, planted in soil. I noted the interchange of the pink and blue flowers, like a newly born anima and a faith in something beyond himself.

But like most of us, Helmut's road was up and down, off as well as on. In late April he dreamt again of the baby girl, again neglected even though now older, about four:

This child stands naked and alone on a dangerous subway platform. She enters a train and curls up, asleep, in a corner. No one pays her any attention. Helmut kneels, full of pity, to care for her and sees that she has vomited in her sleep. What should he do? He worries, then decides to take her to a nearby hospital. He picks her up in his arms, knowing she is his own baby.

Thinking about this dream, Helmut realized the child had grown and was strong now, sure of herself, healthy. She was somewhat androgynous, he felt, and reminded him of his early desires to be a girl, though he had never really wanted female genitals. This child is clearly a girl. How had she been nourished, despite his neglect, he wondered? Who had been taking care of her? He did not feel so guilty as in the first baby dream. He felt this child was his, inside him, and not really his but connected to something outside him. He felt Sophia in the wings.

In May, several dreams called up young women he had had crushes on when a youth. He likened his transference to me to that kind of falling in love, a "coup de foudre," but now these actual women from his life carried that emotion. In these dreams his wife has gone off to the Fiji islands. We talked about the differentiation of this anima part of him as his own, carried neither by his wife nor his analyst. Being in touch with this anima added unmistakable zest and excitement to his life. A final dream, before we ended in June, featured Helmut in bed asleep. His wife enters. "She kisses me and says she loves me. I glimpse Athena in the next room reading peacefully in bed and tell my wife to close the door and lock it."

Summary

The transcendent function working in this man's psyche loosened the grip of what he called his lifelong perversions. They told the coded story of his effort to keep his true self alive by detouring his aggression into a loop of fantasied masochistic submission, fetishistic compulsion, and transvestism.

He entered that inner conversation between a series of opposites— of conscious revulsion and unconscious thralldom, of obsession with belts and struggle to free himself from them, of black and white feminine powers, of analyst and wife, of suffering as against libidinized pain. Out of this tension, a solution occurred "in accord with the deepest foundations of the personality, as well as its wholeness; it embraces conscious and unconscious and therefore transcends the ego" (Jung 1964, par. 856). The little boy, the blue flower, the baby girl who began to grow up—all symbolize life outside the loop of perversion and link Helmut to life beyond himself (Hubback 1973).

Through this inner conversation of the transcendent function within the psyche, Helmut gained access, as we all may, to conversation between the psyche and what lives beyond it. It is as if we think we are conducting a two-way conversation only to discover that it is in fact at least three ways. For Helmut this was symbolized by his feeling some small piece of God had taken up residence within him, which he realized he needed to keep caring for and relating to. Consistent with his love for his mother and difficulties with her, his love for his wife, and his transference and working it through, his image of God was feminine—the divine Sophia.

The November following his June termination, Helmut sent me a dream, writing:

> *A young female student shows me a postcard she received from Athena who did a little drawing in the left corner in red ink. Suddenly Athena is across the table from me. . . . I look long and closely into her face and deeply into her gray eyes and am so overcome by her earnest expression, I have to look away to suppress my tears.*

His immediate association, he said, was that of an encounter with the unconscious. The little-girl anima continues to grow up and is linked to the work of analysis as she receives word—or images—from the analyst. Helmut was most struck by the unforgettable expression in Athena's eyes—visible compassion and admonishment for the future. It was not the real Athena, he said, because of the grey eyes instead of my own actual blue and brown ones. "What moved me so much," he concluded, "was that this was an encounter with my unconscious and this new part of me, the anima."

Helmut had reached a new attitude toward his life and his perversions. It enables him—he now knows in full consciousness—to live more fully before he dies.

References

Bakan, D. 1968. *Disease, Pain and Sacrifice*. Chicago: Chicago University Press.

Berliner, B. 1940. Libido and reality in masochism. *Psychoanalytic Quarterly*, 9: 322–333.

———. 1947. On some psychodynamics of masochism. *Psychoanalytic Quarterly*, 16: 459–471.

Cather, W. 1927. *Death Comes to the Archbishop*. New York: Knopf.

Chasseguet-Smirgel, J. 1985. *Creativity and Perversion*. New York: Norton.

———. 1986. *Sexuality and Mind: The Role of the Father and the Mother in the Psyche*. New York: New York University Press.

Cowan, L. 1982. *Masochism, A Jungian View*. Dallas: Spring.

Fordham, M. 1988. The androgyne: some inconclusive reflections on sexual perversions. *Journal of Analytical Psychology*. 33(3): 217–229.

Freud, S. 1905. Three essays on the theory of sexuality. *Standard Edition*. Vol. 7. London: Hogarth Press, 1973.

———. 1919. A child is being beaten: a contribution to the study of the origin of sexual perversions. *Standard Edition*. Vol. 19. London: Hogarth Press, 1973.

———. 1924. The economic problems of masochism. *Standard Edition*. Vol. 19. London: Hogarth Press, 1973.

———. 1927. Fetishism. *Standard Edition*. Vol. 21. London: Hogarth Press, 1961.

Gillespie, W. H. 1967. Notes on the analysis of sexual perversions. *Psychotherapy of Perversions*. Ed. H. M. Ruitenbeek. New York: Citadel.

Gordon, R. 1987. Masochism: the shadow side of the archetypal need to venerate and worship. *Journal of Analytical Psychology*, 32(3): 227–241.

Greenacre, P. 1969. The fetish and the transitional object. *Emotional Growth: Psychoanalytic Studies of the Gifted and a Great Variety of Other Individuals*. Vol. 1 of 2. New York: International Universities Press.

———. 1970. The transitional object and the fetish: with special reference to the role of illusion. *Emotional Growth: Psychoanalytic Studies of the*

Gifted and a Great Variety of Other Individuals. Vol. 1 of 2. New York: International Universities Press.

Horney, K. 1939. *New Ways in Psychoanalysis*. New York: Norton.

Hubback, J. 1973. Uses and abuses of analogy. *Journal of Analytical Psychology*, 18(2): 91–105.

Jung, C. G. 1953. *Psychology and Alchemy, CW* 12. New York: Pantheon.

———. 1954a. *The Practice of Psychotherapy, CW* 16. New York: Pantheon.

———. 1954b. *The Development of the Personality, CW* 17. Princeton: Princeton University Press.

———. 1956. *Symbols of Transformation, CW* 5. Princeton: Princeton University Press.

———. 1963. *Mysterium Coniunctionis, CW* 14. New York: Pantheon.

———. 1964. *Civilization in Transition, CW* 19. New York: Pantheon.

———. 1971. *Psychological Types, CW* 6. Princeton: Princeton University Press.

———. 1973. *Letters*. Vol. 1. Eds. G. Adler and A. Jaffé. Princeton: Princeton University Press.

Khan, M. 1979. *Alienation in Perversions*. New York: International Universities Press.

Klein, M. 1948. On the theory of anxiety and guilt. *Envy and Gratitude and Other Works 1946–1963*. New York: Delacorte Press/Seymour Lawrence, 1975.

Kohut, H. 1979. The two analyses of Mr. Z. *The Search for the Self*. Ed. P. H. Ornstein. Vol. 4. Madison: International Universities Press, 1991.

Koltuv, B. B. 1986. *The Book of Lilith*. York Beach, Maine: Nicholas Hays.

Lambert, K. 1973. Agape as a therapeutic factor in analysis. *Journal of Analytical Psychology* 18(1): 25–47.

Ledermann, R. 1986. Pathological sexuality and paucity of symbolisation in narcissistic disorder. *Journal of Analytical Psychology* 31(1): 23–45.

Limentani, A. 1989. Perversions treatable and untreatable. *Between Freud and Klein*. London: Free Association Books.

McDougall, J. 1980. *A Plea for a Measure of Abnormality*. Madison, N.J.: International Universities Press.

Menaker, E. 1979. Aspects of masochism. *Masochism and the Emergent Ego: Selected Papers of Esther Menaker*. New York: Human Sciences Press.

Miller, A. 1981. *Prisoners of Childhood*. New York: Basic Books.

Moore, N. 1975. The transcendent function and the emerging ego. *Journal of Analytical Psychology* 20(2): 164–183.

Powell, S. 1985. A bridge to understanding the transcendent function in the analyst. *Journal of Analytical Psychology* 30(1): 29–47.

Proner, B. 1988. Comment on the paper by J. O. Wisdom. *Journal of Analytical Psychology* 33(3): 249–253.

Searles, H. F. 1965. *Collected Papers on Schizophrenia and Related Subjects*. New York: International Universities Press.

Stewart, S. 1972. Quelques aspects théoriques du fétichism. *La Sexualité Perverse*. Paris: Petite Bibliothèque Payot.

Stoller, R. J. 1975. *Perversion: The Erotic Form of Hatred*. New York: Pantheon.

Stolorow, R. D. and F. Lachmann. 1980. *Psychoanalysis of Developmental*

Arrests: Theory and Treatment. New York: International Universities Press.

Storr, A. 1957. The psychopathology of fetishism and transvestitism. *Journal of Analytical Psychology*, 2(2): 153–167. Also in *Psychopathology: Contemporary Jungian Perspectives*. Ed. A. Samuels. London: Karnac, 1989.

Strunk, O. 1982. Moral masochism and the religious project. *The Bulletin of the National Guild of Catholic Psychiatrists* 28: 25–33.

Ulanov, A. B. 1971. *The Feminine in Jungian Psychology and in Christian Theology*. Evanston: Northwestern University Press.

Ulanov, A. and B. Ulanov. 1975. *Religion and the Unconscious*. Philadelphia: Westminster.

Williams, M. 1983. Deintegration and the transcendent function. *Journal of Analytical Psychology* 28(1): 65–67.

Winnicott, D. W. 1951. Transitional objects and transitional phenomena. *Through Paediatrics to Psycho-Analysis*. New York: Basic Books, 1975.

———. 1971. *Playing and Reality*. London: Tavistock.

———. 1984. *Deprivation and Delinquency*. Eds. C. Winnicott, R. Shepherd, and M. Davis. London: Tavistock.

Wisdom, J. O. 1988. The perversions: a philosopher reflects. *Journal of Analytical Psychology* 33(3): 229–249.

Wyly, J. 1989. The perversions in analysis. *Journal of Analytical Psychology* 34(4): 319–339.

PART

II

The Transcendent in Relationships

4

Birth and Rebirth:
The Effect of an Analyst's Pregnancy
on the Transferences of
Three Analysands

Introduction

This paper examines the impact of my pregnancy on the transference of three female analysands. Danger of exposure to German
measles, epidemic in New York City in 1970, made it necessary to
tell my analysands of my pregnancy almost immediately, before my
condition was in any way obvious. Fortunately, and at great relief
to me, no one with whom I was working had been exposed to the
disease, so there was no need to postpone sessions until the danger
period was over. When I made my announcement, I made it clear
that I planned to continue my practice after my baby was born, returning to work a month later than usual after the summer vaca-
tion. The time of the announcement figures in what follows because
when I shared my news with each person I looked the way I always
had, a way I was to continue to look for several more months. Thus
the impact of what I said was communicated on a psychological
level; there was no discernible physical reality of my pregnancy to
which to react.

The three women I present here stood out from the rest of my
analysands because of the intensity of their responses to the news
of my pregnancy. All three lived as if contained in the matrix of the
unconscious, in a state of unconscious identity with a mother figure
(Neumann 1959, 63). In each case the introjected figure was negative. The mother archetype constellated the personal identity of
each woman as a "mother's daughter" (Ulanov 1971, 205).

Each woman received the news of my pregnancy as if it were a
message addressed to her own psyche, rather than as news about

someone else's reality that in some way touched her but still belonged to someone else. It was as if my pregnancy was their pregnancy. And in one sense it was; in each case my pregnancy intensified the mother-daughter complex already present in each woman until it burst into her consciousness with all the force of a birth event, thus occasioning a decisive separation from the matrix of the unconscious. This new consciousness seemed, in turn, to lead each woman to a second birth of a psychic nature; a new attitude to herself and her world.

In discussing these themes of birth and rebirth, I will first abstract a description of each woman and then describe her experience of the mother-daughter complex. Finally, I will discuss the significance of my pregnancy for each woman's birth out of unconscious containment and her rebirth into a new self-image and capacity to relate to others.

Description: Jean

Jean was a single woman in her middle twenties who entered analysis because of anxiety over feelings for other women. She had just asked her roommate to move out because of increasing jealousy and fighting between them. Though genuinely fond of her roommate, she resented being so dependent on her. Jean had initiated a few sexual meetings between them which her roommate had not reciprocated. This lack of physical mutuality reinforced her deep-seated fear that she was unlovable. She feared that the love she wanted to give was doubly dangerous because, while it devoured others, it left her starving.

Jean grew up as the middle one of three daughters of a midwestern family of modest means. She remembered suffering painful humiliation in relation to her mother. When she was five, for example, her mother had scolded her for acting like a baby and put her into diapers as a punishment. While she screamed protests, her mother and older sister laughed at her. Jean also felt her mother had always interfered with her relationship to her father, never leaving them to work out their own style of communication with each other. As a result, she felt deep unexpressed love for her father that left her unconsciously tied to him in her adult life.

Grossly overweight at the time she started analysis, Jean nurtured a commensurately low self-image. She saw herself as fat, sick, and without inner substance or strength, yet also filled with dangerous needs and impulses. Unconscious material terrified her.

She feared her dreams knew something about her that she did not know and thus could gain powerful control over her. She feared others' control over her as well. To protect herself she resorted to denial. She dismissed dreams as nonsense not worth remembering and avoided seeing others as really other than herself. She related to them instead by identifying with them. This maneuvre nullified her fear of falling under their control.

Jean worked as part of a hospital chaplaincy team, a job filled mainly by men. This fact reinforced her feeling of being an "oddball"—less feminine than other women and not really acceptable to men. She gave genuine comfort to the patients but ran into frequent conflicts with those in authority over her. Jean felt her life to be lonely and desperate. Filled to bursting with growing needs for others' affection, she deeply resented being so dependent on them.

Description: Sara

Sara was a single woman in her mid-forties who had had many years of analysis when a colleague referred her to me. Originally she suffered from intense anxiety, ostensibly triggered by doctoral examinations, but in fact stemming from a negative, restrictive relationship to her overbearing mother. In retrospect, she felt her early analytic work helped her to manage her anxiety but did not resolve its underlying source. She passed her exams and gradually built a career as an outstanding teacher of small children and of those trained to work with children. In her personal life, however, Sara felt she had remained a girl.

Sara was the only child of a poor Jewish family from a large eastern city. She felt her mother tyrannized over her all her life, directing her plans, undercutting her self-confidence, and making her feel guilty for any shred of anger or faint wish for a life of her own. As a result, she had built up a capacity for prolonged, passive resistance. Anything in her present adult life that smacked of "ought" or "should" automatically set in motion her stubborn refusal to consent. She defied any feeling demand from within herself or from others with a thrill of independence. But she saw, much to her dismay, that she was erecting a wall of loneliness that was blocking her own desires and excluding other people.

Sara insisted that the best years of her life were over. She particularly regretted never having married and borne children, for which she blamed her parents as well as herself. Her mother judged her suitors as inadequate and her father was passive in everything that concerned her. Sara felt enraged at the memory of her father simply leaving the house when her mother created scenes. He abandoned her, she felt, to the mercy of her unmerciful mother. Though he was now dead, she still felt ties to her father for lack of any vigorous emotional interchange with him when she had been a child. Too much of their relationship remained unexpressed. Her love for her father was, as a result, pervaded by a wistful sadness. Her feelings for men in general took on the same flavor. This combination of girlish wishing and stubborn resistance proved fatal to any budding romance.

In her late twenties Sara formed a brief liaison with another woman. The hope of finding support for her wobbly self-confidence attracted her to this woman, but the sexual tone of their warm embraces repelled her, and she soon ended the relationship. Since then she had made a few friends whom she cherished and treated with tact and graciousness. But she longed, she said, for a more intimate relationship with a man.

Description: Sophie

Sophie was a single woman in her middle twenties when she began analysis. She came from a middle-class suburban background and suffered from intense anxiety, a compulsion to drink, and an inability to function more than marginally, working only three hours a day as a waitress. Her background showed severe emotional deprivation. Her coming into the world, she was told, was an accident. Her parents had already planned a divorce. Both parents obviously favored her two older brothers. She spent her childhood "mothering my mother," as she put it, by cooking and keeping house for her mother and two brothers and trying endlessly to keep her mother from drinking. When her parents were finally divorced, the children were asked to choose which parent they wanted to live with. The brothers chose their father; she wanted to do the same but felt she could not abandon her mother and so stayed with her.

When Sophie was twelve, her mother married again. The first night home after her second honeymoon, she died of a heart attack, with Sophie looking on, trying fruitlessly to help. She connected a number of events with her mother's death; her mother's recent honeymoon and open sexual transactions, including intercourse; her own menarch, which started soon afterwards; and her mother's drinking—she had been drunk the night she died.

After her mother's death Sophie went to live with her father and stepmother. Secretly she looked forward to the chance to have at last a real mother. On her arrival her stepmother said with obvious kindness, but with what felt like rejection, that she could not hope to replace Sophie's mother but that she did want to be her friend. They did get along well at first, but as friends rather than parent and child. Sophie's father treated her coldly and at times venomously, criticizing her looks, her judgment, and her character. His most wounding taunt was to dismiss her as boring.

Three months after her arrival, her stepmother became pregnant. Sophie felt very much left out but, surprising herself, eventually became very fond of her new sibling, a little boy. After a few years, Sophie's stepmother began to suffer severely from mental illness; she was hospitalized at intervals for what was diagnosed as paranoid schizophrenia. A constant cold war had developed between Sophie's father and stepmother which periodically erupted into violent, screaming fights, with dishes thrown and threats of suicide and homicide hurled back and forth. When her stepmother was in her "crazy" periods, she would attack Sophie as "stupid, unfeminine, unimaginative, hopeless."

In fact, Sophie had an original and intelligent mind. A first-class eastern girls' college offered her a four-year scholarship. There she found a few splendidly supportive teachers. Her tremendous anxiety at being found acceptable and accepted, however, led her to drink a great deal and to fall behind in her work. The school sent her to a hospital for psychological tests and agreed to take her back as a student only if she followed a course of intensive therapy prescribed by the hospital. Sophie's father refused to pay for treatment and after a year and a half she dropped out of college.

Sophie had long held an extremely negative image of men as critical and rapacious tyrants. Secretly, she thought men were superior to women and envied them (Deutsch 1944, 234ff.). Her first heterosexual experience, which occurred just after she left college, resulted in a pregnancy and a grim experience of abortion. Her later tentative efforts at building relationships with men always involved immediate sexual contact. She assumed that that was what was wanted, and what had to be, because she did not know what to talk about or how else to relate to men.

When Sophie started analysis she had just begun a lesbian relationship with a woman her own age that was to last several years. This relationship was constructed on a mother-child axis, with each woman alternately taking each role. Near the end of the relationship

physical violence erupted as each acted out her fury at her own actual mother for failing to give support and love and using her daughter for her own needs without concern for the daughter.

The Mother-Daughter Complex

The similarities in the psychology of these three women are apparent. Each was single; each had a negative mother who had ex-
ercised a dominant influence in her life; each had suffered from lack
of relation to her father and had grown up to feel that men were
somehow out of reach. Jean feared she would overwhelm men with
her own needs for affection; Sara wistfully yearned for a Prince
Charming yet also felt men were never there when she needed
them; Sophie felt outright envy and anger at men for thinking they
were superior. Each woman, to a greater or lesser degree, had been
drawn into love relations with other women. In each woman's psychology the negative mother-image played a central role. This leads
us to our next clear focus: the constellation of the mother-daughter
complex in each woman's psyche.

Each woman had introjected a negative image of her mother and
had identified with it. The central life relationship, therefore, was always with the mother. As a result, each woman found herself caught
up in variations of behavior along a mother-daughter axis playing either a mother or a daughter role (Jung 1938, par. 167). None of them
could see other people as they were in their own reality, but only as
mother substitutes or as daughter figures to be mothered, the roles
being expressed in both positive and negative forms.

In Jean's case, the mother-daughter axis showed itself positively
when she unconsciously assumed the daughterly pose of a bright-
eyed enthusiast on the brink of life. At such a time her face would
radiate an unusual zest for living. Her exuberance impressed others and she often elicited a protective response. The positive mother
role that complemented this youthful posture showed itself in
Jean's capacity to support and advise others in need. She gave them
genuine encouragement without a gushing false assurance.

These positive personae often turned sour, however, because Jean
had not sufficiently integrated them into a clear ego identity. Her
zest for life, for example, would frequently spin off into a fantasy
that quickly outgrew any realistic expectations of what others or
her environment could offer her. Unconsciously, Jean always set
herself up for a fall. She failed to take any protective measures.
Time and again she felt betrayed by others who did not live up to

her image of them. She refused to register negative perceptions of her situation or of others but swept them aside in bursts of enthusiasm. She rejected with hostility any attempts by others to caution her, hearing such remarks as critical "put-downs" calculated to mar her new positive self-image. Mixed with her expectant, eager attitude toward life, therefore, was a surge of power: life would be the way she wanted it to be. She dismissed from consciousness anyone who questioned her way.

To be with Jean, then, one had to agree with her. Relationship to her was possible only on the basis of identification with her. In its negative guise, Jean's daughter role was that of a whimsical, spoiled child who had to have her way. When she felt rejected, her girlish posture turned hard and cold. Shutting others out, she would withdraw into a cynical isolation, showing a tough exterior to the world and a depressed, frightened face to herself.

In a similar fashion, Jean's maternal capacity to encourage others to be themselves changed into a negative form. Because the maternal attitude was insufficiently integrated into her conscious adaptation, it always carried with it an unconscious expectation that the object of her maternal solicitude would turn about and do the same for her, or at least show unending gratitude. If the other moved toward self-definition, apparently outgrowing dependence on her, she felt cheated and used. Her motherly inclinations then took on a devouring aspect. She created scenes, pleading with the other not to leave her, as if she were a forgotten child, and berating the other person as a cold, manipulative thief who took what he or she wanted and ran.

Often at these times, Jean acted out this devouring attitude in voracious eating binges. Full of a sense of all that she lacked, she stuffed herself with food, hoping somehow to obliterate her inner emptiness. Her maternal capacity to nurture in herself that which needed support changed into scorn and self-depreciation. She let loose against herself deep suspicions that it was her fault love was not forthcoming. As if to shield herself from this inner suffering, she assumed a tough, caustic, mannish exterior. Existing without males, openly hostile to them, she showed a warrior-like face to the world, fending for herself with bitter independence.

Sara's experience of the mother-daughter roles in their positive forms alternated between the personae of an idealistic maiden on the one hand and a wise teacher on the other. Though in her mid-forties, Sara exuded a youthful innocence and charm. She seemed too young, really, as if not yet touched by life, as if only now ready to be brought alive. When in this mood, she presented herself to others as a daughter, a young girl, to be guided by their more experienced authority. She evoked protectiveness from others, making them feel they should help her in a loving, gentle way, much as a wise mother might guide her daughter into life (Jung 1941, par. 311).

Complementing this daughterly role was the positive maternal role of a nurturing teacher. Sara was highly skilled in training those who wished to work with young children. The small child was to her a small person, with a distinct identity and style of being all his or her own. She taught her students to see this and to mold a school program around all aspects of these young personalities. She also encouraged her students to develop their own individual styles of relating to children.

Sara's girlish ideals and her mature skills as a teacher were not sufficiently integrated into her conscious identity, however. Often, and especially under stress, these capacities split off from the rest of her personality and functioned in isolation from the whole, thus easily falling into distortions. Her girlish idealism turned stickily sweet and sentimental, and she dismissed as routine her talents as a teacher. As a result her talents then functioned mechanically by themselves, as she functioned, without personal relatedness to others.

The negative expression of Sara's mother-daughter roles trapped her in an alternating cycle of roles in which she was either too young or too old. The young side of her personality showed itself in a naiveté so pervasive and untouched by life that she seemed lost on the sidelines. She would go through her daily routine with nothing ever actually happening to her. She made me think of the fairy-tale Sleeping Princess; she was alive, but unconscious; she was there, but asleep. Her involvement with others appeared to consist solely in a sense of quiet expectancy—that they would do or say something that would wake her up. The sweet quality of her innocence was spoiled by the heavy burden she placed on others, making them feel her coming alive was somehow their responsibility.

The old side of Sara's personality presented itself as the direct opposite—as that of a dried-up spinster. At these moments she gave the impression of being over the hill, beyond help and past hope. She gave others and herself the belief she had missed all the passions of life. By not allowing life to use her, she was now used up; no juices flowed; no dreams inspired; no warmth kindled her feelings. She made bitter remarks, impossibly detached observations, sniping comments.

Sophie's positive versions of mother-daughter roles were as gifted protégé and supportive friend. Her creative but untutored mind looked for maternal guidance to enable her to bring forth what she thought and felt within herself. She appealed to others to nurture her creative development and was able to evoke from them an extraordinary willingness to help her. It was as if she had made parents out of her teachers, who then not only believed in her but felt her development was primarily their responsibility. On the motherly end of the continuum, Sophie played the role of supportive friend who pledged fidelity for life, much as a mother might feel unconditional acceptance of her child. In this mode of behavior, Sophie did show remarkable forbearance and an ability to accept the whole personality of others, the bad with the good.

Sophie did not have a firm enough grip on these positive mental and emotional capacities, however. As a result, she frequently fell into their negative versions. The protégé became the helpless dependent, not only with respect to developing her creative talent, but with respect to her every need. She played to the hilt the role of helpless infant. Her fine mind remained undisciplined because she could not take criticism. To her, criticism was a form of rejection, the fear of which blocked all her efforts to develop her thinking and writing. She made her teachers feel her block was somehow their fault because they had been too harsh with her. She gave way more and more to her feeling of helplessness, making her mentors feel they had to support her every single step of the way. In her emotional life as well, Sophie regressed to total dependency on her woman friend, much as an infant depends on her mother. Sophie literally would not go anywhere unless accompanied by her friend. She demanded constant reassurance that she was really loved and really lovable. She wanted a protector from a hostile, menacing world and used her helplessness to manipulate others to revolve around her needs. Yet she found herself manipulated by this helplessness, believing in it utterly and thus utterly at its mercy.

She therefore failed to set any conditions to her friendship and let her friends take every advantage of her; they made her feel their problems were her responsibility and even her fault. Her genuine loyalty to them was contaminated by a pseudo-motherliness that equated love with total permissiveness. By letting her friend take such advantage of her, Sophie accumulated massive resentment. When it finally burst forth, her entire personality was seized with rage and fury. She spat out vitriolic condemnation; her friend was a traitor fit only for excommunication from all human contact. She carped, complained, needled, and baited others as well, provoking their anger and then accusing them of rejecting her. She became the devouring mother incarnate.

Birth and Rebirth

Although each of the three women became aware in her analytical work of her mother-daughter complex, each still fell into spurts of acting out the roles. Confrontation with my pregnancy intensified this awareness to such a point that each woman seemed to undergo her own style of birth and rebirth. Each now really saw just how caught up she had been in her mother-daughter complex. This awareness set in motion her ego's birth from its womb-like containment in the matrix of the unconscious. This "birth" constellated in turn in each woman a sense of her rebirth as an adult female. Though each woman had long ago reached the chronological age of adulthood, each still felt herself a little girl. With this new emergence of her ego, each woman was able to cut her ties of psychological identification with the mother archetype and to perceive herself as a feminine person with her own possibilities of sexual and psychological identity. With the emergence of a sense of self, each woman could perceive others differently; she could recognize and even enjoy their reality as separate from her own.

Central to this whole process of birth and rebirth was each woman's transference to me. Through confrontation with my pregnancy—the beginnings of a real biological mother-child relationship—each woman saw how she had been attached to the fantasy mother she had projected onto me. Through acknowledging the beginnings of a real baby, each woman freed herself from the fantasy that she herself was somehow still a baby.

In Jean's case, for example, the news of my pregnancy helped move her into accepting her own sexuality. We had worked several years together before I became pregnant. During that time, Jean developed a positive transference to me, seeing me first as a good mother figure and later as a model for a more or less whole feminine self. Several incidents, Jean felt, secured her positive allegiance to me and the analytical work we did together. In the first interview she told me in a moving way of her affection for her roommate. Although the situation had grown impossible and had to end, Jean felt she did care about the woman as a person separate from herself. I was touched by the element of genuine love in Jean's feeling for her friend and identified it as such. This small action on my

part affected Jean deeply; she felt relieved from her fear ____
was completely "crazy" and that all her feelings were "bad." ____ ____
amazed that I could have such a reaction. She had expected an impersonal clinical cataloguing of her feelings.

Another incident concerned Jean's weight. During the first
month of sessions she mentioned her excessive weight in connection
with something else. I casually remarked that when she was ready
to lose the weight she would and then continued with what we were
discussing. A year and a half later when she decided to diet, she told
me how much my earlier, casual remark had meant to her. Her
mother had always nagged her about her weight and still did, yet
continued to send her holiday packages of sausages, cheeses, cakes,
and cookies. My remark made Jean feel I had accepted her as fat.
She suddenly realized then that it was her fat, and her body to do
with as she saw fit, at her own pace.

Occasionally, Jean still succumbed to eating binges when she felt
discouraged and angry with herself. I remember my amazement
when she told me that one Sunday afternoon when she had felt particularly empty and worthless, she had sat down and eaten a coffee
cake—a whole one! My astonishment showed on my face and I burst
out laughing. Jean was shocked but then started to laugh, too. Not
until now had the humor of her wolfish eating capacity struck her.

Many times Jean felt intense anger towards me because she could
not manipulate me into seeing her as she saw herself—"A fat, ugly,
angry, hopeless dyke!" It enraged her when I would say at such moments that we must look at those feelings but not identify with them
and that I simply did not agree with her definition of herself.

The year I became pregnant we had been working for several
months specifically on her transference and its dissolution. Jean
felt she was now ready to venture out on her own and to have more
serious contacts with men. She had formed some cordial friend-
ships with a few men, who were themselves homosexual. She
needed to be sheltered from more direct confrontation with her own
femininity and to experiment in fantasy with her own sexual feelings. These men were safe because they "wouldn't move in," as she
put it. But their own repudiation of women as potential sexual partners unconsciously reinforced Jean's doubts about her femininity
and played into her unconscious hostility towards men. Just before
I became pregnant, Jean had changed her job and had met some
new people, one of whom was a man who showed great interest in
her. At this point in her life, Jean was still a virgin.

When I told Jean of my pregnancy, she showed no strong reaction but turned instead to other matters. That night, however, she called me at home. In tears she angrily accused me of abandoning her by having a baby of my own. This proved, she asserted, that she was all the things she had always feared about herself—unlovable, devouring, sick. But one small detail at the end of our conversation showed a new tone. She said, "You know I am happy for you that you will have a baby." At that moment, just before she hung up, she saw my pregnancy as mine, as a fact about me; she recognized me as a separate person. At our next session she reported that when she had hung up the phone she had felt the whole conversation had been ludicrous—that she had simply been knocking herself down. "I felt like a baby and edged out by your real baby. But I didn't like my behavior because I'm not a baby. I wept and grieved and let go of all that crap in me, that wallowing in being a baby. I'm sick of it and everyone must be sick of me. I want to get a hold on myself." The next day, she said, she had gone to see the man at her job who had showed a personal interest in her and they went out for a drink.

During the next weeks they saw each other and began an affair. The sexual interchange was gradual yet very exciting. Jean felt she had embarked on a new venture with herself, as well as with another person, and a new relation to her own femininity. She also dreamt a great deal. She told me this dream at our next session:

> *Two girls and I are involved in some kind of work. I meet a boy on a bus and one of the girls tells me sex is bad. I laugh and say that's not so. Then I go to a cafeteria; there was all this food. I want to eat a fixed plate—that is, not too much, not to gorge myself, but to enjoy some of it.*

My pregnancy occasioned Jean to face openly that she had previously identified herself as my child, even if unconsciously. The appearance of a real child made her feel abandoned, forced out. But Jean also saw this fantasy as totally inappropriate to herself, not only because it was physically impossible, but, more importantly, because it was not what she wanted for herself. She no longer found it suitable to herself to alternate between mothering and being mothered. She was emerging from the mother-daughter world. Dependency and protection paled in their appeal. She wanted her own adult life with its possibilities for relationship that offered different kinds of satisfaction.

That I became pregnant clearly announced to Jean that I was sexually involved with my husband, a "male." Because I still carried for her projected elements of her own fuller femininity, Jean could now conceive of herself as a woman capable of adult sexual relations with men. She was no longer the fat little girl whom only motherly women could love. She herself wanted to experience the world of the masculine.

I emphasize "masculine" because the man with whom Jean involved herself represented a collective masculine world to her more than a person with whom to build an individual relationship. He symbolized to her more of a transition in her own life from being a girl to being a woman, than he did the beginning of a shared life with a man. In Neumann's terms, Jean entered the paternal uroboric world (Neumann 1959, 71). She had given birth to her female sexuality. The task of building an individual relationship to another person, male or female, lay in her future. Nonetheless, at this point in her life, Jean clearly was bringing into her world a new self-image and a wider capacity to relate to others on the basis of reality rather than of unconscious needs.

In Sara's case, my pregnancy helped her to stop hiding in past failures and to strike out boldly for her own future as a gifted, adult woman. Sara's previous analyst had referred her to me when he felt they were stuck in a hopeless impasse.

Analysis had come to replace life for Sara rather than to enhance it. Her relationship to her analyst had become a substitute for a real relationship to a man of her own. Any effort on his part to analyze this impasse or to dislodge it by terminating treatment made her feel angry and give all her energy to holding on. Such an impasse revived painful memories of many such incidents that Sara had endured as a girl with her mother. Consciously, she herself wanted to be done with treatment. But unconsciously she saw termination under these circumstance as abandonment and defeat.

Referral to me seemed a way out. Her analyst thought she might gain new impetus to move her life forward by working with a woman younger than herself, one who was fully involved with her own life, in her marriage, and in her job. Since Sara, too, wanted to be done with her block against any kind of pressure, she and I worked out a plan together. We set a deadline. We would work for another year and then stop, no matter what. It seemed to me that by setting a deadline—much in the Rankian sense—all the conflicts she felt over attachment and separation would surface quickly (Rank, 1968, 14). Our goal was to lead Sara out of analysis into her own life. She needed to risk mistakes, to dare relationships, and to rely on her own authority and initiative.

We got off to an auspicious start. She immediately felt towards me the anger she always felt towards anyone she saw as an authority who might put pressure on her. Rather than settling into comfortable dependency, as was her wont with analysts, she felt active hostility. Her first dream set the tone of our work. In it, I paid more attention to a vivacious woman friend of hers than I did to her. She stood by, feeling furious and left out. Sara consciously felt this new anger; she dreamed about the anger that heretofore had blocked her unconsciously. The dreams also pointed up a lively shadow figure full of the spunk Sara needed.

We worked hard during the first months to make her awareness of this anger more supple. Our planned termination proved helpful in this task. More than once Sara accused me of forcing her out before she was ready to go. She blurred over the fact that it had been as much her idea as mine. This gave us a chance to see how automatically she projected her initiative onto someone else while saving for herself the negative reaction of feeling rejected.

Whereas Jean's transference invested me with maternal support of her feminine Self, Sara's transference cast me on the side of her shadow. This role of shadow ally also held promise of opening Sara to her own Self, but through a different route. In Sara's first dream, as mentioned above, she felt anger and jealousy over the rapport her friend and I, her new analyst, quickly established. Although Sara admired this vivacious friend that she dreamt about, she also thought her selfish and a bit too charming, especially with men. The dream showed why Sara had been unable to integrate these shadow aspects: she was walled off on the sidelines behind her anger. She needed this shadow side to help her to be more openly "selfish"—to take something in life for herself and not always wait passively for her mother or mother surrogates to provide it.

When authority figures fell into this providing role, Sara was not at all pleased and bitterly resented their power over her. When I refused to wield such authority but threw the initiative back to her, her resistance to acting on her own authority quickly surfaced, along with her anger at being put on the spot. As she expressed these feelings, she gradually came out from behind her wall of passive sabotage. She took more action verbally and emotionally, making clear decisions about her life. She showed spirit. The vitality of her shadow side seemed less opposed to her conscious orientation and now seemed to act as a lively counterpoint.

When I told Sara I was pregnant, a lot of important things happened to her, though not all at once. Her first reaction was conventional congratulations and good wishes. She then took up other matters that were on her mind that day. At the next session she said that she had at first forgotten we had an appointment that day. That had never happened to her in all her years of analysis. Then she became mad that we had set a deadline for our work. It was restrictive and pressuring and made her "blank out." When she came to the words "blank out" she started to cry, saying she knew it was my pregnancy that made her forget the session. She had blanked out because my pregnancy reminded her of how much she had blanked out in her life. She wished more than anything else that she had had children of her own. In missing motherhood, she felt she had missed the purpose of her life, which was, as she saw it, "to recreate mankind in the best sense." She grieved, "not the instinctual thing, but the missed years of bearing and rearing children, the experience of my own emotional nature."

That night, Sara dreamt:

> There is a wedding going on of many young women. Most of them carry one bouquet and some are with two bouquets. The women with two bouquets are brides without bridegrooms. One of them gives her bouquets to a young girl in the bridal party.

After this dream, Sara said, she cried for two days. She identified with the groomless brides. They were also brides about to enter womanhood, she said, although on different paths from the usual ones for women. Her feeling about them was sadness. Sara felt this dream described her own way, a way that was different from the conventional path of marriage, home, and children. What this unconventional path held in store was not at all clear, but Sara felt both kinds of brides were undergoing a ritual of initiation into womanhood.

Later that week Sara dreamt again:

> There is inserted in my vagina a hollow clear plastic tube so the menstrual blood can flow through in a constant flow. I look at myself and see that the tube has cut the outer lip of my vagina, which is hanging limp, raw and bleeding.

The dream image of the constant flow of blood from this source suggested many themes to her—that her blood flowed and she was not congealed and dried up; that it was blood connected with giving birth to new life; and that pain was involved in getting life flowing again. Indeed, she had been cut raw. The dream also depicted a kind of sexual penetration of her sexual center—by a tube that would not let her close up again. The flow of blood was to be uninterrupted. The menstrual blood was not to feed an actual child but to flow constantly from Sara into the world. The dream seemed to say that her capacity to give of herself to create new life was to be a means of keeping herself open to the world.

One day in the late spring, when I was already quite big with child, Sara remarked on entering the office, "Well, I hope you don't lose your baby." She seemed unaware of what she had said, let alone of its hostility. When I pressed her, she remembered how her mother used to belittle her. She felt again the pain of her mother's failure really to "support" her. Thus her remark about my losing my baby seemed really to be a way of saying she felt her mother had not carried her long enough—until she was strong enough to stand on her own. Whereas Sara already knew she had identified with me, wanting a fruitfulness she associated with me for herself, she now discovered that she also had identified with my unborn baby, whom she saw receiving a secure mothering that she herself had been denied.

The roots of her hostile remark to me were thus traceable to this sense of deprivation that preceded any sense of loss. She was angry at having thus been deprived, and also sad that it had happened. The uncovering of this deeper context to her anger and her feelings of loss seemed gradually to set them in a different context. She perceived more candidly what had been and what had not been available to her in her life. She saw her parents as fallible human beings conditioned by their own backgrounds and limitations rather than as malicious tyrants or abandoners. This unsentimental contemplation of the emotional and psychological facts of her childhood shifted Sara's stubborn judgment of her mother to a more flexible appreciation of her mother's inability to give what she did not have, probably because no one had given it to her. Sara sensed a bond with all human suffering. This acceptance of human frailty allowed her gradually to accept herself, both her past and her present, and to think less of what was lost and more of what was still to be found.

This movement toward self-affirmation was carried even further when Sara became aware, through others' reactions to her, that she constellated an impression of herself as frail yet bitchy, girlish yet elderly, sad yet hostile, unfulfilled yet rigidly rejecting life. She appeared too young and weak to fend for herself, yet too hard and repelling for anyone to want to get close to her. Sara was astonished to realize all this; she did not feel herself to be old or frail or bitchy.

At this point the issue of pregnancy came into focus. Sara gradually had come to see that she had projected onto a literal pregnancy that was no longer physically possible for her all of her capacity for fruitfulness as a person—her initiative, her power to sustain relationship, her hope for a lively and emotionally rich future. She thus made her creativity inaccessible to herself by projecting it into the past. Onto a literal physical capacity to bear children now denied her, she projected her psychic creativity. She was presenting to others a self-image of a spinster barren in all the areas of her life. Moreover, by projecting her present originality onto a past no longer available, Sara was succumbing to passive resentment: what she wanted had not been given her and now it was too late; she had missed out forever. With a mixture of moping and bitterness Sara fought anyone who challenged this view of herself by refusing to participate in any present ongoing relationship.

Sara finally became fully aware of this self-image and slowly freed herself from it. She ceased to give off the girlish old-maid tonalities that maneuvred others into protecting or avoiding her. Sara genuinely gave birth to a new part of her psyche. She brought into consciousness the neglected shadow elements of initiative, spunk, and emotional responsiveness. Sara's first dream after learning of my pregnancy, of brides entering womanhood by an unconventional route, can be seen in retrospect as a psychic initiation. Her dream of being penetrated and permanently opened so that her blood could flow uninterruptedly into the world can be seen as a remarkable and altogether positive kind of psychic penetration and conception which would issue forth in a new relation to herself and to others.

For Sophie my pregnancy exploded the fantasy that she lived only as a helpless infant within the protective orbit of my personality. When she had begun analysis, six years before, her adaptation was so marginal that I focused entirely on establishing a relationship of trust and security with her. There were many times when she burst out with desperate appeals for acceptance coupled with violent assertions that she could never be accepted. She insisted I prove to her that she was accepted yet concluded that any sign would, a priori, be insufficient. Her early experiences of deep rejection automatically set in motion distrust of anyone who seemed to find her acceptable. Such acceptance also let loose in her what felt like a rapacious hunger to be affirmed by others. This alarmed her.

She felt she could control her violent needs for affection only if she were treated coolly or with hostility. To be treated warmly terrified her, even though she longed for it, because it threatened her self-control. Sophie dreaded the love she desired. She was caught; she could not survive without love, yet she felt love would destroy both her and her loved objects. The way out she devised for herself was hostility. She would attack any person who showed her warmth. But it was so transparent an attack that her helplessness showed through, thus checking the other person's angry responses.

Sophie's transference to me was strongly positive from the beginning—dependent, tenacious. She saw me as a good mother figure. Her outbursts of anger and scorn towards me, when they occurred, were usually connected with her difficulty in accepting that she felt such positive feelings for someone; she feared her dependence on me. Dependency left her helpless and in my control, she concluded. How could she be sure I would be any more reliable than those people on whom she had depended in the past? To try to end her grim anxiety, she would attempt to provoke me into nasty fights. She was alert to any hint of abandonment, keenly perceptive of the slightest change in my moods from session to session. For me, working with Sophie was tense, trying, interesting, instructive, moving, and at times maddening. The vehicle for analysis was, reasonably enough, our relationship, but much more than is usually the case. Sophie's way of becoming aware of herself and her capacities to relate to others seemed to be through experiencing her reactions to me and mine to her.

As our work went on, Sophie's anxiety lessened. She obtained a good job, one worthy of her gifted mind. Later she left this job to do freelance work. Eventually she began a new lesbian relationship. Although still beset with a compulsion to play out mother or daughter roles, Sophie worked hard to build a friendship rather than just act out her conflicting feelings.

We had focused on the transference throughout our work together and had returned to it repeatedly during the last year. By now Sophie had come to accept her own acceptability and my esteem for her. She had given up many of her aggressive maneuvers to manipulate me and others into proving the reliability of our affection for her. She knew she still held me in the maternal role and resented anything about me that threatened that image. One such threat had been my marriage, which had occurred a year before. She felt abandoned, left out. Yet she also felt impatient with her own insistence that I remain in a maternal role. We analyzed the roots of her transference, worked on dreams that brought it up, talked about her conscious reactions to me, and explored her need to rely on nurturing aspects newly developed in her own psyche. Nothing availed. Her transference persisted.

It was at this time I became pregnant. When I told Sophie, she cried and then became angry. "I'm hurt," she said, "and it's obnoxious that I should be hurt. It feels as if you're responsible; therefore, I want to pay you back." She felt flooded with memories of going to live with her stepmother and the betrayal she felt when her stepmother became pregnant three months after her arrival as a new member of her father's family. She had felt left out; there was no room for her. Now she felt with me as she had with her stepmother—all the support was gone just when she needed it most.

Sophie's initial reactions to my pregnancy intensified in our isolation from one other for many weeks after this session. During some sessions, she felt just the deep hurt of being abandoned. She lost her awareness that this was one of several feelings and fell into total identification with her own sense of abandonment. She lived for her abandonment; it was all there was. During other sessions, she was consumed with rage at what she felt was my betrayal of her. At these times she identified with her rage and could find no distance from it. She wanted revenge; she hated the baby growing in me; she quarrelled and picked fights saying I should have adopted a baby if I had any concern for the world's plight—that is, I should have adopted her; she would also say I probably only wanted a boy. In other sessions she would stand back from her feelings of hurt and anger and trace their roots in her own childhood. She groped for a fleeting sense that her feelings for me were not simply those of a child to its parent and that my pregnancy did not threaten the trust between us.

The most striking effect of my pregnancy on Sophie was her shock at how much she had related to me on a transference basis. She said that although we had often talked about her placing me in the role of mother, she had never really seen it until I became pregnant. Not until I was going to be someone's real mother did she see how much she had made me her fantasy mother. The blinding clarity of this insight "smashed to smithereens" her feeling for me as her mother. She could not get over the fact that she had really felt (and still did feel when she had an upsurge of rage) that she was my child and I was her mother. It was incomprehensible to her that she should have made such an assumption with such certainty. For one thing, it was so unrealistic; the closeness in our ages would not support such a feeling; yet she had felt it. Only in what to her was a sudden smashing of her unconscious image of me as parent did she realize to what extent the unconscious existed and influenced her. That there was such an unconscious realm that could so affect her perceptions, actions, and emotions amazed her and filled her with wonder. She said that she felt "an implosion of consciousness"; now she knew what I had been trying to get across to her all these years: namely, that she gave me attributes that belonged to her, and needed to belong to her.

This "smashing to smithereens" of her mother transference had immediate positive effects. Sophie articulated some of them in response to a dream she had soon after the pregnancy news so unsettled her:

> *I am in my family's home. My room has a terrace that faces the ocean. All of a sudden I discover that if I open the window of that terrace onto the ocean, horrible spiders will come into the house. I see one huge one and instead of running as I usually do, I try to kill it. But it is incredibly fast and elusive. I feel and see it run right under my leg, but I still try to get it. I persist, but there are too many of them creeping in. At the back of the house I discover another sort of terrace, only this one is screened in tight and covered over and very gloomy. There is nothing to see from it except a highway with trucks passing. I know that I can stay there and read and be safe from spiders, but I realize what a sealed, dark place it is. I stand there considering my choices; staying safe but in a prison-like gloom or opening the windows onto the other terrace where, though spiders might come in, I can also see the ocean.*

Sophie sensed that the dream images showed her position exactly. The ocean, which often turned up in her dreams, represented to her unplumbed depths of her feelings and of life itself. In commenting on other dream images, Sophie said:

> The windows that might be opened on that ocean of unexplored feelings are openings to me in the work that we do together. Your pregnancy was truly a total shock to me—it opened a window and some hideous spiders of feeling I never knew even existed in me came crawling through to my sight. My alternative to facing up to the spiders of fear is to remain in jail. A good part of me does believe that the spiders—of anxiety, of being unloved, of being abandoned, of being helpless—will kill me, but at least in the dream I was willing to fight them. And I do fight; you just hear mainly of the times I don't fight.

Without a protective mother role transferred onto me, Sophie began to fight her own battle with her anxiety. Instead of wanting me to do it for her, she drew on resources our work had already given her with which to meet these creeping anxieties that her dream depicted as the spider threat, a common and archetypal symbol for the negative mother. I gradually became for her a genuine support rather than someone to manipulate into being a substitute for her own efforts. Heretofore her aggression had exploded into rage at me for refusing to take charge of her life. Now she began to channel her aggression into acts of self-assertion. She stood up for herself, for example, in her work and did not allow fellow employees to take advantage of her by overworking her or passing their work onto her. In her new relationship with her woman friend, she resisted her own temptation to play the baby and to manipulate her friend into the mother role. What is more, she also refused to play mother herself; instead, she struggled to establish a different kind of connection, one based on choice, affection, and the value of their history together.

For Sophie, it was as if my conception of a baby had triggered in her a new conception of herself. Whereas before she saw herself as existing within a maternal womb, or at least desperately wanting to do so, and felt full of bitter, impotent rage because she was too big to go back to that unconscious, tiny state of being, now she accepted that she was really born, really alive. She existed independently of me or anyone else, with her own capacities to breathe, to feel, to decide, to try—even though those capacities often felt shaky to her. Sophie gave birth to herself as a person quite capable of self-support. She could live out in the open, supply her own sources of feeling and self-sustaining commitment.

Of the three women, Sophie was most upset by having to recognize that the pregnancy signified sexual relations with a man, my husband. She could no longer, then, deny the existence of men. The mother-daughter unity was penetrated and disrupted by the presence of the masculine. Sophie expressed contempt for me for "joining the enemy," yet she felt envy, too, and acknowledged it. Men were still distant beings to her, far out of her reach. By conceiving herself as an independent person, she began to feel free to choose the relationship with her woman friend. She remained in the lesbian world, but now more from choice than compulsion. She intensified her efforts to structure her sexual relationship along the lines of true mutuality and self-giving.

Conclusion

Initially the news of my pregnancy provoked negative reactions in all three women. Jean found her identity under what she saw as my motherly protection and felt rejected by the conception of a real child. Sara had identified with me as a woman capable of having a baby and a fruitful life. When I became pregnant, she had to face the full psychological meaning of the fact that pregnancy was no longer a physical possibility for her. Sophie literally had thought of herself as a baby and had indulged in the fantasy that she was my infant. My pregnancy exploded this fantasy; Sophie clearly was enraged at having to face reality, and felt betrayed. All of these women had believed unconsciously that their identifications with what I represented to them could somehow magically solve their problems. Psychologically, they relied on me as a saving maternal figure and saw themselves as dependent daughters. My pregnancy exposed this belief as illusion.

The impact of my pregnancy on the transference of these three women initiated a revolution in each of them. They gave up the daughter role and relinquished their unconscious insistence that I play the mother counterpart. My pregnancy triggered a new self-conception in each of them: each emerged from her all-embracing identification with the unconscious to seek life from the perspective of a feminine ego. With this emergence, each woman gained a new sense of herself and a new style of being in relationship. Each had to nurture this new attitude to self and world just as a mother must slowly bring up a newborn child, and each found herself capable of doing so, in spite of all the anxieties, uncertainties, and fears, so much like those which confront all who give birth.

References

Deutsch, H. 1944. *Psychology of Women.* 2 vols. New York: Grune & Stratton.

Jung, C. G. 1938. Psychological aspects of the mother archetype. In *CW* 9i. New York: Pantheon, 1959.

————. 1941. Psychological aspects of the Kore. In *CW*, vol. 9i. New York: Pantheon, 1959.

Neumann, E. 1959. The psychological stages of feminine development. Zurich: Spring.

Rank, O. 1968. *Will Therapy and Truth and Reality.* New York: Knopf.

Ulanov, A. B. 1971. *The Feminine in Jungian Psychology and in Christian Theology.* Evanston, Ill.: Northwestern University Press.

5

The Search for Paternal Roots:
Jungian Perspectives on Fathering

Jung's theory of depth psychology is distinguished by its emphasis on the unconscious as an objective reality, exerting specific pressures on our subjective consciousness, and so producing compensating viewpoints and directions of development. The unconscious does not determine consciousness in a fixed way, but it operates constantly in the background. Nevertheless, its existence positively demands to be acknowledged. Jung articulated his observation of the psyche's objectivity and its effects on our conscious identities in his theory of the archetypes, seeing the archetypes functioning in our psyches as ready-made forms or possibilities of behavioral and emotional response activated by concrete life situations (Jung 1942, pars. 195–96). In the grip of archetypes, we feel ourselves caught by a force larger than ourselves, accompanied by clusters of images that we come to recognize as falling into certain unmistakable types. We register this kind of event as one of the deep human experiences of our lives.

One such important experience is that of having a father, not just physically but psychically. Our images of what a father is or might be, Jung says, are influenced by our experiences of our actual father, of persons who acted toward us as father surrogates, and of the plentiful images of father figures in our culture. Our unconscious introjection of those father images assures that their influence will continue to operate in our adult lives long after we have ceased to be children. Damaged images and painful experiences of the father also live on in us unconsciously like a bruise that does not heal and that makes us continually vulnerable to fresh woundings. It is precisely to repair such damage that many people seek the intervention of psychoanalysis.

In addition to biographical and cultural factors that help make up the father image operating in our psyches, Jung theorizes that our personal image of the father is unconsciously influenced by the father archetype in which the general human experience of fathering is compounded. Thus our subjective personal notion of "my father" has in its background an objective, impersonal image of "the father" that is called into play by what happens or fails to happen in our conscious experience of father. Hence, when Jung talks about the "father imago" and its influence in our lives, he means three things: our conscious concepts and images of what a father is, influenced in large part by memories of experiences with our own fathers and father surrogates; our unconscious introjection of how we saw our fathers when we were children, which often is at variance with the person our father actually was, a mixture of distorting projections and accurate perceptions; and the archetypal images of the father set into play by our own experiences (Jung 1959, par. 37; Jung 1912, 44 n. 5).

The Father Archetype

The father archetype consists of a cluster of images and associated behavioral and emotional possibilities of response that together convey the human picture of what "father" is and what it stands for symbolically. First among these is father as procreator, prime mover, begetter of new being (Jung 1938, pars. 198–99). In contrast to the tangible material birth process associated to the maternal, the engendering activity of the father is characterized as intangible and invisible, rather more a spirit than a human person. Frequent symbols of this father spirit are the wind, the voice, the spermatic Word, the life breath that enlivens the soul and takes it beyond the limits imposed by the body (Jung 1912, par. 396; Neumann 1973, 189, 197).

The very invisibility of the sort of spirit associated with the father brings with it certain vulnerabilities and dangers. For example, one can easily mock this "spiritual" activity as entirely imaginary, especially if one contrasts it with the palpable fleshy activities of the feminine—conception, pregnancy, and birth. Another equally dangerous temptation involved in the use of this kind of "spiritual" language is to drift off into abstractions and impossibly generalized speculations, altogether forsaking concrete connections to real persons and events. But none of this should make us forget the special values that come with this interpretation of fathering, for in it the father is associated symbolically with a particular kind of consciousness that is uniquely capable of discrimination between self and other. It is a form of consciousness that enables us to stand back from instinctual processes happening within us and to conceive of an individual identity or ego development without falling into the archaic collectivity of the impersonal unconscious (Jung 1953, pars. 92, 159). It is because of this experience of ego differentiation that the father is sometimes symbolized as the very *principium individuationis* (Jung 1938, par. 40; Jung 1959, par. 301).

The father as a symbol of consciousness extends to general cultures as well as to individual persons. In mythology, for example, the king as father of his realm usually represents the dominant type of ego-consciousness reigning at any given time in any given society. He stands for the ordering principle operating within that particular culture, asserting the collective values of his civilization. The king's association with divinity underlines the supreme value of ego-consciousness and its creative powers (Jung 1963, par. 501).

The oft-repeated fate of kings in mythological stories—that they die and a successor must be found among their sons, or that they are ailing and must be regenerated—points to transformation rites that are peculiar to the father archetype and to the way in which this archetype finds its renewal in relation to the son. The father represents the wisdom of tradition, "the precious acquisition of our forefathers, namely the intellectual differentiation of consciousness" (Jung 1953, par. 84). In the guise of the "wise old man," another persistent archetype, the father instructs the son figure in the traditional ways of the spirit that are embodied collectively in the culture's dominant religious, philosophical, or educational systems (Neumann 1973, 173). In this archetypal guise, a father communicates to the young the spirit by which one can live, and the truth that inspires and guides the life-giving activities.

The authority of the father finds constant renewal through being projected and embodied in different symbolic forms and persons chosen, consciously or unconsciously, to fit different historical and societal conditions. Traditional wisdom thus continues to live through its reembodiment in fresh forms that every younger generation gives to values passed on from a previous generation. The spirit of paternal authority is by its nature formless and relative, "an expression of the mysterious dynamic of life itself" that finds ever fresh concretization in the fluctuating development of values within the group (Neumann 1973, 189).

The historical and relative nature of the father figures who embody the father archetype is clearly illustrated by one of its negative manifestations. Instead of begetting and inspiriting the development of consciousness, the negative side of the father thwarts it by a tyrannous refusal to give up power and make way for the son, as the world's literature, folktales, and dramas constantly remind us. Instead of yielding to the process of transformation, the negative force of the father blocks further development of consciousness or pushes it in the wrong direction, insisting on rigid adherence to the old values. Some of the pervasive malaise of our present culture arises from a split between fathers and sons typified in the opposition of the so-called establishment and the radical counterculture. A father may capture and then destroy his son's consciousness by refusing to support its independent development. He feels any innovation of the son as a betrayal. He may have so concretized the values of his own generation that they have become petrified relics for him. If his son complies and identifies totally with his father, he becomes "bound by traditional morality," as Erich Neumann puts it, "castrated by convention" (Neumann 1973, 187). At the opposite extreme, a father may fail to represent and pass on the legacy of his culture's values to his young. He then falls victim to an exaggerated formlessness that concretizes nothing and leaves his children no guidance by which to take their bearings.

If a son is too firmly identified with the formless invisible penetrating spirit of consciousness, he loses touch with the other side of his masculine spirit, which is expressed in the body and the unconscious in the blunt terms one finds in the male force in nature. The father archetype is also symbolized by such natural forces as the heat and the blazing light of the sun that warms the earth and in human terms shows itself as an emotional ecstasy that seizes consciousness, breaking in upon it and lifting it well beyond itself. Thus if a man identifies one-sidedly with the celestial aspect of spirit, living in the name of clarity at a distance from the natural cycles of the body, he loses his roots in the earthy side of the masculine spirit. He is cut off from access to the unconscious and cut off, too, from any strong or significant assertion of his sexuality and aggressive energy. Such an unbalanced development will produce a masculine identity that may be lucid but is also pallid and without emotional vitality. The estrangement from a natural maleness may also appear in its opposite form, where a man falls victim periodically to seizures from the unconscious that manifest themselves as possession by unconscious affectivity through crude bursts of sexuality or aggressive rage that obliterate all consciousness of what is happening to him.

Although Jung strongly emphasizes the archetypal backgrounds of consciousness, he stresses just as much the role of life circumstances that evoke our latent archetypal dynamisms. Thus for him the intrapsychic dimension is matched by the equally important interpersonal and world dimensions that call the archetypes into play and upon which the archetypes must depend for their release. If we suffer the loss of a father, for example, not only do our external lives show impoverishment, but fundamental, if buried, psychic factors do not sufficiently emerge, leaving the soul as wounded as the deprived consciousness.

Two Men Who Lost Their Fathers

The following two descriptions illustrate the effects of the loss of a father on a son's psychic development. For each man, the father archetype was not sufficiently embodied because of early loss of the father, through death in the first case and divorce in the second. Each son suffered great psychic difficulty in experiencing the emergence of his ego from his unconscious and in developing the clear conviction that he would be able to live securely rooted in himself, that is, connected to his unconscious. Each man felt alternatively cut off from the unconscious or submerged in it.

The experiences of these two men also illustrate the startling fact of the objectivity of the psyche, a fact upon which Jung places much emphasis. Just as the father archetype does not exist independently of life circumstances like a psychic mechanism that goes into operation automatically, but rather depends on the stimulus of interpersonal experience for its evocation in a person's life, so do life circumstances depend on psychic factors to complete them. In a deeply damaging situation, where a boy loses his father by death or divorce, the damage is not necessarily irreparable. Not only can a new father figure reevoke the father archetype, but the autonomy of the archetype can also press for its own completion, constellating situations in which the broken psychic connections may be rejoined and allowed to develop in their own appropriate way. Thus the healing process may work simultaneously from within as well as from without. This joining of inner and outer energies to assuage and repair the terrible pain of psychic wounds and to nurture growth typifies the comforting aspect of the spirit often associated with the father archetype. Jung compares it to the action of the Comforter of

Scripture, to God's Spirit: "The Holy Ghost is a comforter like the Father, a mute, eternal, unfathomable One in whom God's love and God's terribleness come together in wordless union (Jung 1942, par. 260).

The Case of Simon

Simon, a middle-aged man, was only five when his father died suddenly from a heart attack. The family was abruptly forced to move back to Europe from the distant tropical country where they had been living. Europe was then in the midst of the travail of World War II, so that as a small boy Simon suffered multiple traumas simultaneously: the death of his father, the leaving of his home in a warm colorful climate for the cold winter of Europe, and the emotional chaos of war. Simon was the only boy in his family, with two older sisters and one younger one. He said that as a child he often felt left out of the family, unable to be an intrinsic part of his sisters' games or the female world they shared with their mother. Simon experienced his mother as rigid and undemonstrative emotionally except for occasional outbursts of rage that only made him feel guilty and frightened. He sensed he could not really touch his mother who "hated to be mussed up." His mother never remarried.

Before his father died, Simon felt rejected by him. He remembered his father as a man accomplished in his profession, as a man of reserved temperament, with little expression in him either of anger or affection. In contrast, Simon thought of himself as a dreamy, curious boy, full of fantasy and feeling. Simon thought as a child that his father did not like his fantasy play with dolls or animals, frowning on it as effeminate. When his father died, Simon felt he now must try to be the "man of the family." But, as he saw it, he failed miserably to fulfill this aspiration. When the family reached Europe they were often on the run and forced to hide from the enemy in their war-torn country. Simon often succumbed to dreadful panic in the face of constant bombing and the recurrent threat of death. He was ashamed of his fear, interpreting it as proof of his own inadequacy and helplessness to "protect" his family in a manly way.

Simon originally entered therapy in his thirties, with a male analyst, out of fear he was schizophrenic. He saw himself as a bundle of split-up parts, drawn simultaneously in homosexual and heterosexual directions and cut off from most feeling, yet periodically possessed by moods of despair or of soaring giddiness and manic inflation. He thought of himself as a highly rational person who could analyze situations logically, yet he longed for some more immediate involvement with life. But any opportunity for emotional involvement with another person simply flooded him with panic. He worked with his first analyst to good effect; he felt stronger and more stable in himself as a result. He chose then to work with me on the feeling and sexual issues that he felt still eluded him. We worked together for two years in both individual and group sessions.

During our work, Simon reported a striking series of images and fantasies that came upon him autonomously. These, he felt, perfectly symbolized his distress. One dominant fantasy theme was mixed with the memory of the boat trip his family took from his tropical homeland to Europe. He felt haunted by his vision of the land slowly disappearing, slipping away from the boat and from him. He saw himself standing alone on the deck, watching the colors of the trees and the ground slowly disappear in the distance. Around him, as far as he could see, there was nothing but endless water and the approaching coldness of the northern climate they were sailing toward. His mother was confined to her cabin with his sisters comforting her. His father's body was in a coffin somewhere on the boat. He was all alone, without even a toy. He remembered being dressed in girls' stockings that had been borrowed as some protection against the cold; he had no winter clothes of his own because he had lived all his young life in a hot climate. This fantasy memory embodied for Simon all his feelings of being cut off from life, sailing alone, feeling homeless, with no clear connection to any other person or to his own identity.

Simon's second fantasy series presented itself in two forms: one being a set of images of his own body, and one being images of a bird. He saw his body in his imagination as half-dead, half-alive. Divided along a north-south axis, his right side was healthy and manly and often colored black, to which Simon associated the vitality and instinctive health of the black persons he had grown up with in his now foreign homeland. His left side appeared as shriveled, inert, a pallid white in color, all but dead. To this side he associated his European nature, his rationality, his civilized personality. His fantasy birds were similarly polarized and frustrated, birds capable of soaring high and yet unable to fly because of a crippled wing. The birds, too, were sometimes colored half-black, half-white. Simon felt these fallen creatures depicted his broken faith in life and his broken spirit. In speaking of them he often broke down into painful sobbing, which, like the birds, was in strong contrast to his usual cool rationality. The grief Simon felt over his father's death and the painful lost relationship to just about every area of his own life overwhelmed his usual cool rational language and accompanying poise. Crying for Simon was not a cathartic relief but a way of losing his safe perch of rationality to fall headlong into the depths of his unassimilated pain.

It was with surprise and pleasure that both Simon and I greeted a new fantasy image that appeared close to the end of the two years we worked together. The image expressed the slow forging of connecting links he had achieved to his undigested pain and the natural life of the unconscious that lay behind it. The new bird image was of a plump, somewhat pedestrian bird that was dappled in black and white. Simon liked this fat creature, felt comfortable with it, and was somewhat amused by its fitting combination of his two "sides." It was a creature of the air yet could walk on the ground. Its color joined black and white and what they symbolized—the instinctive and rational aspects of his own spirit, as well as his associations to his childhood and his acquired European culture. That it made him laugh suggested he was less identified with his pain and less defended from it, less impelled to keep his distance. He could laugh a little more at himself, thus gaining some compassionate perspective on his experience.

Simon chose to end our work when he decided to leave his home in America to return to Europe. One of his purposes for this present journey was to actively reenact his long-ago childhood trauma of the boat trip. Before leaving America, in our last sessions, he dealt with the uprush of memories of that boyhood journey. But this time Simon imaginatively added something new to that trauma. He saw himself now, as an adult man, joining that little five-year-old boy on the boat deck and standing with him affectionately. He felt he had repaired some of his psychic injuries by embodying in the present some of the needed fatherly care and concern for that abandoned boy who had existed so long in a split-off state in his psyche. By connecting himself to his unconscious pain and, bit by bit, trying consciously to suffer it through and digest it, he was no longer unconsciously identified with it or with the abandoned little son. Simon now began to embody some of the father's side of the father-son archetype, reaching in a loving fatherly way toward the part of himself that had gotten stuck in a little boy's pain. Freed from fixation, that left-out dissociated part of his psyche could now begin to grow up to the age and fullness of life of the rest of him.

The Case of Tom

Tom entered therapy when middle-aged. He chose to work with me because he had read my book (Ulanov 1971). He said in our first session he wanted therapy because he felt strangely blocked: "Something holds me back, as if all of me was not living." His first dream after that session was of his father who was then dying of cancer but was denying the gravity of his condition:

> *I am talking intimately and tenderly with my father. His condition of terminal cancer is known to both of us openly. We seem to be reminiscing about the good old days. Then suddenly I see his face full in front of me as it looked thirty years ago. He says, referring to his present physical condition, "It's too bad we can't wrestle right now like we used to." My reaction is total agreement.*

Tom had not lived with his father since he was ten years old, the exact age the dream recalled to him when it depicted his father's face as it had looked thirty years ago. His father had left his mother at that time for another woman, and had not seen Tom or his younger sister in any of the intervening years. The first contact Tom had had with his father after that long period was just at the beginning of our work together. His dying father had asked to see him.

Tom said that in the first ten years of his life, before his parents' divorce, he had felt closer to his father than to his mother. He had many fond memories of sitting on his father's lap or rubbing his face against his father's whiskery cheek. He remembered his father singing to him. Yet he also remembered that he "feared his father's world" and felt his father pushed him too fast sometimes. One such time his father wanted him to put on boxing gloves and fight with him. Tom remembered he did not want to fight, but he finally agreed and struck out at his father, who was in a stooping position to match his son's height. He knocked over his father, who responded with anger while his mother stood by laughing. Tom had many memories of his mother laughing at his father or in some way making fun of him or indicating that he was ridiculous. He felt shame on remembering how often he was drawn into joining with her in mocking and scorning his father. The tension between his parents grew, especially after his father lost his job and was unable to find another during the time of the depression. In many ways he felt that his mother had driven his father away, letting herself get fat, using foul language, being unfeminine and unladylike in comparison to the mothers of his friends. When the divorce came, Tom remembered his mother saying over and over with recurrent panic,

"This can't be happening to us." She began sleeping half the day. It seemed to Tom "as if there were a hole in the bottom of me and all the sand fell out." He felt his mother's sense of defeat very keenly when they had to move in with her mother and live there in two rooms, he the only male in a household of grandmother, mother, and sister.

In his adult life, Tom suffered certain recurring difficulties. One of the most frequent was a feeling of humiliation. He often reviled himself for being "dumb," which did not mean stupidity so much as being unconscious of something happening of which he should have been fully conscious. For example, in treatment with me in both individual and group work, if I said something or if someone in the group said something that Tom did not immediately understand, he felt panic flooding him as if once more he was being "dumb." He mutely endured this attack of self-judgment at first without telling the other group members. Then he would drowse off and even fall asleep. The hostility this behavior aroused in others led to their challenging him. We soon got at what was behind this sinking into unconsciousness. He felt he should have known what was going on or should not have needed whatever interpretation I came to make. He should have been conscious. He resented that the unconscious existed at all. He recalled his boyhood resolution to take care of his mother, grandmother, and sister now that he was the only man in the family, knowing at the same time he was too little to do so. Similarly, whenever the grown-up Tom experienced a number of conflicting emotions at once, he felt humiliated and angry at the confusion that came over him. His falling asleep both provided escape from his painful perplexity and expressed his anger at those persons who aroused conflicting feelings in him. He simply tuned them out.

Another problem of which Tom complained was feeling "disconnected." Sexually, for example, his lovemaking was interrupted by an inexplicable loss of his erection. In his job he frequently alternated between compulsive busywork—in a sense of being an industrious "father" to everyone in his office, giving plentiful advice, always being available—and a contrasting inertia and withdrawal from the work that was his precise professional responsibility. When particularly overextended, he would break down in exasperation and desperation that too much was asked of him. He feared he was unable to give a woman he loved what she wanted and feared that in general he was not masculine enough, that he lacked discipline in his work or sustained determination to see anything through to a clear conclusion. He longed then for the kind of unconditional loving he associated with his father, "that kind of benevolent love you want just to happen to you gratuitously and overwhelmingly."

As with Simon, the main direction of analysis with Tom was to forge connections between his conscious confusion and his unconscious feelings of panic and anger when he judged himself inadequate to a given situation, between his wish to be a father and his unfulfilled need to be a son, between his love for his father and his anger at his father's desertion.

Reconnection with the Father Archetype

Although Simon and Tom were very different people with different cultural, economic, and educational backgrounds, they both suffered a similar wounding in relation to their fathers. Both illustrate the kinds of problems a male may have when his psyche is cut off from its paternal roots, in whatever form. They also illustrate how a natural healing process is set in motion once they find reconnection to the father archetype. In these cases, such reconnection was effected not through the transference of the father role to me nor by way of conferring on me a mothering function. Rather, to use Jung's terminology, I seemed to embody the connecting function of their own psychologies, the anima that connects a man's ego to the deeper regions of his unconscious. Let me illustrate.

Both Simon and Tom felt only "half-formed." Simon depicted this feeling in his split body-images and fantasies of half-dead birds. Tom felt "dumb," unconscious where he should have been conscious. Thus both suffered a drastic abridgement of the begetting function of the father archetype, which they experienced sexually as fear of loss of virility, actual impotence, or confused sexual identity. They experienced that abridgement generally as a failure to sustain involvement with otherness—in Simon's case with another person, in Tom's case with his work. They both felt their egos as weak, without secure masculine identity, and deeply feared the strong pull of the unconscious. Simon feared he would be engulfed in his own pain if he allowed himself to feel. Tom feared he would sink more profoundly into the pervasive sleepy confusion he knew so well.

Both Simon and Tom tried to be fathers at an early age, when still in fact boys and sons, as if to protect themselves from the terrible loss of their own fathers. Both grew up to enter fatherly professions, where others came to them to learn, to get comfort and advice. Both felt that their work was threatened by the unsatisfied longing to be a son. Hence, they both became rigid and compulsive father figures, stuck in their roles without promise of renewal.

The two men felt weighed down by responsibility and inwardly impoverished, as if there was no one to offer nourishment to them. Turning to women availed little and their sexual difficulties soon arose, because what they needed was sure connection to a generative source of meaning and order that would support their own ego development and not a mere sexual acting-out. Both men needed a conscious connection to the transforming dynamism of the masculine, symbolically depicted as the renewal of the father through the son—that is, renewal of the more developed ego parts of his psyche (the "father") by fresh new contents (the "son") always coming from the unconscious. Lacking the connection, both men alternated between playing the exhausting role of father figure for others, giving away more than they had to give, and the equally enervating role of the rebellious son who defied those in authority without receiving any nourishment from them. Simon frequently felt trapped by rules and regulations, against which he vented his anger. He said at those times he "was flying high, free!" No one could touch him. Similarly, Tom often sabotaged his own work by not giving reports on it to his superiors, simply ignoring their requests, whatever they were. Each man was riveted to his identification with either the father or son aspect of the father archetype, with little understanding that these were simply two sides of the same reality and either of them could become the means for the experience of self-renewal.

Instead of their strong emotions recharging them or pointing the way to new patterns of behavior, each man felt his aggression and his sexuality split off from the rest of him, with no hope of renewing the structures within which he lived. Each felt threatened. Each thought he had to choose between an ordered existence that was half-dead or a tumultuous and chaotic one. Simon, for example, at times succumbed to instinctual orgies of one kind or another— eating great quantities of highly seasoned food, dancing wildly far into the night, or engaging in sexual tempests with little or no sustained relationship to his partners. When let loose, his anger took giddy unrelated turns, poking sadistic fun at his adversary, leading him into manic expenditures of energy as if he never had to come down to earth again. Tom, on the other hand, would let himself go in periods of inertia and messiness. His aggression would find a passive route to its target, either masking his sense of omnipotence in a desire to help everyone or forcing him or the other person to hold on tenaciously even when he had registered signals that the best thing to do was to quit the situation. In both cases, the sex or aggression did not lead back into the center of their lives but rather moved away from it, reenforcing the feeling of ego weakness and of being undermined by forces from below. As a result, each man came to distrust the unconscious. They had little connection to the comforting aspect of the masculine spirit that conveys the unit of instinct-backed emotions and life's order and meaning. They both had lost hope of ever achieving a deep accommodation of consciousness to the unconscious and felt themselves therefore unconnected and unsupported.

Inwardly Simon and Tom suffered a gap where there should have been a connection between consciousness and the unconscious, just as they had suffered the great gap left by their departing fathers. The forces of their unconscious feeling lives—of sex and aggression —had not achieved sufficient humanization but had simply burst out in episodes and then receded out of reach of their egos. Because each felt his mother to be more rejecting than nurturing, to each the maternal birth-giving aspects of the unconscious seemed very far away from conscious use. Each man held at bay a large store of repressed material. Simon, who consciously felt rejected by his father and angry at him, had repressed what love he and his parent had shared. Mixed with his pain at having lost his father was the love he felt he and his father had shared but not openly expressed. Tom, who retained memories of an open love for his father, needed to face and to feel consciously his strong outrage that his father could have left him and not asked to see him again until he was actually dying.

It was at the point of making these connections that each man's work in analysis found its strength and clarity. My principal role in each case was as an agent of connection to the unconscious. Neither man related to me as if I myself were a parent figure and neither transference was dominated by sexual feelings. Unlike a maternal surrogate who would be identified to her analysand for a time as the unconscious, I seemed rather to be experienced by each man as a receptive and focused awareness of the unconscious. For quite a while I carried this function for each man in our work together. Then gradually each man took it over for himself. Simon began to let himself consciously feel pent-up pain that he had repressed. He began to see how he could use his fine rational powers to be compassionate and eventually to understand his father's point of view. Increasingly, he felt that his reason could live alongside his feelings, each stimulating the other. In allowing himself to feel this pain, Simon began to feel as well the pent-up caring he had in general withheld from life. He felt lighter, happier, on the way to risking more feeling involvement with others. Tom became more aggressive in our sessions, trying to shape their focus and outcome in a direction he chose. In the group he relinquished his overeager concern with others and concentrated upon what he wanted to get for himself. This act of connecting to himself brought him into authentic contact with the rest of the group members in much the same way as he had begun to connect his outer and inner selves, his conscious and unconscious lives.

Tom traced the source of his anger to his own unconsciousness, indeed to the fact of the unconscious existing at all. He had always felt he should not be unconscious; he should know the things he did not know. What came to light was not Tom's unwillingness to accept limitations, but rather his angry disappointment that his father had not been there as he grew up to instruct him in things, to teach him how to live. His father should have been there; he could not accept the fact that there were things he did not know because his father had not taught them to him. It was not, he finally realized, the unconscious that should not exist; it was the absence of his father that should not have been allowed.

Both Simon and Tom, then, in the course of their analysis, effected reconnection to lost paternal roots. After initial periods of mistrust toward me and the split-off unconscious I symbolized, each began to make the painful descent to the dead, the confused, and the trapped areas of their own psyches. As indicated above, the primary role unconsciously entrusted to me by both men was that of a responsive, present, alert, reacting, personal connecting link to the repressed traumas and cut-off areas of a functioning life held fast in the unconscious. Each man gradually took back to himself this present, alert, and caring attitude toward his own psyche, thus bringing the split-off contents into direct relation to his ego-consciousness. The growth of their egos allowed them to be fed from the unconscious with the things they needed, such as emotion, focus, and some guidance for the future. Moreover, each man now needed less energy to enforce repression and hence had more energy available to him to be released into relationship and work. Reforging connection to the unconscious restored their hope in life and renewed in them a sense of life's possibilities.

Both Simon and Tom had had to develop too early in life a man-sized kind of male responsibility, or at least they had thought they had to do so. Now they had the beginnings of psychic maturity and some of the connections that came with it. They began to grow roots downward. They felt more grounded in being; their confidence in themselves increased. They each felt something like sureness. Simon chose to embark on another journey across the sea to try to see if his roots were there in his second homeland in Europe. Tom came to understand his former rejection of the unconscious and now willingly allowed himself to connect to it in periods of dreamy imagination and meditation. His confidence grew with his ability to make connections in his own way and with his own authority to his work, to the people he loved, and to the meaning he found in life. His dreams reflected a buoyant sense of renewed life in such humorous examples as the following dream. In it different aspects of longing and aggressive self-assertion are united in the same psychic reality; a down-to-earth humanity is linked up to cosmic aspiration.

> I was talking to D., who is a big strong Bronx kid with a warm personality and soft heart. He is saying either, "I want to be a major," or "I want to be in charge," or "I want to be a bear." I say to him, "You are big enough to be Ursa Major—that's the big bear in the sky—that would make you Major Bear."

The experience of both these men led to the heartening and surprising discovery that when the connecting links to their own paternal roots were reestablished, the inner psychic momentum of the father archetype was again set in motion. The missing father was, they saw, to be found within them. Something interrupted and disconnected was once more joined. This restoration of the father archetype at the center of their lives helped guide each man toward better inner response toward outer situations and strengthened masculine identity. Each man felt more confident of being able to make use of basic life situations that could nurture him and make him grow comfortably within such situations, thus connecting to other persons in a much more vigorous way.

Conclusion

These two cases illustrate a major Jungian conviction: the strength of fathering patterns lies in being open to the ways of bringing together inner and outer life that are distinctively masculine. The full significance of this conviction or perception, based on examples such as these, is still, I think, to be fully grasped. For the present it may be necessary simply to record one analytical experience after another in the exploration of archetypes, so that we can develop that familiarity without which any serious grasp of fathering in the sphere of depth psychology will be impossible. The world of the father has obscure and subtle dimensions that escape easy verbalization. That should not keep us from working attentively and meditatively with its mysteries.

References

Jung, C. G. 1912. *Symbols of Transformation*. CW 5. Princeton: Princeton University Press, 1952.

———. 1938. Psychology and religion. In *CW* 11. New York: Pantheon, 1958.

———. 1942. A psychological approach to the Trinity. In *CW* 11. New York: Pantheon, 1953.

———. 1953. *Psychology and Alchemy*. CW 12. New York: Pantheon.

———. 1959. *Aion*. CW 9ii. New York: Pantheon.

———. 1963. *Mysterium Coniunctionis*. CW 14. New York: Pantheon.

Neumann, E. 1973. *The Child*. New York: Putnam.

Ulanov, A. B. 1971. *The Feminine in Jungian Psychology and in Christian Theology*. Evanston, Ill.: Northwestern University Press.

6

Follow-Up Treatment in Cases of Patient/Therapist Sex

When we begin treatment with a woman who has been sexually involved with her former therapist, we are immediately faced with certain kinds of problems. First, superimposed upon the problem that originally led the patient to seek treatment is now the burning issue of sexual activity with her previous therapist. Establishment of rapport and trust between the patient and her present therapist takes place, or fails to, around discussion of the issue of the patient's sexual affair with her former therapist. Some patients feel they must protect the old therapist and may as a result be unable to register any negative reactions to the sexual encounter. Other patients may be altogether consumed with negative reactions to their old therapist and may then be unable to investigate any part that they may have played in establishing the sexual connection.

A second crucial problem is the countertransference reaction of the present therapist to the events of sexual involvement of the patient and her previous therapist. Of course, countertransference reactions occur to some degree in any treatment, but in this situation they spring up almost immediately and more strongly than usual. Potentially, therefore, such reactions can be injurious to treatment, preventing an easy beginning of the solid affective connection between therapist and patient that is so necessary to the work of therapy.

Typical countertransference reactions include all sorts of anger that such patient-therapist sex had occurred in the first place. If the present therapist is a woman, she may feel some degree of identification with her patient as a woman and genuine outrage at her having been taken advantage of. As we all know, the patient-therapist relationship is not an equal one. Regardless of the circumstances in which sexual activity has occurred, the patient's is the weaker position. In addition, the therapist may feel anger at the violation of professional therapeutic standards in such a case, where acting out not only occurred but was encouraged instead of analysis. We are angry when such a breach of standards damages the integrity of our profession. We feel let down by a colleague.

We may sometimes feel compassion for the former therapist for landing himself and the patient and now us in such a complicated mess. We may feel judgmental toward the former therapist, attempting thereby to protect ourselves from the threat that this kind of thing might also happen to us. By projecting the danger onto our colleague and condemning it there, we avoid directly facing the problem of handling sexual feelings for patients that may occur in ourselves. We may also find ourselves caught in a gossipy interest in what happened between the patient and the previous therapist, an interest that defends us from such a touchy issue by reducing it to petty curiosity. Whatever our reaction, we must deal with it early in the treatment, both in working out our own feelings and in deciding which, if any of them, need to be shared with the patient.

A third problem facing the patient and her present therapist is not only the task of sorting out the original presenting problem from the screen issue of the recent patient-therapist sexual activity but also the tedious procedure of tracing the way back to that point in the previous treatment when therapy stopped and sexuality intervened. To put the same thought another way, we must work back to the point in time where sexual fantasy failed to be treated as fantasy and was taken instead as a substitute for reality. We must recover the sexual fantasy as fantasy.

The Symbolic Nature of Sex

Sexual fantasy is particularly well suited to convey unconscious psychic contents to consciousness. Sexual fantasy enlists the instinctive needs of the body, and its qualities of desire very well express affective longings for satisfactions and security. In addition, its non-rational imagery communicates the yearnings of the soul to unite with something or someone beyond ourself. Our sexual imagery carries our hope to be accepted as we are, for all that we are. In this imagery, we reach beyond ourselves to connect with a transcendent quality of life—with its otherness—through intimate relationship with a concrete other, with a person.

As Medard Boss points out, all patients mature enough for a sexual relationship will find it outside the therapeutic situation (1963, 258). A sexual edge arising in the transference invariably creates an unreal intimacy that masks something else. It is the work of therapy to discover what that something else may be, so that the patient can relate to it consciously.

In general, we can say that sexual imagery that is strongly present in a transference points in a double direction, being at once regressive and prospective. To look at the regressive first, sexual attraction expresses a patient's as yet undifferentiated need to be seen and accepted and valued for whoever she is. The sexual overtones convey the pleasure when one is found to be not only all right, but a unique and cherished person. Whereas in ordinary life this experience makes up part of the wonder and sheer fun of falling in love and being loved in return, in a therapeutic relationship a patient's desire for sexual contact with the therapist expresses a need for a safe place where the patient can work on integrating her sexuality so that it may be made available to her in a real love relationship.

In general, women who feel strong desires for their therapist somewhere suffered damage to their ego-identities in their childhood years and some degree of dissociation of their sexuality from their ego-functioning. Their sexual desire, which inevitably turns up in treatment, comes to symbolize an incestuous longing for union with a parent who is represented in surrogate fashion in the person of the therapist. This longing for a parent mobilizes the patient's energy and desire to repair the past damage done to her ego and to strengthen its relation to her sexuality by reaching back as if to grow up all over again, with better results if at all possible. The interweaving of symbolic meanings shows the delicacy and complexity of the matter. A woman's sexual desire for her therapist contains her longing for a good parent figure in relation to whom she can heal the damage done to her feminine identity.

We can see, then, the enormous harm that can be done to a patient if these sexual feelings are taken literally instead of being appreciated for their symbolic value. Symbolically, they carry to the patient's consciousness her own sexual longings and her own efforts to heal the breach between her inadequate ego and her sexuality. Not only is the chance to undo previous injury lost, but the previous damage is simply reenforced and perhaps made permanent. We can easily empathize with the fury some women feel after sexual activity with their therapists. They know they have been betrayed both by the therapist and by themselves.

What is needed here is analysis of the regressive aspects of this sexual material. How does the material symbolize a woman's dissociated sexuality? How does it suggest the inadequacy of the patient's ego? For example, the content of a woman's sexual fantasies may center on a little girl wanting to please her father. Then the therapist and patient will be presented with a direct line to a major source of the difficulty in her past relationship to her father. Another woman may fantasize about her power to seduce the therapist, thinking how she might "get him." Hidden in her sexual fantasy is a power fantasy. In turn, the power fantasy may conceal a woman's weak ego trying to compensate for her feelings of helplessness by using power ploys that will make her therapist feel helpless. Guggenbühl-Craig (1971, 61–62) suggests that a patient's efforts to seduce her therapist may mask a wish to destroy the therapist in his professional role as therapist.

The regressive aspect of the sexual symbolism in such a patient's fantasies will always point to the salient relationships and experiences in the patient's past that need to be analyzed reductively. The compelling sexual imagery must be reduced to its originating causes. Having been sorted out and consciously integrated, these patterns no longer need repeat themselves compulsively. The patient's conscious execution of choice may now intervene.

Looked at prospectively, the incest motif hidden in a patient's sexual fantasies about her therapist functions symbolically in itself. As Jung emphasizes, the incest symbol in any one of us expresses our unconscious urge to unite with our own being—to become a self, one and indivisible and self-originating (Jung 1946, pars. 460, 471). Because this urge toward individual wholeness is so vital in us, its symbolic structures exert a fascination on our consciousness, vividly conveyed by insistent sexual tonalities.

The prospective aspect of a patient's sexual transference gathers up more than her drive toward ego-repair and the reliving of past relations to her parents or parent figures. The prospective direction of the symbolism leads a patient's ego to reach beyond its own borders to connect with her whole psyche and its non-ego elements. Jung talked about these elements as archetypes, as unconscious capacities to respond to elemental human experiences. Concrete life circumstances and relations evoke these capacities, which evidence themselves as clusters of spontaneous imagery. These then arouse instinctive emotional behavioral reactions in us toward those elemental human experiences.

A woman, for example, who unconsciously looks for a better fa-

ther in her therapist, in order to repair damage done to her feminine identity in her relationship with her actual father, may work
through this "father complex" in the transference setting. At the
core of the complex lie images of a father principle that exceeds the
dimensions of her therapist's personality, just as it did her own father's personality. Both father and therapist are finite human beings who cannot concretize in a personal relationship all the images
of the masculine in its fatherly roles, roles with which a particular
woman may need to come to grips. She must build her own relation
to those archetypal images of the masculine. Some women, for example, who get involved sexually with their therapists know that
more is at stake for them than either a personal relationship to
their therapist or the working through of the experience of having
a good father that was missed in childhood. They sense the sudden
burgeoning of what can be called "ultimate issues." They project
onto the therapist a larger-than-life significance, giving him authority over their souls, so to speak, feeling as if summoned,
through him, to be and become their true selves. These feelings
are—as they always have been—prototypical human associations
to the powerful impact of fathering at its archetypal best. Clustered
around the image of the father are emotions of being called out of
comfortable identification with a protecting womb (such as, for example, mother, home environment, accepted ideology, or religion) to
set forth toward the goal of discovering who one is in oneself—
individually, not on the basis of inheritance—and to discover what
actual value beyond oneself one is called upon to serve.

The analysis of this level of a patient's sexual fantasies does not
ask reductively where this fantasy came from. Rather, the analysis
must proceed synthetically, as if asking where the fantasy leads.
What, we want to know, is it pointing towards? Mixed in with the
patient's sexual longing is her urge to become her very own self,
with direct connection to elemental human experiences forged between her adult ego and an archetypal element, no longer mediated
through a parent figure or his surrogate as of necessity was the
case when she was a little girl.

The synthetic quality of this line of analysis focuses on piecing together a woman's present and past experiences, and her conscious
ego-knowledge with archetypal elements in order to construct a
larger center of personality, that core of being that Jung calls the
Self. A mature woman can connect and relate to the masculine in a
more direct and personal way than a young girl can—not by proxy,
not simply through unconscious images of her father, brother, or

the "male." She has grown up from a girl who placed the authority outside herself into a woman who finds her own authority deep within.

This synthesizing work may produce several practical results. By integrating her images of the masculine into her own working ego-consciousness, a woman tends to project them less onto men. A loosening of sexual stereotypes follows, and her ability to appreciate individual men as they really are may increase. Instead of rehearsing old complexes in relation to the male, a woman can now build her own individual relation to dominant images of the masculine that are properly central to her own psychology. Her own style of uniting masculine and feminine—either in relation to actual men or to characteristics of her own psychology that she calls masculine—becomes surer and more flexible. She discovers the symbolic side of her sexuality, where it functions as a metaphor to unite opposite sides of herself—as, for example, in linking her conscious feminine ego-identity with unconscious images of the male.

Preventive Measures

In the training of new therapists as well as in the practice of established therapists, it helps to conceptualize different kinds of countertransference. Winnicott (1947, 195) sums up the three types:

Normal countertransference consists of "identifications and tendencies belonging to an analyst's personal experiences and personal development which provide the positive setting for his analytic work and make it different in quality from that of any other analyst."

Abnormal countertransference consists of "feelings and set relationships and identifications that are under repression in the analyst." These require the analyst to seek more analysis.

Objective countertransference consists of the "analyst's love and hate in reaction to the actual personality and behavior of the patient, based on objective observation." These reactions may offer clues to the patient's experience and the problems the patient herself is trying to work through and solve.

Jung, as Michael Fordman points out (1974), adds a further distinction between personal and archetypal levels of transference or countertransference. The personal level refers the therapist's attention back, regressively, to people and feelings in his own biography that unconsciously he has been projecting onto his patient. For example, when Jung speaks of a therapist getting entangled in an anima projection onto his female patient, he is indicating that one part of the countertransference must be analyzed reductively in hope of uncovering a still unconscious piece of the therapist's experience of and association to particular women in his own personal life—say, his mother or sister or first love. This unintegrated piece of personal material would be that part of "abnormal countertransference"—in Winnicott's terminology—that requires further treatment. (It is on the basis of this conceptualization that suits of malpractice may be brought against therapists who get sexually involved with their patients. The therapist is lacking in sufficient "consciousness" or training to avoid being tripped up by unworked-through pieces of his own personal psychology. He is "practicing" badly—"unethically" or "illegally," as the judging vocabulary may decide—as a result.)

The archetypal level of the countertransference refers to the core image embedded in a personal complex that can be unearthed in its own right only as the therapist becomes conscious of the shell of personal material surrounding it. So, for example, a therapist who projects onto his female patient the image of a helpless, sensitive, feeling woman, estranged from the rich resources of her own femininity because of a negative mother complex, may be unconsciously and vicariously repairing a wound to his own feminine sensibilities which were helpless in the face of his own overbearing mother. He may, on the other hand, be drawn by an image of the female that is unclouded by maternal overtones and therefore promises to put him in touch with a range of sexual and feeling values that he thought belonged only to the poets and philosophers who write of woman as the "soul" or speak of love as union with one's "soul-mate." He may feel the chance now of being born into a heretofore unrealizable dimension of spiritual fulfillment.

Here the therapist himself is caught up in the usual symptoms of an overactive countertransference—an exaggerated anticipation of his hour with the patient, agitation of feelings about her, and a sense of being unduly muddled about "the case." In addition, the therapist will almost certainly feel pulled by an unknown force that surrounds the patient in his mind like an aura and exerts a constant fascination for him.

For this level of archetypal countertransference, a prospective view and a synthetic analysis are required. If the therapist is to help his patient, he must himself be firmly related to and not just fascinated by the archetypal images that are constellated; that is, he must be related to images of the feminine as a mode of being in its own right, uncontaminated by the aspects of the feminine embedded in maternal instincts. He needs to build conscious ego-connection to these images of the opposite sex and to all that they could mean to him if he were to be put in touch with them. Intrapsychically, this means opening his ego-identity to non-ego elements, represented through the image of the non-ego "otherness" of the opposite sex. This synthesizing operation—putting together new pieces of experience in addition to recovering to consciousness the missing pieces of the past buried in the unconscious—takes place under much larger prospective questions. How does he, the therapist, relate to the unknown mystery of life? How does he reach out to that which lies beyond his ego-circle and his ego-control? In addition to repairing the wounds of the past for better ego-functioning in the present, this connecting of the ego to the non-ego elements in the unconscious demands a tough-minded questioning of the whole idea of "functioning"—functioning for the sake of what? What is the "whole picture" of which anyone's ego is only a small part?

We can see how necessary it is for the therapist to be grounded in his own relation to archetypal elements in this matter of transference-countertransference sexuality. If a therapist endows his patient with archetypal significance, and the patient on her side sees the therapist not only as a larger-than-life parent figure, but as a spiritual guide—or another archetypal image of the masculine, such as a princely figure who awakens her sexuality from its unconscious slumber—the transference-countertransference becomes fraught with an unmanageable intensity that seems compelled to move into sexual enactment.

There are, of course, preventive measures that can protect the process of therapy against such compulsive enactment. The best measure is simply that the therapist live his own life as fully as possible. Where his patient's transference touches unlived aspects of his life, he needs to confront the material frankly, even painfully, and then to work it out in his own life—but not with his patient. These contents would pertain both to the "abnormal" and the "personal" levels of his countertransference.

The "objective" level of countertransference raises some special aspects in the handling of all transference levels. So-called "objective" reactions arise in the therapist in response to what is going on in his patient. They give valuable clues about the nature of the unconscious material the patient is trying to integrate. The therapist may receive from the patient a "transferred" sexual reaction that the patient is not yet able to feel for herself. By noting his own sexual reactions, the therapist can come to recognize that the patient is beginning to permit herself sexual responses. The therapist's task, then, is to hold in his awareness these sexual signals until the patient is ready to claim them as her own. The patient may endow the therapist with archetypal significance and potentially find access thereby to the archetypal core of the personal complex besetting her. The therapist's task again is to hold in his awareness a sense of what is going on, of what kind of archetypal image is being constellated, until through manifold interpretations he can assist the patient to construct a relationship to the archetypal images and signals.

In both kinds of examples, the therapist's attention to his own countertransference reactions is essential. Having been analyzed himself and introduced in his training to the textures and guises of the unconscious, he can be clear about when his own personal complexes are being touched by a patient's transference. He should be able to tell if an archetypal dimension is involved in the transference-countertransference interplay by an odd sense of feeling moved in reactions that are not entirely made up of his own personal feelings. He may feel, for example, in response to a patient who endows him with the role of spiritual guide, an unfamiliar impulse actually to play this part rather than to stick to the more mundane work of therapy. To act out this impulse would be to steal from the patient her potential awareness of and ability to come to terms with this image of truth-giving guide that figures in *her* psychology, not *his*, and which it is not his role to enact. But for the therapist to avoid noticing that he does experience impulses to play this part is also to steal from the patient her chance to become aware of this need for values as part of her psychology.

What is needed is the usual strenuous requirement of all therapeutic work: to make a space in consciousness to allow unconscious material to emerge. The making of this enabling space requires a trustworthy human relationship in which the distortions and defacements of the unconscious through patient-therapist sex simply can have no place.

References

Boss, M. 1963. *Psychoanalysis and Daseinanalysis.* New York: Basic Books.
Fordham, M. 1974. Jung's conception of transference. *Journal of Analytical Psychology* 19(1): 1–21.

Guggenbühl-Craig, A. 1971. *Power in the Helping Professions*. New York: Spring Publications.

Jung, C. G. 1946. Psychology of the transference. In *CW* 16: 163–323. New York: Pantheon, 1954.

Winnicott, D. W. 1947. Hate in the countertransference. *Through Paediatrics to Psycho-Analysis*. New York: Basic Books, 1958. 194–204.

7

Transference/Countertransference: A Jungian Perspective

Transference and countertransference are universal in human experience. Defined most simply, transference is a phenomenon that occurs when one person becomes the carrier for an unconscious content activated in another person. That content carries into the present moment conflicting and unassimilated feelings about figures in the past that distort the perception of the present person or situation. Countertransference describes a similar phenomenon flowing in the opposite direction (Jung 1966, 64; Stein 1971, 40). Jung notes that the carrier need not always be a person, but could "be a book, a piece of hearsay, or a legend" (1975, 504). And we are all familiar with transferences to places and things, such as childhood houses, pieces of furniture, kinds of food, schools we loved, and so on, transferences that can invade our perceptions of present surroundings and set them askew.

Analysis is a situation in which the phenomenon of interlocking transference and countertransference is examined with particular care. In recent years this phenomenon has become a center of attention in psychoanalytic literature of all schools of thought, not only as a clinical tool used in the daily work of analysis, but also as a metaphysical concept used to think about the nature of human beings and their relationships to each other and to what they value.

As a clinical tool, the transference-countertransference interaction becomes a focus for investigating the early stages of a relationship. By registering the way an analysand makes him or her feel, the analyst can give back insight into what the analysand is unconsciously transferring into present relationships from unresolved past conflicts. If, for example, the analyst feels the analysand is subtly controlling interactions by standing back and searching the analyst's face for clues indicating how to react, the analyst can say so in appropriate form to the analysand. What may come to light then is the analysand's discovery that this is the way he always felt with his mother; he *did* withhold his spontaneous responses in order to adapt to her expectations. Such a wounding of self in order to please another blights our capacity to be a full person. Kohut's work on the narcissistic, idealizing, and mirroring transferences explores such early damage to an individual's ability to esteem the self and carry it forward into life (1971, 37, 78, 116, 203). Kernberg examines the rage and envy that defeat formation of a self capable of relating to another self (1975, 60, 69, 322). Searles suggests that the assault an analyst feels in the primitive love and hate in the transferences of patients suffering from schizophrenia shows, in grossly exaggerated forms, the tasks all of us face in relating to each other. We all must come to know and to tame these forces of love and hate in ourselves, and we can only do so in relation to another person (Searles 1965, 273–283; 1979a, 22; 1979b, 53–54).

As a metaphysical concept, the transference-countertransference phenomenon has been used as a way to conceptualize the human tendency to personalize any relationship, even one to transpersonal realities such as God, society, or the values and truths held to be of supreme worth by individuals or groups. No human relationship can avoid the impact of the human unconscious, whether it is deemed a positive or negative contribution. Freud, for example, understood the father transference as the psychic root of religious belief. Loewald, a Freudian, understands transference to be the root of psychoanalysis itself, a discipline he considers to be a value system in its own right and one that has, in this country, strongly influenced our understanding of the construction of human values (Loewald 1977).

Hans Dieckmann finds a nonpersonal, collective theme dominant in any transference-countertransference interaction, and suggests that it is fundamental in shaping the way personal issues between analyst and analysand come up and are resolved. Thus he reverses the usual direction of thought in which an analysand's personal conflicts lead the analyst to speculate about the human condition. Instead, he sees certain universal human themes as arranging the kinds of transference-countertransference conflict that occur between analysand and analyst. For example, the unconscious human tendency to cast the authoritative figures of the analyst in a parental role activates in the analysand a father transference (Dieckmann 1976).

Fordham posits progressive stages of transference, in which a shift occurs from earlier, ego-centered concerns to the eventual displacement of the ego in favor of a more comprehensive center of the psyche that Jung calls the Self (Fordham 1978, 87). For example, an analysand's concern about whether or not the analyst likes the analysand can move through the memories of early attempts to gain a father's approval into deeper layers of the human longing for a felt connection to some power at the source of life. What is at first sought as approval from the analyst becomes a move to establish a secure relation to life itself, to a center that is not felt to belong to either analysand or analyst. The analysand can now see through the whole interaction with the analyst around the issue of approval to a deeper purpose—that of securing a durable emotional connection to an inner authority that is no longer projected onto the analyst or any other individual. Jung would call this view a glimpse of the Self.

Despite differences of approach among analysts of conflicting schools, firm agreement exists in two areas. The first is the uniqueness of every transference-countertransference relationship. As Jung puts it, each case is "pioneer work" because of the unrepeatable nature of each person (1946, 177). General trends are evident, but each transference has its own singular quality. Winnicott (1977, 189–190) captured this uniqueness in his exchange with a three-year-old girl as treatment drew to a close:

Winnicott: So the Winnicott you invented was all yours and he is now finished with, and no one else can ever have him. . . .

Gabrielle: I made you.

The second area of agreement focuses on levels of transference and countertransference. As noted above, Winnicott (1975, 195) describes three levels of countertransference (1975, 195): "abnormal," meaning those areas arising from the analyst's past unresolved conflicts that intrude upon the present analysand; "normal," meaning those reactions that describe the idiosyncratic style of an analyst's work and personality; and "objective," meaning those reactions evoked in an analyst by an analysand's behavior and personality that can provide the analyst with valuable internal clues about what is going on in the analysand. Transference reactions would customarily fall into the "abnormal" category, but the other two categories are never entirely excluded.

Jung adds a fourth level of transference-countertransference interaction—the archetypal. It is upon this level that I will concentrate. I will not, however, altogether exclude the other levels and the analytic systems that stress them (Fordham 1974, 6; 1978, 83), for, just as Jung built upon the work of Freud and Adler (Jung 1966, 41), seeing his own emphasis as adding an extra dimension to their systems, so many Jungians today use the insights of workers in other schools to deepen their own.

The "extra" element Jung and Jungians see operating in transference is the archetypal. In addition to the projection of infantile conflicts onto the analyst, transference activates what Jung calls the archetype-centered process of individuation (Edinger 1957, 33; Paulsen 1956, 203). In this process, the ego is radically changed as it comes into increasingly cooperative relation with the Self, that center and goal of the whole psyche that Jung describes as

> both ego and non-ego, subjective and objective, individual and collective. . . . the "uniting symbol" which epitomizes the total union of opposites. . . . not a doctrine or theory but an image born of nature's own workings. (1946, 474)

Individuation involves the transformation of the analyst as well as the analysand, stirring up in his or her personality the layers that correspond to the analysand's conflicts and insights (Jung 1946, 176; Fordham 1957a, 62; Fordham 1958, 172; Lambert 1972, 33). In the midst of infantile issues, the archetypal core breaks open, calling the analysand not only to resolve issues of personal identity and functioning in the world, but also to come into a better relationship with potentialities that are not properly the possession of any one person but are part of a shared human culture. The analyst then will find personal issues constellated in response to the analysand's material. Ideally, those issues will be familiar to the analyst and nonobtrusive in the treatment because of the analyst's own long work as a patient. Archetypal dynamics will affect any analyst, but particularly one whose life is not fully lived and needs to be (Jung 1975, 172).

An example can be given from the analysis of a woman who suffered from intense anxiety stemming from a negative mother complex. As she was growing up, her mother criticized and belittled her harshly. As a result, her self-confidence was severely blighted and she became aware of radical self-doubt. She also harbored a lot of repressed anger, of which she became aware only as the treatment progressed. In the transference, she needed now to please me in the way she used to try to please her mother. The whole mother issue was there with us and I could feel different parts of the mother role in its archetypal form come alive in me at different times. Sometimes I would find myself wanting to react as the good mother the woman never had. Other times her frantic anxiety aroused in me the thought of brusque responses with which to put a swift end to all her dithering. Other times, such as the day the patient greeted me at the door with "I'm sorry" before she even said hello, I wanted to laugh and just get out from under the whole mother constellation.

The analysand's transference took her back into her actual relationship with her mother in the past. Because the analysand perceived me as different from her real mother, she could risk facing her repressed angry reactions to her mother. In addition, she came to see how her mother's criticism continued to live in her own belittling attitude toward herself.

The issue of relating to the mother archetype arose in the midst of all of her personal struggles, for around associations and memories of her real mother, and mixed in with transference feelings to me as a mother figure, appeared images, affects, behavior patterns, and fantasies connected to relating to the archetypal mother. The analysand reached to feelings of happy dependence, which she had not experienced with her real negative mother, but which can be an authentic response to the mother image. She reached to a deep sadness that her mother was so anxiously distressed herself that she could not be a secure refuge for her child. Thus she went beyond her own bruises to perceive her mother's damaged state and to feel genuine compassion for her parent. The analysand could wonder about where all this led, at moments seeing her mother problem as an important thread in her own destiny, setting her specific tasks to solve. She could accept the relationship now, with all its hurts, as an essential part of her own way of life.

On the countertransference side, I found my analysand's material touched some of my issues with my own mother, some of which were finished and easy to keep from intruding upon the treatment, and others which needed more work and attention so that they did not interfere. The life issues around "the mother," good and bad, were posed for me as well, to think about, to feel again, to work on.

Jung lays great emphasis on the importance of the relationship between analyst and analysand, which accounts for his sitting face-to-face with his patients and confining sessions to no more than three a week. (Some Jungians of the English school, influenced by Freudian and object relations theory, do use a couch and a greater frequency of sessions.) In transference-countertransference, archetypes are constellated and both personalities are changed in the process of coming to terms with them. The aim of Jungian analysis is to secure greater connection to all the contents that properly belong to a patient's ego and to connect the ego to the Self, the center of the whole psyche. One needs a setting that mirrors the otherness of the Self in the otherness of the person sitting across from oneself and time between sessions to digest the effects of archetypes in the analyst-analysand relationship. Jung says of the connecting process, "That is the core of the whole transference phenomenon, and it is impossible to argue it away, because relationship to the self is at once relationship to our fellowman and no one can be related to the latter until he is related to himself" (1946, par. 445; see also Edinger 1957, 41; Fordham 1974, 15; Plaut 1970, 19).

Jung's recognition of the pivotal place of the archetypal element in transference, or in any content of analysis for that matter, accounts for his development of the synthetic-constructive method of interpretation. The method addresses the archetypal potentiality hidden in a vexatious symptom (Jung 1944, 80). In practice, we feel this archetypal element as an unknown, as "something" that seems to us precious and on no account to be lost sight of even when embedded in gross perversion or degrading compulsion (Hillman 1972, 186; Khan 1979, 14). Awareness of this archetypal component quiets the clamor of judgment in both analyst and analysand and makes room for the analysand to breathe. We can discover the archetypal element urging the potential for growth that has been hiding in the distress of personal dysfunction.

Awareness of that element reveals what Jung calls the prospective function of the psyche (1948, par. 493), one we experience as a power that summons us, if it does not drag us, in a certain life direction. With sufficient consciousness of this power, we come to ask basic questions. What does this problem make me discover about my whole direction in life? What does it show me that must be dealt with if I am to go forward? To what banished area of life has this distress sent me back? We cannot undervalue the importance of this perspective, not only in building a bridge between the ego and the psyche's archetypal contents, but also in rescuing for the ego a sense of its dignity in the midst of a humiliating illness. The illness has a purpose and was not to be avoided, even if one had had just the "right" attitude, the will power, or better luck.

In the transference, this perspective can yield particularly good working space. An example is an analysand who asks what purpose can possibly be served by the intense attraction he or she feels to the analyst, who is clearly not available for any romantic or sexual relationship. Unfinished entanglements with parent figures from the past can be reductively analyzed. And the value of such an apparent impasse for the analysand's growth into a realistic maturity can also be underscored.

The fact that the analyst is not available for social or sexual relationship turns out to be the centrally important fact. Only where outer action cannot be taken does the inner demand for greater consciousness urge itself upon the analysand. In the analytical relationship, the projections of anima and animus can be worked on directly, so that the analysand becomes more aware of what attraction to the analyst represents in the analysand's own psychology.

Jung remarks that the sexual attraction is always used by the unconscious to represent the urge toward reconciliation with split-away parts of ourselves (1976, 173). The sexual transference, then, is a spontaneous way by which the psyche seeks to bridge a gulf between the analysand's ego-identity and the contrasexual contents projected upon the analyst (von Franz 1970, 3–4). What would otherwise be a humiliating fixation upon the analyst is redeemed by its hidden purpose—to bring to light the analysand's relation to the anima or animus, depending upon the sex of the analysand. Analysands in this position, then, need not just go on feeling foolish for desiring someone they cannot have and indulging in childish sulks, mopings, or resentments when refused gratification. Instead, such analysands see the task set them by this welling up of emotion, impulse, aspiration, and the sense of soul with which they cloak the analyst figure. When analysands long for the analyst, it is their first direct experience of their strong longing to be reconnected to a missing part of themselves, to some aspect of their own souls.

It is precisely in matters of transference that Jung's distinction between subjective and objective levels of interpretation makes its worth felt (1948, 266), for the analyst figure makes visible and accessible heretofore unconscious affects and value-laden instincts. The analyst also embodies aspects of the analysand's psyche that must be claimed as part of the territory of the analysand's own depths (Jacoby 1971, 17). When after the first session a male analysand dreams, for example, that he is having a session while a female analyst is seated in a tub having a bath, interpretation must follow two lines, each with its own individual effects on the analysand's ego. It must look backward into the analysand's attitudes toward his mother that may be recaptured or corrected in the dream image, and it must look forward to discover a solution that has some significant connection to the dreamer's life attitude.

In the reductive stage of analysis, such an analysand withdraws his projections onto the analyst and assimilates them to his ego, an action that enlarges his ego and his responsibility for his own psyche's contents. In the synthetic stage, the analysand is called beyond his ego concerns to build a stronger connection to his anima. He relies on his ego as one pole in the developing relationship. The analyst figure in the dream must be interpreted objectively as a real person to whom the dreamer is transferring unfinished issues with women as well as a personification of anima content in the dreamer's own psyche. Amplifying the symbolic connections of this dream to include the symbolic meaning of bath, immersion, water, cleansing, baptism, and so on will clarify the content the unconscious urges upon the dream-ego (Jung 1944, par. 220; Edinger 1978, 34). One possible meaning of such an intimate dream scene might be to compensate for the dreamer's actual life attitude. In actuality, his too-strict compartmentalizing of his responses to women and to the feminine parts of himself segregates them from the rest of his life. In the dream, sitting with a woman while she bathes suggests easy intimacy, relaxed interchange, and, in the image of water, a dissolving of separating formalities and uncovering of feminine presence.

Fordham correctly warns us against the tendency of analysand and analyst alike to use the symbolic-synthetic perspective as a defense against uncovering the infantile roots of a complex (1978, 84, 93; see also Guggenbühl-Craig 1971, 65). Jungians can easily waft themselves upward into mythological spiritualizing, with talk about "the goddesses" and "the gods," and thereby avoid the tough work involved in analyzing the anger, the envy, the sexual attraction, the embarrassment, and so on that may be present in the transference. For example, when an analysand dreamed of me as an embodiment of presence and love, I was too quick to reject that projection. I insisted upon seeing the projection as an aspect of his own inward reality, something he should claim for himself and not project onto women as if it were to be found only in and through them. He quite rightly caught me up, sensing my unwillingness to see and deal with his feelings about me. I thought of Searles' point about parents who deny their children the experience of all-out lavish loving, because their own low self-esteem cannot tolerate it (1965, 230, 232–33), and of Jung's point about the archetypes of king or queen that lurk in the midst of parental images. But we do not get to such understanding except through the concrete details of specific personal relationships.

It is also fair to say that the fascinating work of exploring the early dynamics of introjected objects can be used as a defense against the pull of the archetype on the ego to get it out of placing itself, its wounds, its past, and its purposes at the center of the analytical universe. The product of this exaggeration is not a positive cooperation of ego and Self resulting in generosity to others, but rather an increasingly narrow and narcissistic concentration on the intricacies of the psychic process.

The reaching of the ego toward relation with the Self is the central issue in analysis for Jungians, whether with negative or positive effect. The movement of ego toward Self is involved in any transference, but nowhere so strongly as when the contrasexual anima or animus is activated, stretching consciousness to make space for all that arrives from the unconscious. The contrasexual archetypes galvanize the deepest issues of individuation—that process of differentiating out of unconsciousness one's individual personality in relation to other persons. Whether a mess or a grand experience, a source of connection or disruption, a relation of love or one of hostility—our sexual life is a constant drama in which the contrasexual archetypes play a major role. These are the archetypes that open onto the Self in the individuation journey. They touch all aspects of human life: our past experiences and future hopes, our sexuality, our bodies, our souls, our sense of purpose or purposelessness. An indication of how profoundly anima and animus reach into us in the transference-countertransference relationship can be seen in the way they constellate the backward and forward strivings of the incest motif.

Anima and animus introduce a sexual tonality into the relationship that symbolizes the urgency of the underlying impulse toward "union with one's own being . . . individuation or becoming [one's] self" (Jung 1946, par 419). To become all of one's self means to connect consciously with unconscious parts of one's personality, such as personal memories from one's childhood that have been forgotten and need to be remembered and impersonal unconscious contents like images that arise spontaneously in the psyche to accompany autonomous instinctive processes. The joining of the opposites of anima or animus and ego that Jung calls the *coniunctio* pulls the analysand backward into his or her personal history through incestuous longings to be joined once again to those large and fascinating parental figures, with their interesting shapes, smells, tastes, and textures. The analysand feels again in the transference the strong pull of small child to large adult, of infant to containing parent, of dependent self to encompassing other.

The sexualized tone of these feelings underscores their urgency by enlisting the body instincts in the movement of the psyche's longings. Sexual imagery is particularly well suited to conveying unconscious material, for it is a preverbal, nondiscursive language of images, emotions, and body drives. It includes autoerotic imaginings alongside efforts to build intimacy with another. It is almost impossible to forget a sexually charged dream!

The transference of anima or animus to analyst pulls the analysand forward into the crucial work of *coniunctio*, the inner marriage of ego and contrasexual archetype that "brings to birth something that is one and united." Longing for "union on the biological level is a symbol of the *unio oppositorum* at its highest," of finding how to put together into a whole all the parts of oneself (Jung 1946, par. 458–460). The contrasexual archetype is particularly well suited to personifying contents of the collective unconscious, because it is so vivid in its appearance in the images of those "other" humans, those of the opposite sex. They are both so like us and so unlike us. Relating to contrasexual figures demands that we somehow put at our ego's disposal identification and differentiation, the psychic processes that encourage acceptance of sexuality in its entirety, our own sex and its opposite, both in ourselves and in others.

If the analyst receives the full transference of the contrasexual archetype, a most intense and flammable situation will ensue. This is the case regardless of the analysand's level of psychic development. The Self—the center of one's potential wholeness—is elicited and the ego feels its pull. The contrasexual archetype, though differently presented from stage to stage, will nonetheless always display its potentiality to connect ego and contents of the objective psyche, that realm of unconscious psychic life out of which the ego originally emerges (Hubback 1980, 231; Fordham 1978, 87). To illustrate this connecting function, I will take an extreme example, one that amounted to a transference psychosis. That is a particular danger in this sort of transference, just because the anima or animus opens onto the Self, which then may threaten to overpower the ego. The analysand feels the Self is at stake—in its smallest terms as personal ego functioning, in its largest terms as the center of authentic being.

A woman barely established as a person in herself entered treatment with a male psychiatrist and fell totally in love with him. She experienced herself as an infant coming to her divine parent, as unawakened female coming to her hero-prince, as love-starved middle-aged woman to her soul-mate. The treatment ended and a sexual relation ensued, but it soon dwindled to infrequent meetings. When she entered treatment with me, she felt all but crazed by the experience. Our work for many months centered around her feelings for him, her intense transference. She felt that her love for him represented her most essential, true self, which she needed in order to exist at all. She felt he connected her to the center of life. But now he was withdrawn from her. The withdrawal recapitulated with explosive force deprivations in her early life. She felt in danger of annihilation, either from loss of him or from her rage over the loss.

She had not just transferred to her psychiatrist the animus that might connect her to that authentic Self. He *was* the animus; hence, the delusional aspect of the transference. The experience was so powerful that it threatened to overwhelm her ego. The Self was glimpsed before the ego was strong enough to relate to it. She saw the promise of being loved and of loving, of feeling alive and real, of being connected to what she experienced as life's meaning and truth. But the promise was broken. It fell apart in ruins. The ego was then in danger of being plowed under, swept away, or invaded by rageful animus opinions. Some unlived part of the psychiatrist had also apparently been ignited in the dynamics operating between them. The analysis was lost and with it the relationship between them, and for her, the relationship to her own inward center.

Acting out the transference-countertransference, instead of analyzing it, is one of the greatest dangers in the transference of anima or animus, for in the long run the analysand is robbed of the analytical container in which to forge connection to this inner "other" (Ulanov 1979, 101–4). In such acting out, analysis presumes to replace a life relationship. As a result, analysis loses its own rightful place and only very rarely does a real personal relationship develop.

The other major danger with such a transference is that of talking it to death instead of experiencing it (Guggenbühl-Craig 1971, 65; Newmann 1980, 122). That, too, is a sort of defense, but it is done verbally, with an excess of theorizing and an amplification of imagery that seduces the analysands into a symbolic bond that sucks the libido out of all their intimate life relationships (Ulanov 1979, 109). Where acting out the transference robs the analysand of realizing its symbolic significance, talking it to death steals the analysand's right to experience instinct and affect and put together a creative solution (Winnicott 1971a, 57). Both impede the potential transformation of the analysand because, from different sides, both split apart the instinctive and the spiritual urges. The opposites are sundered instead of united.

Proper handling of a transference-countertransference that takes shape around anima or animus requires more vigor than either of the negative extremes of acting or talking it out. I will give some examples of anima transference in which one central theme is constant. In each, the anima acts as bridge between ego and objective psyche; it mediates the contents of the objective psyche to the ego; it functions as a connecting point; it opens the ego to experience of otherness. Personal concerns get linked to life concerns. One's conscious sexual identity gets in touch with opposite sex characteristics in one's own personality. Ego purposes and values—all that one asks of life—are confronted with what life asks of oneself. We meet up with less familiar parts of ourselves, sometimes parts that are unknown to us but that nevertheless belong to us and that we must accommodate. This changes the whole. Thus in the transference, the analyst who receives the anima projection is experienced, whether positively or negatively, as one who facilitates the connection of the ego to its own deep resources in the Self.

When a man gains consciousness of anima contents, his ego changes. It enlarges and becomes more spacious and more flexible. His ego opens to contents that are not properly part of his masculine identity but that his ego houses, so to speak, letting these contents enter and pass through. He does not identify with them. He experiences the anima contents as quite other than himself, yet as part of his larger personality. His ego becomes more flexible as he simultaneously takes notice of the anima qualities and impulses and stands aside from them. He sees them but does not become them; he holds them but does not possess them and is not possessed by them. He can look them over as something both within and outside himself to be considered alongside his own more familiar points of view.

A man dreamed that he came for a session with his analyst, and she made him wait while she attended to a frail girl who had worms in her hair (Ulanov 1981, 72). In associating to the dream, the man evidenced that peculiar doubling up of consciousness so character-istic of coming into awareness of unconscious contents. It is particu-larly true of anima contents, because they present themselves in forms so different from the dreamer's ego-identity, so opposite from it. The man saw himself in the dream as robust, purposively di-rected, healthy, and male. He saw the anima figure as sickly, de-pendent, with disgusting hair, and female. Yet she touched him. She irritated him by keeping him waiting and yet stirred some re-mote and painful sense of dependency in himself. She belonged to him, he felt, though he did not want her. The analyst took care of her in the dream, thus previewing the fact that this phase of the analysis (and transference) would be much occupied with this fig-ure of otherness. He did not identify with his anima, but his ego-awareness enlarged to make room for her and her side of things, so opposite to his own.

Another man's experience in a session illustrates the flexibility this doubling up of consciousness engenders in the ego. He spoke of his pleasure in beginning a friendship with a man whom I knew and whom the analysand knew that I knew. Suddenly, the analysand thought I had some reservation about this mutual ac-quaintance. He asked me point blank and I said no, that in fact I liked the man. The analysand, long used to dealing with his own projections, was astounded by the contrast between the certainty of his intuition and my reply. He felt simultaneously two opposed re-actions. He saw in me a response that he had projected onto me, which contrasted sharply with the response to this man that he had thought was the only one he had.

In fact he had two responses: while he was consciously pleased, his "other" reaction was fearful, hesitant. We explored this second response in the context of an anima figure who recurrently ap-peared in his dreams as frightened, even disturbed. I commented that "she" might find the new friend's directness overwhelming and intrusive. Again, suddenly, the analysand's experience repeated it-self. He had been sure this was my reaction, but he knew that it was not, that it was his own. For the moment he cloaked me, the analyst, in the reactive guise of his anima. By claiming my own re-action, I enabled the analysand to see his anima's view. He saw it, then lost it, then saw it again, experiencing that doubling up of perspective—his and the anima's—that occurs when one becomes conscious of the opposite that dwells within each of us. This simul-taneity of experiencing and standing aside, of owning one's own view and perceiving its opposite, develops flexibility in the ego.

The connecting function of the anima can reveal itself from the countertransference side, too. For example, I felt my attention wandering in a session, which is uncharacteristic of my reactions. I reviewed whatever complexes in me might have been touched off by what the analysand was saying, but that led nowhere. Then I considered whether my reaction was being evoked by something going on in the analysand himself. My sense of wandering evaporated, but I got no further than feeling negated, as if my own consciousness, comments, and interpretive remarks were being cancelled by the analysand's refusal to connect to them. The "wandering" revealed itself now as trying first this way, then that, to reach the analysand, but no door opened. I felt connection between us was being nullified. I held this feeling and did not use it for interpretation at that time.

A few days later I received a letter from the analysand in which he wrote of a painful insight that came to him soon after our session. He too felt disconnected. Tracing that feeling, he came upon an envious destructiveness in his attitude toward me that resented my having anything good at all to give him. By not taking in anything from me, he in effect cancelled my goodness. It was as if his anima made her presence felt negatively by disrupting the connection between us, spurred to do so by envy of the nourishing role in which he had cast me. His insight proved most fruitful for our subsequent work. Klein comments that envy of the opposite sex can sometimes be a split-off mad part in any of us that would destroy or spoil the goodness that one missed getting from one's mother (as was in fact true for this man), so that no one else can have it either (Klein 1975, 208–11; see also Winnicott 1971b, 73–75).

Just as a man's ego is changed by admitting anima contents, so we may hazard that the anima is changed by connection with consciousness. It is the securing of the ego-anima connection that comprises *coniunctio*. That is the way we achieve the inner marriage that opens us to the Self, beginning a process "whose goal is complete individuation" (Jung 1946, par. 468). The ego changes. It is no longer center stage nor entirely intact. It has something like a permanent hole in it that opens onto another center. For some people, the original hole in their ego-identity, which caused so much suffering and pathological distortion, is precisely what becomes transformed into an opening onto what Gerard Manley Hopkins called the "yonder, yonder, yonder" of being, for the sake of which, finally we live (1948, 53–54). The anima also undergoes transformation, becoming less blurred and more defined in character. Moreover, "she" may take a more vigorous role in dreams or active imagination in order to get her point across.

For example, a man who was given to angry outbursts of critical judgment against a woman with whom he was deeply involved discovered, after some painstaking reductive analysis, that these scenes always erupted from his own hurt feelings when he felt his own sensitivities had been utterly disregarded. Who had disregarded them, however, remained the question. He berated his woman friend for this crime, while remaining clear in himself that she was a very important friend and a beloved companion.

His recounting of these episodes left me with my own puzzled reaction. I felt anger passing through me, anger at being left out and a sense of "What about me?" that I could not account for in my personal reactions to this man. Nor did I find any significant abnormal transference of activated complex from my side. I felt as if I were having someone else's reaction, not my own. I was feeling, I believe, the reaction of the analysand's most sensitive anima, a piece of objective countertransference originating in the analysand. "She" felt jealous of his increasing affection for his woman friend; "she" felt left out, not taken into consideration, not dealt with directly by him. He was unconscious of this missing part of his own reactions and projected it onto me, and I found myself temporarily identifying with it. Fordham calls this "identifying with a patient's projective identification" (1978, 92; see also Klein 1975, 11). For the moment, I was carrying a piece of the patient's psychic reality of which he was not yet conscious and so could not experience as his own inner conflict.

This bit of objective countertransference gave me a valuable clue as to what was going on in the analysand and his resultant behavior. No matter how solicitous his woman friend might be, the possibility of his feeling utterly disregarded remained, for he was himself the culprit in his dealing with his own anima. Working on this led to a change, summed up best by a dream fragment:

> Someone knocks angrily at the door. The dreamer opens it and is confronted by an angry woman who says that she wants to come in, that he has left her out and not cared about her feelings. She wants to know what he is going to do about it. (Ulanov 1981, 57)

The change this dream signified was the initial mending of the split in him between sensitive feelings and angry attack. Both arise together and are clearly connected with each other, instead of the anger hiding the hurt. The woman says right out that she is hurt and angry. The issue is clearly between him and her, no longer split into pieces, some of which are projected onto the woman friend and some of which remain with himself. He was connected now with an element of himself, and the anima had made connection with him.

A last example illustrates an extreme anima transference that took shape around the anima's function of connecting the ego world to the otherness of the ego-transcending dimension of the psyche. Here both analyst and analysand were opened to the otherness of death. The analysand had worked intensively in analysis for several years on a radical split-anima condition that was being lived out both internally and externally (Ulanov 1981, 168). A dream best sums up the extreme nature of this split and its seeming insolubility.

> *The dreamer sees himself in a room between two other rooms, in each of which stands a woman who represents one of the opposite poles of his anima fascination. The rooms are so arranged that the woman can see him and see each other. Each woman holds a revolver in her hand, threatening to shoot either the other woman or the dreamer, yet each is stayed in her action by the fact that the other can see her take aim and perhaps shoot first. The dreamer is trapped between them [in a menacing and divisive relation to different figurations of his anima].*

The analysand's transference to me was to anima as a trusted sister or colleague, even as a spiritual guide, who made space for both sides of the anima split. After some years of work, this split softened. The dreamer felt, at last, that he could live with it, a very different feeling from his attitude when he entered treatment. At that time, he had felt close to suicide, desperate over the gap between his public life—where he was respected by all and was, in his small sphere, famous—and his secret private life.

Against my counsel, the man terminated treatment, feeling he had gone as far as he could go at least for the moment, though he kept in touch over the ensuing years until I was again brought into sustained contact with him. That contact was initiated by his phoning to announce that he had just learned he was gravely ill with an incurable and fast-moving disease. Indeed, he was to be dead within three months. The transference now moved into the deep waters of spiritual direction, as the man put the question to me bluntly of whether or not he should kill himself before the disease ravaged his brain and made him psychotic, which was its predictable course. Then I was crowded with questions about the ultimate value of life, proper preparation for death, and the fate of the soul after death, particularly one that had contemplated or even committed suicide.

As in the examples above, this case also recommended itself for reductive analysis and synthetic-constructive treatment. On the personal level, the man feared his long-held, secret anima complex and behavior would be what would spill out from him for all to see if he became psychotic before death. His thought of suicide was a defensive maneuver to protect his secret. Locating his fear and defining it brought him some relief. The prospective question, however, of what to do then and how in fact to move toward death loomed all the larger.

For my part, I felt the impact of larger questions about the value of consciousness, analytic methods, countertransference reactions, and so on. I found in myself deeper convictions than ever about the value of these activities, which really are important to me, and yet at the same time saw their emphasis shift, not in the sense of any loss of value, but loosened from their moorings, less fixed, less simply defined. I saw the positive qualities involved in giving over, opening up, remaining less anchored in method or procedure. This was a small mirroring of my analysand's great loosening of his hold on his life, with all its rich values. His dying and, particularly and centrally, his manner of resolving the issue of suicide, affected me in a permanent way. We asked the synthetic questions: What might the meaning be? To what end still not clearly in view might this particular disease's threat of psychosis be tending? What could be the purpose in the threat of exposing a long-hidden secret life, with which he had worked so hard to live yet had not fully accepted?

In the midst of these groping questions, another way opened. He voluntarily—and completely—gave up the escape route of suicide by offering it up to the source of life from which he had come and from which he had received all that he had known of life. He felt this as an intensely personal offering of what he had to give, of all he feared and wished for, back into the hands of God, of life. He offered even his sanity, letting go of everything—his fear of losing his sanity, his fear of exposure—and releasing all to the power that had created him. In dying, he reached a depth of acceptance he could not reach in life. He reached beneath the split of public and secret life to deliver himself over utterly as he was, fears, splits, and all.

One could say it all would have been taken from him anyway, which is true, for the disease took one function after another—his balance, his sight, his muscular coordination, his hearing, his voice. The difference occurred as a result of his voluntarily bringing what he had and offering it up, all of it. That difference manifested itself outwardly in the surprising fact that he did not become psychotic before his body gave out, that, far from falling apart in spirit or psyche, he held together magnificently. Thus he was spared what he most deeply feared, but only because he faced the fear and willingly submitted to it. For my part, since this experience, there always has been a space between the analytic methods I cherish and my commitment to them, an empty space where questions can appear that may challenge the whole analytic endeavor while at the same time confirming it.

References

Carotenuto, A. 1980. Sabina Spielrein and C. G. Jung: some newly discovered documents bearing on psychotic transference, counter transference, and the anima. *Spring* 1980: 128–145.
Dieckmann, H. 1976. Transference and countertransference: results of a Berlin research group. *Journal of Analytical Psychology* 21(1): 25–36.
Edinger, E. F. 1957. Some manifestations of the transference phenomena. *Spring* 1957: 32–45.
———. 1978. Solutio. *Quadrant* 1978 (Winter): 32–44.
Epstein, L., and A. H. Feiner, eds. 1979. *Countertransference*. New York: Jason Aronson.
Fordham, M. 1957a. Notes on transference. *New Developments in Analytical Psychology*. London: Routledge and Kegan Paul. 62–104.
———. 1957b. Note on a significance of archetypes for the transference in childhood. *New Developments in Analytical Psychology*. London: Routledge and Kegan Paul. 181–188.
———. 1958. *The Objective Psyche*. London: Routledge and Kegan Paul.
———. 1974. Jung's conception of transference. *Journal of Analytical Psychology* 19(1): 1–21.
———. 1978. *Jungian Psychotherapy*. New York: Wiley.
Groesbeck, J. 1978. Psychological types in the analysis of the transference. *Journal of Analytical Psychology* 23(1): 23–54.
Guggenbühl-Craig, A. 1971. *Power in the Helping Professions*. New York: Spring Publications.
Hillman, J. 1972. *The Myth of Analysis*. Part 2. New York: Harper & Row.
Hopkins, G. M. 1948. The leaden echo and the golden echo. *Poems of Gerard Manley Hopkins*. London: Oxford University Press.
Hubback, J. 1980. Development and similarities, 1935–1980. *Journal of Analytical Psychology* 23(3): 219–237.
Jacoby, M. 1971. A contribution to the phenomenon of transference. *The Analytic Process: Aims, Analysis, Training*, ed. J. B. Wheelwright. New York: Putnam. 10–17.
Jung, C. G. 1944. *Psychology and Alchemy*. CW 12. New York: Pantheon, 1953.

————. 1946. Psychology of the transference. In *CW* 16: 163–323. New York: Pantheon, 1954.

————. 1948. General aspects of dream psychology. In *CW* 8: 237–280. New York: Pantheon, 1960.

————. 1966. *Two Essays on Analytical Psychology*. In *CW* 7. 2nd ed. New York: Pantheon.

————. 1968. *Analytical Psychology: Its Theory and Practice*. New York: Pantheon.

————. 1975. *Letters*. Vol. 2. Ed. G. Adler and A. Jaffé. Princeton: Princeton University Press.

————. 1976. *The Visions Seminars*. Vol. 1. Zurich: Spring Publications.

Kernberg, O. 1975. *Borderline Conditions and Pathological Narcissism*. New York: Jason Aronson.

Khan, M. M. R. 1979. *Alienation in Perversions*. New York: International Universities Press.

Klein, M. 1975. *Envy and Gratitude and Other Works, 1946–1963*. New York: Delacorte.

Kohut, H. 1971. *The Analysis of the Self*. New York: International Universities Press.

Kraemer, W. P. 1958. The dangers of unrecognized countertransference. *Journal of Analytical Psychology* 3(1): 29–43.

Lambert, K. 1972. Transference/countertransference: talion law and gratitude. *Journal of Analytical Psychology* 17(1): 31–51.

Loewald, H. 1977. Transference and countertransference: the roots of psychoanalysis. Review essay of the *Freud / Jung Letters*. *Psychoanalytic Quarterly* 46: 514–527.

Moody, R. 1955. On the function of countertransference. *Journal of Analytical Psychology* 1/1: 49–59.

Newman, K. D. 1980. Countertransference and consciousness. *Spring* 1980: 117–128.

Paulsen, L. 1956. Transference and projection. *Journal of Analytical Psychology* 1(2): 203–07.

Plaut, A. 1970. "What do you actually do?" Problems in communicating. *Journal of Analytical Psychology* 15(1): 13–22.

Racker, H. 1968. *Transference and Countertransference*. London: Hogarth.

Searles, H. F. 1965. *Collected Papers on Schizophrenia and Related Subjects*. New York: International Universities Press.

————. 1979a. *Countertransference*. New York: International Universities Press.

————. 1979b. The self in the countertransference. *Issues in Ego Psychology* 2(2): 49–57.

Spiegelman, J. A. 1980. The image of the Jungian analyst. *Spring* 1980: 101–117.

Stein, R. M. 1971. Transference and individuation: reflections on the process and future of analysis. *Spring* 1971: 38–50.

Ulanov, A. B. 1979. Follow-up treatment in cases of patient/therapist sex. *Journal of the American Academy of Psychoanalysis* 7(1): 101–110. Adapted and republished as chap. 6 of this book.

————. 1981. *Receiving Woman: Studies in the Psychology and Theology of the Feminine*. Philadelphia: Westminster Press.

von Franz, M.-L. 1970. *Interpretation of Fairy Tales*. New York: Spring Publications.

Winnicott, D. W. 1971a. Playing: creative activity and the search for the self. Chapter 4 in *Playing and Reality*. London: Tavistock. 53–64.

———. 1971b. Creativity and its origins. Chapter 5 in *Playing and Reality*. London: Tavistock. 65–85.

———. 1975. Hate in the countertransference. *Through Paediatrics of Psychoanalysis*, New York: Basic Books. 194–203.

———. 1977. *The Piggle: An Account of the Psychoanalytic Treatment of a Little Girl*. New York: International Universities Press.

8

Self Service

The play on words in this title points to two ethical issues we face in analysis. At one extreme lies the use of others to serve our own needs. At some unconscious level we treat them like a gas tank; they are there to service us, to give energy to our self. At the other extreme lies service to something beyond us—to the Self, to a meaning which gathers and constructs itself as we find and create it, which we find ourselves experiencing in a devotional way. No analyst, unless suffering from severe sociopathy or dissociation, sets out to do violence to an analysand, but rather falls into it through entanglements of complexes which distort perception and thought. Despite the pertinence of R. C. Zaehner's pithy reminder about the wickedness of evil (1981, 27), the problem can be seen as equally large on the opposite side when we remember that "even the very disease takes on a numinous character" (Jung 1973, 377) and that for analysts, as Winnicott says, wickedness is illness (Winnicott 1963a, 103). It needs to be treated, not simply condemned.

We know enough now about the danger of acting out transference and countertransference into physical exchanges between analyst and analysand, and about the equal and opposite danger of talking to death the hot feelings that pass back and forth between the two (Ulanov 1979, 101–4, 109; Ulanov 1982, 77–78). Are there alternatives to those twin dangers? Can we take in and make sense of the powerful constellations of archetypal and personal affect, image, behavior that surge upon us in intense transference-countertransference couplings? These intensities, we know, can arouse hate as well as love, and rage as well as tender rescue; they can bring into play the mother complex or the twin, the wise old figure or the child. Indeed, any archetype can galvanize any out-sized figure or emotion.

The fact is that we need our complexes to play their proper role in order to sustain the arduous work of a long and successful analysis; but if we work only within our personal complex, trouble must come, if not from imposing our own issues onto the analysand's, then from remaining locked into the personal levels of the material. Then the treatment will peter out because the personal level is finite and gets exhausted; it simply is not enough. To move to the Self level in analysis is to raise issues of life-and-death importance that push us through our personal complexes to their underlying archetypal depths, as we respond to a particular analysand's reality.

The questions still stand. Are there alternatives to acting out and to repressing or rationalizing a tremendously strong archetypal constellation? What can we do when the emotions stirred involve the strongest and most tempting of the constellations, sexual love? In it lie the treasures of *coniunctio*—a uniting of opposites as strong as love and hate deep inside us, between us, and in the world, too, so that in lovemaking we may feel that we are contributing to a greater good, not just succumbing to quick individual gratification. Sexuality is peculiarly suited to carry almost all levels of psychic life, from a child's dependence to an adult's profound spiritual longings. It delivers us into an immediacy both before the other and ourself. Its preverbal, body-based, emotion-laden language of image, affect, and instinct makes it well suited to convey our longings for union with split-off parts of ourselves, with a soul-mate found in another, and even with the Transcendent. The intensity of our desire thus carried in body, heart, and soul recalls something as directly religious as the first commandment given by Yahweh to Israel and often repeated by Jesus: to love God with all our heart, mind, soul, and strength. When an erotic sexual archetypal constellation occurs in the transference and countertransference, analyst and analysand find themselves in the most flammable of situations. Any glance or word, let alone action, can ignite an acting out. The fear of such intensity can drive both into sterile denial and rationalization.

Recent work has been done on the primacy of the intersubjective field (Stolorow 1987) and on the necessity of imaginal seeing in order to avoid mechanically rendering into projection and counterprojection the original organic wholeness in which both analysand and analyst are held (Schwartz-Salant 1989). This work shows us how the dangers of ignition or denial increase if we equate the field with the Self. If the intersubjective field becomes idolized we quickly forget the necessary limits of the analytic relationship. It is not, after all, one between equals, for one person sets the fee and the other person pays it. However much the two may be on a par as human beings and however much the analysand may in some respects be superior to the analyst, an analyst like a surgeon is an employee hired by an analysand to perform an operation. The hiring and the payment "for services rendered" is a permanent component of the relationship, such that even as the two concentrate on the field between them, one is more responsible for what happens than the other. An analysand's dependence underscores this responsibility. Sexual feelings in analysis make a person especially vulnerable, not only because its language carries our heart and soul along with our instincts into communication, but also because sexuality brings us in bodily terms as close as we come in adulthood to that fullness of presence—where we are open without covering or camouflage before another's gaze and touch—that we knew as infants with our parents. In such moments of intense sexual feeling we cast off our defenses. Our capacity to be hurt is greatly enhanced, and we depend on the analyst to see and protect us (Winnicott 1963b, 249–50).

When we focus on the intersubjective field, we meet the role of the feminine as a major factor in the analyst-analysand relationship. The feminine tendencies are to relate by being in-the-midst-of, by being at-one-with, and by taking the downward-going-road beneath the clear abstractions and differentiations of the masculine mode of being. These tendencies all lend themselves to working with skill and comfort within the intersubjective field (Ulanov 1971, 169–79; 1981, 76–80). Still the question remains: who is responsible for holding the situation, for holding the sense of the analysand's being, both in the present and in potential? I say that the analyst is responsible. Guidance does not come from the field, nor from the analyst, but from the Self, which acts through the field and through the persons, and to which all parties—but especially the analyst—must listen. That greater acuity of hearing, experience, and skill which an analyst should have developed is what the analysand is paying for. If we make the field the Self, then the analytic couple assumes primacy over the real life of both analyst and analysand and also over the ego-Self couple that is growing in the analysand (Ulanov 1992a, 52). That assertion of power is a major betrayal of the analytical process, for the analyst then is not available to the analysand to inculcate a sense for living a real life.

The alternative of working with the erotic sexual field without acting it out, denying it, rationalizing it, or making it the Self lies, I believe, in both parties putting themselves under the authority of the Self and following its lead. This means making sacrifices for both analyst and analysand, but in unforeseen ways, thriving, too. Happily, the two meanings of my title meet. Service to the Self turns out to answer our most particular personal needs as well as those of a commonality beyond us. We are thus reassured at a deep unspoken level that devotion to the transpersonal moves through and fulfills the personal. The two are not split. Rather, one orders the other (Ulanov 1971, 341).

Sacrifice sounds a familiar note that both analysand and analyst can recognize, for each knows that the limits of analysis make impossible their involvement with each other outside analytical sessions. What the anima or animus constellate must be integrated, not projectively identified with each other. When the analysis goes deep into early and painful wounds and explores fearful places where madness threatens, the borderline enactments of the anima or animus figure emerge. They stand with a foot on either side of the borders between ego and archetype, reasonableness and passion, sanity and madness. They bring with them gusts of archetypal emotion as they put their finger on the precise spots of ego-vulnerability. The danger looms of being emotionally overwhelmed.

One man, for instance, speaks about his attraction to his analyst and says he wants to carry her off to another country. He feels the burden of the one-way street of analysis, where the analysand must tell all the stories, reveal all the secrets, speak all the feelings, while the analyst remains comparatively unknown, stories untold, feelings unvoiced. This man knows the courage it takes to make something out of this asymmetrical relationship. But he suffers the sacrifice of a felt sense of dignity as he goes on revealing his secrets and relinquishing his reserve, telling all without a comparable return from the analyst. He feels he is sacrificing his natural urge to live out his attraction—and at great cost. He comes to see, however, that the momentum to go on making himself vulnerable springs not from the analysis, but from whatever it is beyond the analysis that he really loves and desires. He takes his experience in analysis and lets it feed his outside life, his real life shared with loved ones, with friends, with work. He takes what bubbles up in the consulting room and lets its currents flow into his day-to-day living.

When a person lacks relationship to others in life outside the analysis such sacrifice becomes harder, and the analytical situation much more tense. For the real seems to flourish only within the analytical relationship. The urgency to live it right there becomes more compelling and the sense of vulnerability all the more risky. The required move remains what it always must be—to experience the passion well within the holding container of the analytical relationship and see where the current can be made to flow into one's own real life. Hidden in the urge for sexual gratification is purpose: the energy is going somewhere and we must bend our will to the task of discovering just where and why.

Sometimes the person finds the climate of desire too hot to handle and breaks off treatment. To see the work suddenly chopped off in mid-life is almost as hard to bear for the analyst as for the analysand. Sometimes, fortunately, the person comes back to pick up the work or at least to find better closure (Ulanov 1992b). A supervisee involved in a difficult case said she watched the man she was treating become more and more of a human being, uncovering his capacity to love, but then he quit. That was it—the treatment was over. She felt unfinished. She discovered in working on herself that her bond with this man—a bond that sprang from contacting an arrested child-part in him—touched unresolved pain suffered by her own inner child. Once she had come to that realization, she felt able to let the analysand's treatment go, unfinished as it was. Synchronistically, the man then contacted her for more sessions that brought their work to some conclusion.

Sometimes an analysand sets out at some level of consciousness to snare an analyst into an affair. I have come to understand this as a move of desperation when persons feel only power can secure the split-off parts of self they so ardently seek (Ulanov 1979, 104). Often mixed into this power-play lies a wish to defeat the analyst, even to wreck his or her career. The analysand simply refuses the sacrifice that analysis as a way-station to the Self imposes. Feelings of revenge or rage triumph over all. It is for the patient as if the sacrifice is reified and projectively identified with the analyst so that only the analyst has to pay the price.

On the analyst's side there is a matching vulnerability. It is not the same as the vulnerability of transference-love. It is related in kind, however, for the analyst, opened and exposed to feeling, very much wants the analysand to take what is given or found or created in the analysis into fully lived life. That feels like a kind of love for the analysand in which the analyst is made use of quickly enough and left behind. That is what countertransference-love often becomes on the objective level.

On the subjective level, an odd dialogue may occur between the complexes and wounds personified in the anima and animus figures of each person. These archetypal figures press for fulfillment in their roles as thresholds for the Self, and do not hesitate to press for full expression even in their most damaged forms (Ulanov and Ulanov 1994, chapter 1); but whether damaged or in good shape, the archetypal anima-animus couple will mirror and be mirrored by the analyst-analysand couple that forms and dissolves and forms again around the soul's desire to reach the center and heal the past. Analysis becomes a paradoxical exchange that is at once full-bodied and chaste, emotional and yet held within the limits of analysis. Those are the limits that make depth of feeling permissible. Each person addressed by the Self must face a tremendous energy suddenly let loose. When the male analysand discussed above, for example, was working on his feelings for me, I dreamt of a tiger, powerful, lustrous in its fur, and demanding that I drive it around the driveway of my house. With great exertion and concentration I manage to do it.

Both analyst and analysand know their feelings for each other can be lived symbolically but not literally either inside or outside the sessions. The thriving offered each person consists precisely in what flows into each of them from encounters in an intense erotic intersubjective field to be lived in their own separate ways. We must understand that when we confront an anima or animus issue it sets off reactions on two levels: an ego level, where we are faced with a precise problem with which to struggle; and an archetypal level, where we are ushered into the energies of the Self which demand to be realized and lived.

This last, deep level of Self-living, when really engaged, will rearrange all other aspects of personality, of object relations, and of our life in the world. At the ego level, we are handed specific tasks to solve. At the shadow level, we are directed, not just to go on uncovering shadow bits we would rather bury, but, perhaps surprisingly, to get at them by recollecting and claiming the good that already belongs to us (Ulanov 1993). We must remember what we love in order to reach what we hate. We must claim what we construct in order to tackle destructive elements (Winnicott 1960). Finally, our anima-animus personifications transmute into bridges to lead us into Self territory. New objects come into being. We feel generating in us the beginnings of ideas, new ways of feeling, and insights that fuel new belief in what matters. We are bound to be deeply moved by how much is given.

All of this takes a lot of work. It asks an energy sustained by a complicated set of devotions. Hence the thought behind my title— that ethical issues ultimately resolve into service to the Self. Two examples must suffice. In the first, a supervisee, a male analyst, says that a woman analysand speaking of her love for him had accused him of denying the fact that he really is in love with her. "I'm not in love with her," he said, "but then I wonder." He felt hypnotized. What struck him with great force was this woman's "feminine courage" in not hiding her vulnerable love for him and in not accepting his denial without challenge. But did he too easily lose his own boundaries and merge his with hers? Still, in that part of him that could be so open to another, he experienced "joy" and felt pulled into union. Was this infantile striving to return to the womb, he asked; was it some comforting illusion to withstand the harsh reality of an ultimate loneliness? Listening, I heard what he said as the anima speaking, expressing a basic orientation to reality, and showing him the particular way he perceived exactly what he saw, with both its positive and negative pulls. A conflict entangled him. He felt an urge to live in kinship but also felt contempt for that urge. "You look down on this urge to union," I told him, "and then feel it persecutes you by tempting you into trouble." This remark triggered memories of his mother, who had never had the centering courage he found in his analysand, but had instead always seemed to fall apart at the center, weeping and collapsing whenever she and his father disagreed and fought. He felt his mother was not reliably there for him, because she could not reliably be present to herself.

In contrast, there stood his analysand, fragile like his mother but able to hold and center herself and speak out to the man upon whom she felt dependent, willing to expose her feelings and challenge him. She was, in psychoanalytic jargon, a woman who possessed her own penis. She had her animus within her as part of her being. He felt hypnotized because she had touched a wound in his anima. For a moment, she was his mother but now repaired, able instead of disabled, in possession of herself instead of dispossessed. When he saw this and really knew it, he could see and not despise his own urge to union and find his way to respond to his analysand along different lines. He could support her and ally with her ego in attempting to penetrate him with her own phallic thrust. He allied with her as a whole woman, in contrast to his mother, who had such an unmistakable hole in her and clearly could not adequately mother him. This inadequacy had left him feeling a matching hole in himself, an emptiness instead of his own anima well within him.

His drive to union with his analysand was in part an urge to go back and do it all over again correctly with his mother and in part the result of a lavish admiration for what she, the analysand, had accomplished in her speaking from her own center. At this moment, in the work of this analytical couple, a piece of his wound in effect repaired itself as he allowed himself to feel the impact of his analysand's loving center and what it led him to find in himself. He was then able to aid her in sustaining herself in her own newfound strength to speak from that center and to be more of the woman she was meant to be. It was a moving exchange of feeling and understanding that arose through discussion of an ethical issue, all of it made possible because of open service to the Self.

The experience, on the other hand, in which the impersonal suddenly becomes personal is often deeply puzzling to analysts (Ulanov 1982, 81). Induced or objective countertransference helps us map such an experience, but the puzzlement remains when the countertransference endures despite all our efforts to work it through. We know that our personal reaction is really not personal to us, yet we feel it. It lives as if dissociated from the rest of our reality. In that way it mirrors a dissociation in our analysand, which we know at first only hypothetically, though we are sure we must live with it, sometimes for months and months, as if it were a reaction drawn from the center of our person, though we know very well it is not. Most ethical violations, I believe, come from such a situation, heightened when wounds in the analyst are touched. Then the analyst feels the pain and the contradiction intensely and cannot clearly mark out what belongs to whom, believing that what addresses her also addresses the analysand and that the two of them are held in a gripping field that transcends both of them where it would prove a failure of nerve and of faith to refuse to experience it. It feels all but impossible to differentiate the induced reaction from the analyst's own feelings. It is then that we should consult a colleague. The failure to do so touches the shadow side of Jungian analysis, I believe, and perhaps a weakness in all schools of depth psychology. We fear incomprehension and judgment and do not count on professional kinship. We do not trust what the great field of archetypal energy and of feeling might yield to a particular treatment or to general analytical understanding. We forget how much we can learn and should want to learn from such sources.

I speak of analytical intimacy as an odd, wonderful, paradoxical fact about this work. Analysts are, after all, closely involved in the most personal places of another human being's life, their confusion, fear, rage, sexuality, prayers, vision of death, originality, creativity. We participate in our analysands' lives while not living at all with them outside our sessions. Still, we do live a history with each person that must affect and change each of us, analyst as well as analysand.

The alternative to repressing or acting out an erotic field lies, I think, in orienting the analysis around one summarizing question: What is the Self engineering? This orientation alone, in my experience, is strong enough and has enough of its own passion to contain erotic transference or countertransference and to allow its energies to support research into the ways we allow ourselves, analysts and analysands, to be used as servants of the process of living toward the Self. Because the Self is not a monolithic content that drops like a stone into the treatment or onto the heads of the participants but offers rather a warm and engaging center of life, to work under its authority means to discover or to create the Self in that work. The Self is called into being by strong ego-attitudes, by efforts of inquiry and of sustained passionate interest in Self-life and Self-purpose. That is where erotic passion should go. A general sense of purposiveness—that all this is not for nothing, that if such an erotic field blazes into being it is to reach something—gives the ego a sense of the Self every day, in every session. For the analysand, an analysis fueled by an erotic field means a large overhauling of the personality, rather than simply reparative focus on one aspect of one's person. When anima or animus shapes a major part of the transference, a person's whole orientation to being will be called into question. An anima, for example, will make sure that she is seen and that a man will become conscious of the lens she can provide through which he can view reality. Becoming conscious of that lens will effect changes on every level of the man's life.

In the last analytic experience I wish to discuss, an erotic tinge characterized the transference-countertransference field for a long part of a long analysis and then, amazingly, disappeared completely, as if folded into the integrated textures of analytical intimacy. It was like cooking. The erotic factor was a separate ingredient, always on the counter there before us, for months, but not really part of the mixture of the analysand's personal life or my own. We spoke of this erotic factor from time to time, and I used it to show the analysand how he found himself positioned with that eroticism toward others. But my interpretations did not seem to yield much change. Looking back, I now see that each effort of interpretation was in fact part of a long process that issued finally in an integrating resolution. When the man integrated this erotic factor, it disappeared between us, as if folded at last into the analytical soufflé, no longer separate or even discernible, just a necessary part of the mixture, like egg whites whipped for a long time, an essential if not quite visible ingredient giving lightness and air to the dish.

The case I refer to is that of the man I introduced in chapter 1 (see pp. 17–19). His example will illustrate the puzzling difficulties and the amazing resolution of an erotic transference-countertransference field when we ask what the self is engineering. This was an artistic man in his forties who dreamt that his anima ideal, a "goddess possessed of angel hair," as he described her, was handed over to him by her husband, who personified for the analysand the most crude and brutish aspects of his own shadow. Following that dream-encounter, he dreamt of his own father as needing the loving care he, his son, could provide, rather than as the judge who had always defeated his son's self-confidence by his severe judgments. At that point, he risked writing out his most intense and most repeated sexual fantasy and, in showing it to me, transferred onto me the self-loathing that accompanied it. He was then, inevitably, enraged at me, expecting that I would condemn him for that raw transference; but the dreaming went on its crusading way. He dreamt now of being captured and set to an ordeal of religious testing by four men of a different religious faith. When he accused them of going against their god, one of the men offered to take the sins of the other three onto himself. The dreamer then thought of Jesus, who had taken on the sins of others, and reached to put his hand in Christ's as he faced the promised ordeal.

There was a strong erotic tinge in the field between us, the purpose of which at this time became clear. I was carrying the hyphen, so to speak, between the dissociated elements in the analysand, that is, between a ruthless aggressiveness expressed sexually—what he called "impersonal archetypal sex" that just gripped him and all who participated with him while quite ignoring everything about their persons—and his genuine concern both for himself and for others. He needed the ruthless aggression, especially to throw off the condemning father-voice, and in fact he did live the human personal dimensions of his life with much kindness and generosity to others. I carried the connection between these separated elements because I did not echo his condemnation of the sexual fantasy but rather endorsed its positive energies and excitement. Neither did I turn away from or rationalize the eroticism in the field, even though its dissociated elements might have seemed to conflict with the reality of my own commitment to those I love. I just held the eroticism in its appropriate place and bore the strain it brought. My role was to prepare the way for the experience of connecting up ruthless aggression with a genuine "capacity for concern" (Winnicott 1963c). The analytical field held both aggression and concern and the analysand could then finally integrate the two. Our analytical relationship connected the two halves. It was at the point of integration that the erotic tinge simply fell away, its purpose accomplished.

What then followed was what the earlier dream had called "facing the ordeal." This turned out to be a reordering of every level of the analysand's being. On the ego level, specific tasks faced him to be worked through with specific women in his life. The tasks took time, effort, money, thought, and physical labor. On the shadow level, a wonderful dream image showed the chthonic energy now available to him in the figure of an enormous bull with flamingoes on its head which he could summon by dancing a little jig. Cantering over, the bull would stop on his side of the line between them, ready to heed the man, who did not yet know where to direct this energy suddenly at his disposal. To him this image was raw aggression and sex, yet was somehow connected through the birds to spirit. The shadow tasks unfolded gradually, involving him both in differentiating himself from mother and father voices that still exerted powerful control over him, and in facing his own eagerness just to avoid any confrontation. At the anima level, he both engaged his beliefs about life, issuing in a formal commitment to the church, a step he had long considered, and openly acknowledged his despair about the inner emptiness, laziness, and suicidal depression he found in himself. The energy to sustain all this work, which I understood as living in service to the Self and accepting it as life's center, came from the transformed erotic field. He was taking up the opus of *coniunctio*, unifying the disparate parts of his being, uniting with others in his life and creating and finding his own path to the Transcendent.

To reach this unfolding conclusion to analytical work something very specific is required from the analyst, well beyond simply remaining in the field, erotic or whatever, until its purpose comes clear. What is also demanded is belief in the reality of the symbol, knowing that the psyche really does exist, and that we serve its reality. The symbol is not a formula laid over something. It is not a "this" standing for a "that" but both a "this" *and* a "that" dwelling in the analytic moment. Archetypes are basic forms of being which once created go on forever (Lampert 1944). Symbols which emerge in analysis bring together elements of being, as the symbols which arise in the field of erotic transference-countertransference also do. We cannot accept the reality of the moment when these symbols appear if we do not accept the being that the symbols configure. Being in all its reality should be embodied to begin with in the analyst's belief; the analyst's work confirms its reality, enabling the analysand to see it also, and to recover the analytical moment as itself a symbol. It is that belief and confirmation which draw analysts to lives of open service to being. Serving in this way, they not only believe, but see and know the reality of being.

This is the ontological premise of the analytical method. The service of analysis to Being is the grand alternative to the negative processes involved in either acting out or denying the erotic field which analysis so often enters. We are in the field, clearly, unmistakably, and ethically accepting what is there—its consequences, its openings to truth—and facing it with attitudes of directness. This is real; this is reality (Jung 1963, par. 754). We are not outside it, appreciating the experience aesthetically but not really believing in it, thinking we can take it and then leave it. In the elements of belief, in entering into the reality of the archetype from which symbol and field arise, the healing processes of our work are made available to us and to our analysands. The reality itself achieves this great end, not the analyst, not the analysand, not the field; but to accomplish this end, we must believe in this reality and live in it with all the necessary disciplines the belief brings with it.

Believing this way, as against acting out, means knowing reality as a constant presence and knowing that it knows us. The emphasis is on this *it*, so much larger and more positive than Freud's *id*— on its relating to us, on how we relate to it, and on how in time the analysand comes to relate to it. The intensity that first shows itself in an erotic field is released into these many relations to psychic reality. What the erotic tinge offers the analyst is not the *frisson* of sexual fantasy or the entanglements of sexual acting out, but penetration to psychic reality. That is where the passion is destined to go and the place at which it finally arrives, where sacrifice becomes thriving at the deepest levels of life. For, like our images of heaven, each of us receives exactly what we need in our own idiosyncratic being. There can be found all the room that is needed for the intensity of reality to communicate itself and do its uniting work. Igniting or rationalizing the erotic field is a destructive and altogether unnecessary detour from the path of service to this reality whose flame of Self-communication never goes out.

References

Jung, C. G. 1963. *Mysterium Coniunctionis. CW* 14. Princeton: Princeton University Press.

———. 1973. *Letters*. Vol. 1. Ed. G. Adler. Princeton: Princeton University Press.

Lampert, E. 1944. *The Divine Realm: Towards a Theology of The Sacraments*. London: Faber and Faber.

Schwartz-Salant, N. 1989. *The Borderline Personality: Vision and Healing*. Wilmette, Ill.: Chiron Publications.

Stolorow, R. D., B. Brandschaft, and G. E. Atwood. 1987. *Psychoanalytic Treatment: An Intersubjective Approach*. Hillsdale, N. J.: The Analytic Press.

Ulanov, A. B., 1971. *The Feminine in Christian Theology and in Jungian Psychology*. Evanston, Ill.: Northwestern University Press.

———. 1979. Follow-up treatment in cases of patient/therapist sex. *Journal of the American Academy of Psychoanalysis* 7(1): 101–110. Adapted and republished as chap. 6 of this book.

———. 1981. *Receiving Woman: Studies in the Psychology and Theology of the Feminine*. Louisville: Westminster.

———. 1982. Transference/countertransference: A Jungian perspective. *Jungian Analysis*. 1st ed. Ed. M. Stein. LaSalle, Ill.: Open Court. Adapted and republished as chap. 7 of this book.

———. 1992a. Disguises of the anima. *Gender and Soul in Psychotherapy*. Ed. N. Schwartz-Salant and M. Stein. Wilmette, Ill.: Chiron Publications. Adapted and republished as chap. 9 of this book.

———. 1992b. The perverse and the transcendent. *The Transcendent Function: Individual and Collective Aspects*. Ed. M. A. Mattoon. Einsiedeln, Switzerland: Daimon Verlag, 1993. Adapted and republished as chap. 3 of this book.

———. 1993. Spiritual aspects of clinical work. *Jungian Analysis*. Ed. M. Stein. 2d ed. Chicago, Ill.: Open Court, 1995. Adapted and republished as chap. 1 of this book.

Ulanov, A. and Ulanov, B. 1994. *Transforming Sexuality: The Archetypal World of Anima and Animus*. Boston: Shambhala.

Winnicott, D. W. 1960. Aggression, guilt, and reparation. *Deprivation and Delinquency*. Ed. C. Winnicott, R. Shepherd, and M. Davis. London: Tavistock, 1984.

———. 1963a. Morals and education. *Maturational Processes and the Facilitating Environment*. New York: International Universities Press, 1965.

————. 1963b. Dependence in infant-care, in child-care, and in the psycho-analytic setting. *Maturational Processes and the Facilitating Environment*. New York: International Universities Press, 1965.

————. 1963c. The development of the capacity for concern. *Maturational Processes and the Facilitating Environment*. New York: International Universities Press, 1965.

Zaehner, R. C. 1981. *The City Within the Heart*. New York: Crossroad.

The Transcendent Here and Now and Beyond

9

Disguises of the Anima

The Bridge

Through experiences forced on me by my clinical work, I have
come to the idea that the anima or animus maps routes to certain
experiences of the Self which bring us more into life, and make us
face reality. Anima or animus forms a bridge across which the contents of the Self come to address the ego, to put questions to our
very existence. These questions seem to issue from an other—
personified as an anima or animus figure—who says, in effect: You
must deal with me, confront me, respond to me, even if it is to reject me, but here I am and you cannot escape.[1]

These Self experiences make us feel that life is worth living. They
color our perceptions with excitement and awe at the very fact of
being.[2] It makes no difference whatever our age or sexuality is, or
whether we are single or married, celibate or divorced. We all must
face and answer the other who confronts us from a sexual departure point opposite to our conscious gender identity. We all share
the task of putting these parts of ourselves together to make an
identity for ourselves, with its possibilities and tribulations.

In focusing on the anima/animus bridge, I am expanding on
Jung's notion of these archetypal figures as "unwelcome intruders"
who compel our attention through their irresistible and indefinable
attractions as dream and fantasy personages or, in projected form,
through their lure to other people. By making the personifications
of these complexes conscious, "we convert them into bridges to the
unconscious. It is because we are not using them purposefully as
functions that they remain personified complexes" (Jung 1928, par.

399). To the degree that we actively try to understand them, "the personified figure of anima or animus will disappear. It becomes a function of relationship between conscious and unconscious" (Jung 1928, par. 370).

Where then does the bridge take us? Right to the Self, bringing us, as conscious and unconscious move toward each other, to a closer meeting with life and the reality made available to us when our psyche is opened up. We are more pliable and open to ourselves. Reality beckons in our own particular colors. The image of bridge helps us to focus on its function of linking the ego world, and its ways of operation following the laws of directed thinking, with the Self world, characterized by nondirected thinking. Each, ego and Self, has its own aims and values; they link through the contrasexual factor.

Anima and animus provide not a set content but rather a dynamic function or process. When we slap the animus label onto people, as if it always meant the same thing, we are articulating a dysfunction of the bridge. It has, in fact, broken down. The animus, for any given woman, can never be made to fit reductive generalizations; it is always highly individual. For example, a professional woman with postdoctoral training found that her animus figures— whether in dream or reality—consistently appeared as big, silent men, utterly non-verbal, who stood calmly next to her or gently lay over her, to "earth" her, to connect her to her "deeper self." Another woman, who felt herself dumbly inarticulate, married her husband because of his ability to talk brilliantly. Years later, she sought analysis because she thought that if he did not shut up and listen to her, she was going to kill him.

We share among us the same function of anima and animus as bridge between ego and Self. Where we differ is in the contents that walk across that bridge, even though we can describe them in general as issuing from another departure point, opposite to our conscious gender identity. The anima and animus are not just types of consciousness, as some revisionists suggest, insisting that we all possess both (Bachelard 1969, ch. 2; Whitmont 1980; Hillman 1972; Kast 1986, ch. 8). That makes the content a set one, always the same no matter where or in whom it turns up. But the anima/animus contents that cross the bridge insist on their individual particularities. They do not permit reduction to the terms of culture-bound prejudices, and they are not merely the products, as some feminists assert, of Jung's own sexism (Reuther 1983, 190–273, n. 9; Miller 1976, 78–79; Goldenberg 1976).[3] Both of these views miss the epochal nature of Jung's insight, however "clumsy" it seems to be, even to him.[4]

As we know, one foot of the anima or animus complex stands in the personal world, shaped by introjected objects and images—the significant persons of the opposite sex in our early life, images of the masculine and feminine in our culture, and our inherited physical makeup. The other foot stands in the objective psyche, functioning according to its laws of contiguity, similarity, association, simultaneity, and the range of physical to spiritual poles of the archetype (Jung 1912). Here the contrasexual figure confronts us with particular archetypal images that constellate the objective psyche in relation to our personal, physical, and cultural life. That is why, for example, when an animus content replaces that of the adapted ego in discussion, we feel invaded by something wildly irrational, with tinges even of madness. We've got hold of a fish out of water, the animus that swims in the unconscious. When we recognize it as such, its tendency to throw opposites together takes on a revelatory light, rather than a crackpot dimness or frightening disruptive glare.

The contrasexual bridge functions to connect the worlds on either side, not to merge them. The contrasexual are border figures, taking us from one to another sexual departure point, and from the personal to the collective, the conscious to the archetypal, the ego to the Self. So what seems spiritual—in effect, whether we live with meaning or futility—shows itself as all mixed up with the sexual: in effect, how we put ourselves into shared existence with others. What seems private turns out to be social, for our struggles to connect with an other at our own center also has roots that extend from a center far outside us. In this struggle, we feel not as if on some isolated journey but intimately bound up with other people, a woman with other women and with womanliness and, even though a woman, like a man identified with men's points of view, almost in the skin. At the same time, we know that the other sex, however we experience it, also feels bound up with us.

The spiritual expands the sexual view to a wide and flexible contemplative gaze onto all kinds of coupling, while the sexual draws the spiritual into the most specific here-and-now interaction with another concrete human being. Sexuality both forces us toward incarnation and pulls us across the borders of our ego identities toward otherness, toward the center. The Russian philosopher Solovyev said that only sexuality is strong enough to counter our egotism (Solovyev 1945, 25, 35, 77).

Sexual responses, then, have a spiritual function as well as a bodily one. They act to pull us through into another center, bigger and more encompassing than the ego, which is what we Jungians call the Self. But this anima / animus region where sex and spirit tangle and conjoin can also be the place where heart and soul get broken, become addicted, and become compelled to do things against their best interests. We fear this place. There we can be hurt. There betrayal can strike us down. In defense, we make steely vows of revenge against betrayers and against ourselves for opening so far. The sultan in the famous *Arabian Nights*, for example, would have fulfilled his vow to execute every woman with whom he lay, had it not been for the help of Scheherazade. She stopped him by appealing to his imagination with her thousand tales on a thousand nights. She slowly opened in him a space of interior contemplation.[5] As long as we resist finding such a helper in each of us, we will go on reading headlines in newspapers across our world that tell of a woman who hires a thug to kill her husband, of a man who beats his girlfriend to death, of elders sexually abusing children, of rape, of contempt between the sexes. Anima and animus affect our society as well as our spirit and our sexuality.

People come to us Jungian analysts because of the difficulties in these areas. They feel unalive, deeply frightened by a seeming inability to make intimate contact with another, or in an urgent state where they feel split almost in two. They think that if something does not change quickly, they will kill themselves. The psyche brings these dilemmas, and all sorts of fitting images to express them as well as body symptoms to their resolution. We ask the psyche where its energies are heading, what it is trying to bring about.

It is possible to map the territory of these experiences that speak of Self, whether achieved or approached or missed, through anima and animus. I find this map of great practical usefulness in my work. It cuts through dense fields to move toward the point of it all. I find myself, in relation to this theory, trying to do what Vladimir Horowitz said about his performances: "I play music behind the notes. I search for it and play from this other side."[6]

I am interested in the way anima and animus usher in the Self and in the space of emptiness behind the notes of the theory, where our God-images stop and the presence of the Holy is evoked by the Self. I see, in the two case examples I am about to give, that I have always been interested in this space, for these examples span more than twenty years. Work with the first man, whose case I introduced earlier in this book (see pp. 138–40) began in 1968 and was finished, finally, with his death in 1975. Work with the second man, the son of the first, began just recently and, although interrupted, will continue. The anima/animus theory made it possible to map these men's experiences so that one could die without going mad and the other could live because he confronted and chose his life.

Disguise

What makes these cases of father and son of special interest is that both men, allowing for individual variation, suffer the same disguise phenomenon of the split anima. This disguise presents itself to a man's ego at first as an almost intolerable conflict of choice between two females, the wife and the other woman.[7] To be caught between two women and be unwilling to choose is a choice in fact— for death. Life hangs in the air, unlived. The man is caught in suspended animation. The anima in retreat represents death; her disguise, a shroud. Yet, in both these cases, we can see the anima engineering through the split a way of coming to the Self, of making a bridge to that other country, so foreign and so enticing to the ego.[8] Each of these men moved from suspended animation to real election, choosing to receive the feminine in himself. In this way, analysis informed by the idea of anima and animus shows itself as much more than interesting material. It is life-supporting; it speaks for life, not for death.

Both men, in their transference, used me as the anima bridge.[9] This use allowed them to come into relation with the unconscious contents that had sought their attention. The contents were of such importance that they not only disrupted their lives but threatened to end them if left neglected, unintegrated. As the men met the task their psyches set them, they could begin to dispense with me. Their anima was functioning as an inner bridge across which ego and Self were meeting (Ulanov and Ulanov 1994, chapter 1).[10] Something large is demanded of the ego in such situations, or more accurately, everything is demanded. The ego must venture on that bridge and cross over to Self country, but it cannot do so securely until the anima becomes a sturdy connecting link.

The father sought treatment at the age of forty-three, after twenty years of marriage and three sons. The son, youngest of the three, sought treatment at age thirty-one after ten years of marriage and no children, although in the course of treatment he had a son who died the day he was born and who was named for the father. The father came to me through referral from a colleague treating his wife;

the son sought me out because his father had spoken of his work with me and told him to see me if need arose. Need did arise for the son, fourteen years after his father's death. The father came for two hours of individual work a week for three years, then for group therapy, with irregular individual sessions, for another three years. The son came one hour a week for eight months. Both traveled from several states away to undertake analysis.

Both men were deeply unhappy, although they expressed their unhappiness differently. The father said that if it were not for his children he might consider suicide. He and his wife got along as friends, but were hopelessly locked in sexual struggle, he wanting it, she feeling the demand excessive. He quickly saw his need for affection as exorbitant and put the hard question to himself, "Am I a taker, not a giver?" This was painful since he had committed himself to a helping profession, knowing it as his vocation. Bouts of guilt laid him low. He was uneasy in not having discovered his vocation until after his marriage in work his wife hated, work which robbed her of her hope of working together in the wilderness, as they had planned. He felt guilty about his sexual desires, and about the anger his wife aroused not only by denying him sexually and saying she found him unattractive, but also by her general deprecating attitude toward him, "telling the truth when it does not need to be told." His wife wanted him to be celibate; he felt he could not and would not be, and then he felt guilty because of the resultant affairs. The aggression with which he was not in touch turned against him in dreams of pouring gasoline on himself to destroy himself or of going into a house where he might be castrated. In these dream plots lurked the motif of son-lover sacrificing his manhood to mother-goddess.

The son expressed his unhappiness directly, saying he had the fantasy of living a life where he would be "true to himself." In a dream at the beginning of analysis, he was in a plane that would not take off for lack of fuel. His mother was on it, too. When it flipped over and he fell out, a man who was there did not help him. He struggled out of the plane to find himself "on thin ice." He felt dissatisfaction with his marriage. He and his wife were good friends but lacked sexual passion and all the excitement about living together that came with it. He felt anger at his wife's moody withdrawal and negativity about herself, which made her "not nice to my friends." He did not feel guilty about his affair; but he did feel torn apart, desperate that he was unable to decide what to do, which woman to choose. At one point, suicidal feelings threatened him, as they had his father. He presented his problem as a conflict over two women, which his father had known, too, but the son saw clearly that he was "being dragged somewhere" and that "the answer was within," even though he could not yet find his "own truth."

The principal disguise of the anima in both men was an insoluble conflict concerning two women.[11] The father felt bound to his wife for the sake of his boys and his profession, a public one where he was passionately committed as well as very successful. He did find sexual happiness with another woman, and more—laughter, sensuality, intimacy, emotional expression, intensity, and, above all, acceptance of all of him. He felt life was not worth living without the sexual connection.

The son felt bound to his wife by the security of their home and the land which he had worked hard to purchase and through fear of breaking his wife's heart. She was "sad and depressed" and he had worked hard to help her, leading her to face her feelings of abandonment by her father and going abroad with her to see her father after many years of separation. Before their marriage, while they were at different colleges, he had tried to break off his relationship with her but had found no better alternative and could not bear to hurt her. Yet he still had "no desire to kiss her," had "no woman feeling about her." He wanted to sleep with someone else before relocating from the city where he worked. Then he fell passionately in love with this other woman. He knew it mattered to him to be important to her ("not just a dick"); indeed, he wanted to try to change her life, too. With her, he felt pressed to know where he was and what he felt, not to "fall asleep" in his life. "I feel like a man with her," he said. A level of primordial sexual fire ignited between them. He said she could not "control" her sexual response to him; it would overcome her. "She smells me and responds." This he found deeply exciting and reassuring.

The split anima for both men set security, life investment, loyalty, consideration, and responsibility to children against igniting sexual fire and spiritual aliveness accompanied by a feeling of being unhoused and ungrounded. The father's conflict accented the strain between his persona—his beloved profession—and his secret sexual life. The son's conflict was lodged more in his ego and in the question of what his true path was. Although for both men the affair lasted for some time—for the father, off and on for five years and for the son, intensely for two years—neither could choose that sexual option. The father, for example, had another brief fling and then a more sustained relationship before he ended his marriage and went to live as a single man. The son struggled slowly toward realization of the anima fire within himself, toward a real life in himself rather than in either woman, and chose to test his marriage by recommitting himself to it. He did not want to start all over again with another woman, for he felt he had never really chosen his wife in the first place. He had "to give 100%" to the marriage before he could discard it. Thus the anima disguise, when it dissolved and functioned within each of the men as his own bridge to the unconscious, led to a greater sense of life in oneself rather than that sense being carried by a woman. One man chose to live alone, contrary to anything he had ever expected of himself, and, in his sudden confrontation with death, he found himself wholeheartedly choosing the Self. The other chose for the first time to be really married, although he had been married in name all along.

The split-anima disguise can best be summed up by citing two dreams, both of which were dreamt after much analytic work. In the father's dream, as cited earlier (see p. 138), two women, armed with revolvers and personifying the opposing parts of his anima, hold him and each other captive. Each woman might shoot him or the other woman, but each is halted in a stalemate because her opponent might fire first. The father felt trapped, as well as pulled apart. But he also felt a change in himself in this dream. He saw he had shifted away from asking, "What can I do to end all this?" He no longer felt a suicidal temptation. He now asked, "What is the meaning of this suffering?" He was living consciously with the tension of the split. He even felt that his suffering helped him to help others through his work (see Ulanov 1982, 82). In the son's dream, the other woman came to his home, where his wife was. "They were forced to converse, or at least be in very close proximity." The two opposing sides, security and instinct, began to draw together.

The Wounded Feminine

Behind this split in the anima lay a wound to the feminine. The father experienced it with his wife; the son, with his mother. The mother, in her turn, suffered the wound to her feminine self through her own father. In cases like this, we can see the suffering of generations, who pass on wounds that have not been healed. We also see the difference consciousness makes. The son's analytic work began at a better place than the father's, thanks to the work his father had done in his own analysis. He bequeathed his son a psychological legacy.[12]

Growing up, the father had felt himself to be his mother's confidant. She had loved him, he said, in a positive way, but with something sexual missing. His father, he remembered, had been demonstrative and affectionate but ruthless in business and spoiled and worshiped by his mother. In analysis, he began to see how he had lived in thrall to the Mother in her archetypal manifestations. He had depended on his mother's approval, remembering no fights with her or any need to gain his independence. Now he found it intolerable when the woman in his extramarital relationship was mad at him. He felt "doomed" when his wife told him that she felt "blah" about him. On the other hand, he felt cheered and rejuvenated when he was accepted and loved by a woman. He saw, after a while, that he was at the beck and call of the woman's responses. Even his suicidal feelings or self-castration dreams came to seem to him proof of his bondage to the Mother. Gradually, he was able to distinguish between his feelings and his needs. He stopped whimpering and became strong enough to face his wife's anger and her own affairs and the other woman's anger and hurt that he was not going to marry her.

Looking back, he felt wonder at having been drawn to his wife, whom both his parents had urged him to marry. She was so opposite to his mother, not at all the approving, accepting, maternal type, but rather a girl-woman, a sort of Artemis figure, confident in nature and of her own athletic prowess. We could speculate that the marriage had promoted his differentiation from his boy-to-mother stance and permitted him to incubate the opposite sex in himself. Suffering his wife's sexual rejection, he could begin his journey to free himself from endless orbiting around the feminine-as-mother. He would no longer renounce his ownership of his own sexual impulses. Thus he smashed the son-mother containers, both in his wife and with the other woman.

A second woman with whom the father had a long and important relationship was a young prostitute, some decades his junior. Sexually, he said, she reminded him of his first extramarital partner; but the terms were clear and up front from the beginning, although the relationship soon became personal. He brought her to his house and into his community after he divorced his wife. He wanted her to see his world and to meet his sons. When she did, she said there was no way she could compete with all of that. The match could not become a merger, so eventually they parted on good terms. What struck me was his effort to bring the opposites together and let each side know the other, to own both of them. The effort helped heal the wounded feminine in him, which had led to such enslavement to the mother that his own anima had barely emerged, leaving him for so long in his split-anima condition.

The father's wife had originally attracted her husband, I think, because she had approached him from a departure point radically different from his mother's. She came as an equal. She was bold and adventurous as she moved through the world and into nature's wilderness. She prized honesty over acceptance or approval. She got mad and froze him out in disapproval of what she saw as his hypocrisy—his enjoyment of an excellent reputation in his community while conducting a secret sexual life. She owned her own affairs and felt she was not representing herself publicly as a paragon. She felt that his heavy-handed sexual needs robbed her of her own lightness of being. She linked her husband in her mind to her father, who had scornfully criticized her as a woman and as a wife, finding her woefully inadequate on both counts. Her father ignored his own marital difficulties which had ended in estrangement from his own wife except for a persona face they presented to the world together, playing the role of the proper couple. Everywhere was secrecy, betrayal, withholding of warmth, sexual unhappiness. Hurt piled upon hurt.

The wife was wounded in receiving and then again in trying to present all of her feminine self. The wound first came through her father's scorn of any female person and her mother's impotence in asserting an alternative. To receive an other, a woman has to be someone in herself, must be able to meet and inquire about herself. The wife felt this self-possession in the woods, but not with her husband, her sons, or her lovers. She was always looking for it and wanted to find it. Her wounded femininity resulted from her inability to possess and present the full feminine self for which she longed. Her animus did not function as a bridge between her ego and the Self; and so, in her ego, she felt insecure as a woman, while the raw animus pronouncements filled in all the deficits. Her insecure feminine presence was no help to her husband's unemerged anima and left her son only the more depleted.

All these wounds to the feminine descended upon the son's life. As the youngest in the family, with his brothers away at school, he bore the brunt of his parents' unhappiness as they struggled toward divorce. Even prior to that time, he had felt himself "a self-sufficient child," independent of his mother, neither giving nor receiving affectionate hugs and kisses. He saw his mother always struggling under the burden of living up to her father's respect. He did not feel she protected him. Even living with her after the divorce, he felt it was he who took care of her: "I knew my responsibilities." It was what his father wanted him to do: "It was right to do it and I was happy to do it." He felt she had a special relation to him, but not he to her. At the age of seventeen, after his father died, he was already independent of his mother, although pulled in to advise her as she contemplated a second marriage. He described himself as being matter-of-fact in his role of advisor, not overly compassionate. He had "removed" himself, feeling that his life was "together" and hers chaotic by comparison. He did not want her advice when he fell into his own torments. Dependence was not possible: "She never pays for dinner when we go out."

He felt angry at his mother's lack of self-confidence and later at her trying so hard not to be a burden to him and his wife when he married in his early twenties. He found himself impatient with her low self-esteem which resulted in "attracting all the energy and attention to herself." He admired her capabilities, which were apparent whenever she was in the woods or at her job, but which altogether vanished in personal contacts. When his own son died, after one day of life, he had to tell his mother to stay with them at the hospital. "We needed a parental figure there at a moment of parental despair. But I had to tell her how to do it."

He felt his father never had to be told how to be a father. His father had given him a real conviction of what life was about, and, in the way he had dealt with his dying, had freed him from the fear of death. His father made him feel special and loved for the person he was. He knew his father's pride in him for enjoying and participating in life. His father had, in fact, told me, many years before, that this son was a "lovable, genuine boy" and very much "his own person." He felt that he was important to the son and worried, when he was dying, that the boy had to "carry such a load."

Father and son shared a football metaphor for the "game of life." The father, when a senior in college, played on the junior varsity football squad because he loved the game. The son, when he failed to make the starting lineup on his high school team, knew he had not disappointed his father—because, for his father, life was a game to be entered into, no more, no less. In contrast, his mother's father had played only to win. The son knew about his own father's sexual troubles, although not in great detail, and thought his father stupid and lazy in the way he dealt with them. He "ought to have resisted." During analysis, the son dreamed about being chased by a grizzly bear in a mink coat; this image recalled a boyhood experience when his father's young prostitute friend had kissed him goodbye at the end of a visit, wearing a mink coat. He remembered the touch of her soft lips on his mouth and knew in a flash what drew his father: "I wanted to sink into the coat." When later he fell passionately in love, he felt he really understood his father.

When his father died, he saw that his father had forgiven himself "for being who he was"; he saw that his father had "celebrated himself as human, faults and all." For the son, death's destructive blows had come earlier in life, when his beloved dogs were killed by cars. His father had always felt he would die young and had often spoken of it to his sons, saying he felt prepared. The father had suffered an early heart attack, discovered, he said, because "my heart hurt," but the father and I also approached his premonition of death in terms of the archetype of the son-lover yielding up life to the embrace of the Great Mother. After his father died and his ashes were spread, the son felt his father constantly with him: "I have a foot on the other side; part of me is on the other side. And yet part of him is here. I feel comfortable where I'm going, so I'm not afraid of death; it comes back in how I live life." His father gave him, in death, an anima bridge to life. The son took it and grew a womanly receiving presence in himself.

The son's capacity to embrace life stood out in the midst of his grief over his own baby's premature birth and death. He named this son after his father, accepting it as the darkest time, one of great sadness. Yet he was able to gather his family and friends around him and his wife, and to know "confirmation of all that light you felt from everyone coming back to you." He felt "held by all those people" and said, with great feeling, "Confidence is allowing yourself to be indebted to others." He felt his little son's gift to him was the determination to talk openly with his wife about their relationship. He would not risk another pregnancy until things felt right between them.

The son's ability to depend on his family and draw from their love increased, I believe, as a result of his analytic work. We had discovered that he had hopped over the trauma of his parents' divorce mainly because of the wound, the split in his own image of the feminine. The mother image for him broke into the familiar division of what Jungians have called the elemental and transformative feminine, what Winnicott calls the environment mother and the instinct mother (Jung 1912, part 2, chs. 5–7; Neumann 1985, ch. 3; Winnicott 1965a, 75–80). As a child, he held himself to "self-sufficiency." What dependence he allowed himself he transferred onto the house. After the divorce, when he moved away with his mother, he missed the house deeply. This dependency, in turn, transferred to his wife, the land, and the house he felt an urgency to own and worked so hard to buy, complete with family dog. The holding function of the feminine—its grounding aspect, which can be depended upon to support one in being—he transferred into his relationship with his wife and their home. After the rupture of his parents' divorce, he turned to his wife-to-be and became a member of her family. It provided a holding environment. He dealt with the unmothered part of himself by mothering first his mother and then his wife. Part of the intense urgency he felt in trying to hold himself together over his split between two women was feeling, on the one hand, that he would "be orphaned" if he gave up his wife and home and, on the other, that he would lose some essential piece of his soul if he gave up his affair.

Some of the reliability of the feminine on which he could depend transferred to me. When the other woman got angry and said she hated him because he would not see her, he panicked. Later, he told me that he knew he could call me, but then said "knowing I could meant I did not have to; I felt attuned to inner feelings and confidence in myself." I think he was able eventually to let things fall apart with both women because his dependency need was reliably met in the analysis.

He discovered the instinct side of the feminine only with his partner in the affair. He had not known it before either in himself or with a woman. But it was like a soul; it could not be lost.[13] In contrast, he and his wife lived like Hansel and Gretel. With this other woman, he reached across an inner split between security and aliveness to embrace the spontaneous impulses that felt truly personal instead of staying in his usual identification with the defenses that controlled them.[14] I think the other woman reflected back to him the validity and value of those impulses, allowing him to claim them joyfully. He risked aggressive feelings with the other woman, letting himself really want experiences that colored outside the lines of his defined security. That he could only find access to these impulses outside his marriage, in the breaking of convention, symbolizes the outlaw status of these impulses within him. More controlled than lived, these impulses fell into his shadow and could only be contacted again through shadow behavior. He allowed himself to experience desire, recklessness, aggressive pursuit, and intensity of sexual expression and satisfaction. This heightened his sense of the split between his craving for the security of a known framework and his seemingly uncontrollable thirst to follow where his passion led.

He reached a pivotal point in the analysis when he could no longer hold the split together. Consciously, he relinquished control and let things "fall apart." In the midst of the pain he felt in making his wife suffer and hurting the other woman, too, what surfaced was grief over his parents' divorce and his lost home. He took the risk of feeling all his mourning, for his mother and his father, for his childhood house, for his wife, for his woman friend, for his dead son, for himself and what he had missed as a boy. He concluded, "This is the biggest change. I can let things fall apart. I don't have to control everything." He faced all of his reality.

Around this time, two dreams signaled deeper change. In one, the son was trying to reach a place farther down the coast where there stood a Greek temple, "like Sounion, in Greece." He had been there on a trip with his mother at a time when he did not have to take care of her but was free to have his own experiences. The temple's location recalled the poignant moment in the ancient myth when Theseus forgot to hoist the sails on his ship whose color would signal to his father that he was returning safely after killing the Minotaur. Aegeus, his father, not seeing the right signal, thought his son was dead and dove to his death in the sea. My patient related to this myth, saying:

> It is about a country divided against itself and that is me. Two women battling for me, but it's really my battle manifesting itself in two women. Why didn't the father know, or see the colors? It's such a tragedy. It makes me think of the hair colors of my two ladies, for they are opposites like the black and white sails of Theseus.

I thought, here is a man facing the split anima in himself, finding a way in his masculinity to hold the feminine in himself. I wondered then if the allusion to the king's death signaled the death of the son's attachment to his father, so that he could now find his own solution to the split-anima problem.

The second dream, a week later, seemed to confirm this guess; in the dream, two porpoises approach him as he is swimming in the water:

> *I am flanked on each side. I reach out and hold onto the dorsal fin of each one. I am being carried over the water by the two powerful porpoises. I can feel the water rushing all about me as my arms are opened as far apart as can be. The water is made turbulent by the speed and the power.*

Immediately, he thought the two fish were the two women and saw his split between them in a new way. If he let go of either fish, he would sink. He had needed to hold both to "keep from going under." But they were fish and not women, and so the image led him to see the two as aspects of the one. We asked what the psyche intended in changing the women into dolphins. He felt that it was to get the projection off the women. For me, the dream dolphins seemed to correspond to the usual symbolic meaning of a psychopomp, destined to carry the soul to the realm of the dead, to ultimate reality, and thus to be associated with the redeemer.

The son's wound to the feminine consisted in the split between the holding and instinctually enlivening feminine. What died was the projection of those two aspects onto the two women. What was redeemed were the psychic realities he was now able to find within himself. He had changed his life in many remarkable ways, showing the transformations that can happen when the ego faces the conflicts brought by the anima. Changes occur to the ego (which includes others), the shadow, the anima, and the Self (which includes other people, too, in a collective way).

Transformation: The Father

In all psychological work, no perfect answers develop. But subtle and decisive changes happen if the work goes well enough, and so it was here, with both father and son. For each man, the anima came to function as bridge between ego and Self, and this affected them both in urgent, life-and-death instances. For the father, it made possible what might be called a blessed death. Not only was he at peace with himself, given over to the source of life, but (to follow the traditional notion of a blessed death) other people who came in contact with him then felt they had been blessed with something peculiarly their own. For the son, it meant taking hold of his life in a new way, consciously carrying his own wounds and seeking his own path. These two lives show us, I believe, both the ragged imperfect state of human solutions to problems and the somewhat larger-than-human effects of an integrated anima functioning as a bridge.

Both men's egos changed, enlarged. They found their missing pieces hiding in the shadow. Thus, the shadow changed, too. The ego integrated bits of it. The anima aided the task by pushing shadow parts under the ego's nose all the time and thus differentiating itself as articulator of the unconscious, as in the *albedo* stage in alchemy (see Jung 1984, 53, 55, 258; 1944, par. 333–35). The father's dream of the two women with guns showed him that he had to deal with two anima carriers full of murderous hostility, each to the other. In life, he had to deal with his wife's confrontations of his hypocrisy in protecting his public persona by hiding his sexual activities and with the other woman's refusal to carry his sexual life for him, her threats to expose him, and her pressure on him to face up to his waffling and need to please. I stood on the anima bridge, so to speak, pointing out how each woman carried the burden and the effects of his secret split for him. He, instead of his wife, needed to carry the strain of his conflict between his public reputation and his private sexual life. He, instead of the other woman, needed to face the stress of his conflict between trying to please all parties and choosing among them. In his work in group therapy, others took the same tack, always pushing to make him see his evasions of what the split meant, his use of the women, and his hiding behind an image of affability.

What he found when he looked at the split was bits and pieces of missing aggression that belonged to his ego. Dreams tossed up images of guns. He was shooting and killing; or he had the enemy in his sights and was supposed to kill him and found he couldn't; but then the enemy shot his best friend, which made him sob with remorse. In other dreams, he was once again in military service, going back "to the man's army," living in communal barracks and urinating in a huge urinal that took up one whole wall with cascading water; or, he had to deal with a raucous group that drove a giant diesel locomotive through his place of work. He suffered seeing how much energy he devoted to weaving and dodging his ego tasks in order always to please, to make no one mad at him, to be the good boy pleasing to the other whom unconsciously he cast in the role of all-accepting mother. He had to face that he was negating life with his suspended animation. He dreamt of another of his sons (who he feared was too "good" and who, interestingly enough, joined the Marines), telling him to stir up the fire on which they would cook their steaks. And then, "rats came out from everywhere."

He tried hard to deal with all the rats, which toughened his ego, making it more realistic, and benefited others in his life. He stopped blaming his wife for his sexual problems and took responsibility for his own actions, realizing it was not just her rejection of him that set him off into an affair but his own dissatisfaction with their relationship. He faced the other woman's wrath and pain, decided not to marry her, and told her so. He managed to see it through enough with both women so that, although he made them angry, they also saw and respected his firmness in deciding he could not go on with two lives, and, surprisingly, they won through together to a level of genuine cordiality. He bought a motorcycle and enjoyed it hugely. For once, his enjoyment did not depend on his community's approval, although in fact they did approve. He made public his decision to separate from his wife and their subsequent joint decision to divorce and carried the consequences for that to his reputation and work. Altogether, he felt more independent, not "swept all over the place."

The reduction in his fear of aggression freed up more energy which went into his work. That, in turn, deepened and flourished. Being more realistic about his own disabilities made him both tougher and more compassionate of the weaknesses of others. It is not too much to say that, at this time, he had a formidable and often decisive impact on people's lives.

Instead of trying to get a woman to fill deficiencies in himself, to stuff her into the holes in his being, the father received and held his deficiencies like an empty space inside him that he could increasingly accept and allow to be empty. He began a new relationship with a woman who, it seemed to him, combined in herself the opposite qualities of his wife and the other woman. He decided for the time being not to marry nor even to promise that he would in the future, but simply to allow himself to be, a single man, a man in his own right, holding his empty space himself. The anima projected itself much less and came to function much more as an internal bridge to the Self. He had reached a place of emptiness where his God-images could leave off and the presence of something other could make itself known, which showed dramatically in the way he met his death.

When the anima begins to function as a bridge, we see a change not only in the ego and shadow but also in the anima itself. The ego toughens; the shadow becomes more integrated; the anima projects less onto others and becomes more of an articulator of the unconscious, and that is what puts something different into the world. The anima functioning as a bridge strongly and distinctly affects the ego, making it more masculine, with the anima's own special spiritual qualities connecting the ego to the Self and social elements as well, changing others' lives, and helping them across their bridges to reality (Ulanov and Ulanov 1994, chs. 6, 16).

When shadow aggression is not integrated adequately, as was the case with the father, external reality is not external enough. As a result, a man tends to use others, principally women, as characters in his own inner drama of needs and shoring up. In bouts of sexuality, a man is apt to approach his partners essentially as self-objects, props for his fantasies. This is a nonlife, a shrouded life, a disguised one. He is not apt to take in much of what comes his way or to take advantage of what reality brings him. He then wastes life and its great opportunities. Caught in a consuming attitude to counteract the inner emptiness he fears, he uses and disposes of rather than really lives and feels gratitude for life. Gratitude, after all, is a positive force and an essential one in our lives, gathering all of us into our shared existence. This father was, I believe, a good person, and so his benefits from analysis were not only shared with others, which happens automatically in such a changed personality, but also brought to others because he so much wanted them to benefit from what had happened to him. This accounts, in part, for his "blessed death." He ended up alone, but with a remarkable long day's dying that gave much to many people.

In the lengthy dying, he completed the task on which he had worked so hard but had not finished in his living. He was suddenly struck down by a rapid, rare brain disease. It opened up all of the troubles that had initially brought him to analysis. The prognosis of the disease was that it would ravage him, causing psychosis before death. My analysand feared that his long-contained, secret life would spill out into the public when he became psychotic, as the disease threatened he would.

Suicide once more presented a solution. There he was again, back at the beginning, fearing for his reputation, keeping secrets, afraid of disapproval, tempted to defend by destroying. We worked sporadically at this point because of his need for constant physical treatment and his increasing disability. But we worked enough to see how all the great differences had been put into place. The old problems jumped up again, ready to assault him; he was back in the same old place. But the man himself was different because of all the work; this new man reacted to the old threats in a new way.

He used his aggression. A teaching hospital heard of his affliction with this rare disease and wanted to examine him. He did not like the way they treated him, which was as simply a thing to be tested, not as a person facing the end of his life. He contacted his sons and made them take him away, back to his home, where he wanted to die. With me, he was able to locate and articulate his fears and link them up to the old ones we knew so well, despite the increasing loss of all his physical functions that I recounted earlier in the book (see

p. 139). He drew openly on his past work, and he drew on me to reach further into his present reality. This brought a relief of pressure, but suicide still beckoned. He had some dreams that helped. In one his watch stopped, which we took as referring to his impending death. Describing another, he said:

> *There is a bad guy in the trunk of my car. Should I turn him in or keep driving? He's tried to get me. Now I've got him.*

He dreamt of being in "the worst battles of North Africa [in the Second World War, in which he had served], wounded, hot, face down in the sand with no water."

His transference had been to me as trusted guide and colleague, not mother or hoped-for sexual partner. Those parts were fully cast. Now the urgency of his illness pushed me into spiritual issues of the most intense kind. He drew on me and on our analytical connection to lead to real life, not to enactments of fantasies that would shut him up against life. We asked basic questions: What meaning might be assembling in the face of this illness? Was there a purpose, still unclear, toward which the threat of psychosis in this disease was moving him? What was the threat of exposing his long-held secret aiming at?[15]

In the midst of grappling with these open-ended questions, he spontaneously made a lavish gesture which, paradoxically, both surprised him and confirmed his struggle. Gathering his fears of insanity and exposure and his temptations to make a getaway through suicide, he renounced control and sacrificed his escape route. He spontaneously handed over this bundle of dreadful emotions to a presence beyond himself. He just gave everything he was to God, withholding nothing, not even his sanity. At the uttermost boundary of death, he came into accepting his life fully. With gripping directness, he confided himself to the power that had created him.

I saw him the day before he died. Although he could no longer speak, I knew he knew me as I spoke to him and read him a favorite psalm. He made whalelike noises, as if hailing me from a great distance, from the midst of the "blue fog" he lived in now, which he had spoken of on previous occasions. What amazed us those last days was that he did not become psychotic. His was the only one of the recorded cases to have missed that fate. Thus he was spared what he most deeply feared, because, I believe, he faced his fears and willingly submitted to them and offered them up.

In Jungian language, the anima that functions as bridge to the Self engenders faith that the Self can be reached and trusted and relied upon. It will hold the ego. When it is reached, the Self is always shared. We do not know the Self in isolation. As Jung put it, where the Self is genuinely constellated, it creates a group, a true gathering of persons.[16] And many people did gather around this man's bedside. Some members of our therapy group came to see him, and his death was written up in the national press. From all these sources, I saw how his reaching the Self gave others access to their experiences of the Self, too, in the most individual, idiosyncratic, and deeply felt forms. For myself, I knew a permanent shift in my commitment to the analytic methods, theories, and practice that seek to enlarge consciousness. They remained valuable, but less as methods that achieve outcomes and more as methods that frame the mysterious meeting of our psyche and its author.

Transformation: The Son

Faith in the Self showed in the son's analysis, too, although not in any form of dying but in an increase in the living of his life. The largest change in the son's ego was that it grew big enough to hold as its own the split anima, formerly projected onto two women. He now wanted all of his life to be available to be lived in an unmistakable reality. He saw the split as between security and sexual needs, between a long line of continuity built up with land, house, home, and wife, and the spiritual explosion of seeing and being seen as an assertive sexual man. In his outer dilemma of having both a wife and another woman, he was searching for an inner way to heal the split between his dependency need for a reliable other and his need to live from his personal impulses instead of controlling them.

Claiming the split as within his own psyche changed his treatment of the two women. He saw that he had taken his wife for granted, bundling onto her a whole fabric of projections centered on his own mother needs. He saw, too, that helping her with her bad moods was just more of the same. He discovered now that he had always been a bit afraid of his wife's moods and that he felt bound to "her leash," even though he had helped tie it. He was angry, "tired of pulling feelings out of her," and wanted to "cut the leash" and "bring the woman out in her." He understood now that he had not "chosen her" when they married. I understood this to mean he had simply assumed her presence in his life, much as a boy counts on a mother's presence behind him as he goes out into the world. This assumption accounted, I think, for his lack of guilt about his affair. When he told his wife that he had not "chosen" to marry her, she took off her wedding rings, not wanting to put them on again until they both chose to be married. She also, he said, dropped her moodiness. It just fell away, she told him, because when you lose a child and maybe a marriage, "moods just don't compare."

Early in his analysis, the son had wanted his wife to see an analyst, making it a condition for continuing the marriage. Then, as he took up his own problems, he let go of all his conditions, leaving his wife to decide about her own psyche. He shifted to a larger ego; he ceased being his wife's mother and started to carry his own wounds.

His wife's reaction to his affair, he said, was grief, and, it is not too strong to say, a kind of unconditional loving. She gave him, he said, "a gift of forgiveness." She wanted to hold onto her relationship with him and made that clear from the start of his disclosures. She was hurt by his betrayal but managed to carry it, leaving him free to find his way back to her or away. This deeply moved him and allowed him to go further with the removal of his projections onto her. He found he was holding nothing back from her now in the sense of saying, "This is who I am." He did not report details of his activities with the other woman; he only reported the emotionally significant fact that he loved her. The energy that used to go into taking care of his wife now returned to him, and he told his wife that he wanted her to say what she wanted and thought and felt sexually for him, and he wanted to be and do the same with her. Nothing less would do for them both. The death of their baby gave him, he felt, a deep resolve to relate truly to his wife before they risked another pregnancy. It was a "rebirth based on honesty." I saw him addressing his wife, as if saying, "receive yourself and come out to me with who you are. Find out if you want me and me you."

He chose to give his wife "one hundred percent," as he put it. If that did not work, he would leave, but he could not leave without having ever arrived. He was closing the wound to the feminine, passed to him through his mother, who did not receive all of herself and could not present it to him because of her father's scorn. Feeling connected to his own sexual passion, no longer projected onto and lodged only with the other woman, he wanted to see what might ignite with his wife. His way was unsafe, quite unguaranteed. He did not know it would turn into a renewed relationship. But this was what he had to do. He even seriously entertained moving out of the house and off the land, terrible decisions for him. He was afraid he was "just settling in" because it was too hard to let go of his wife and home. So he allowed himself to think and talk about moving out and that broke the unconscious tie. "That was sufficient."

With the other woman, he went through much guilt and pain. In the jargon of the trade, his wife was the environment mother and the other woman the instinct mother (Winnicott 1965b, 182–83). He used the latter to risk a ruthless experience of his instincts toward which he had not reached before. This was her gift to him. He remembered that at the beginning of the affair he had wanted to have such an effect on her that she would live differently after knowing him. He said he wanted to change her, "impact her," "know that she had a vision because of me." He felt he knew, as he put it, "what was important and what was not because of Dad and the way he died; it changed me forever."

He loved this other woman and went on loving her and felt deeply distressed by her pain and his own at their parting: "it tore me apart." He felt they had both learned and had both given a lot to each other, but he had to face both himself and her with the fact that he did love her but not enough to change his whole life. He talked with her whenever she needed to reach him, but chose not to see her. He felt depressed and very sad, feeling they had met at the wrong time in their lives. He went on loving her but no longer lived the love with her.

One of the reasons for his choice was that his ego now owned his sexual passion instead of having to project it on the woman. He knew it now as real in himself, as an integral part of himself, and as something that could leap up in response to other women as well. It was no longer attached only to this one woman. From this he knew he had to contend with it directly. Changing his life around to start another marriage and build another home was not going to change the task that confronted him. He could imagine a good and compatible life with this other woman, but it would not differ much from what he presently lived with his wife. He took up the management of his sexual and spiritual passion, rather than making the woman its keeper.

He had made direct contact finally with his sexuality and with his guilt over using the other woman to do so and then not staying with her, and he faced as well now his depression over losing her. Other shadow bits pressed to be integrated into his ego. Aggression and anger came up on the job with his boss. He did not mind being called down for something he did wrong, if he was spoken to calmly and rationally, he said, but he hated being yelled at. I saw that the split between the sense of the feminine he depended on to hold him in being and the feminine that instinctually aroused him left him identified with controlling, rather than experiencing, his spontaneous impulses. Faced with yelling, he would first get hurt, then explode with rage. This linked up with the bear in the mink coat that had threatened him in his dream (see pp. 169–70). Although the image of the bear recalled the impulse to surrender to the soft lips touching his mouth, it also evoked terror at the bear's power: it could devour him! This led him to speak of how he differed from his father, thus reaching out for some of the bear's power. In addition to the bear symbolizing a positive mother or, like Artemis, fostering the growth of the young, all its masculine associations came to my mind. The bear can represent a warrior's strength or military energy, a kingly beast. The bear can stand for a mediating figure between heaven and hearth, as well as symbolize the obscure *nigredo* or *prima materia* in alchemy. In the dream, the bear chased him and he had to defend himself and fight back. He contrasted himself again with his father. He wanted to integrate the passion; his father could not. He saw his father as reaching passion but never integrating it. His father seemed compelled to respond if someone said they needed him, whereas he, the son, wanted to understand things in his own terms and choose accordingly. It was important to him, for example, that the other woman know he loved her even though he was choosing not to build his life with her. He was all the personages in the dream and wanted to own them all—the hunter, the hunted, the female in the coat, the man who could fight.

Claiming the anima within him affected not only his ego and shadow but also his living toward the Self and his transference to me.[17] His transference was not unlike his father's to me as neither mother nor lover, but rather as a sort of guide standing on the anima bridge. I offered a perspective leading to reality, to life. I represented a counselor whom increasingly he came to see as within himself. Sometimes he wanted me to assume an answer-giving function and was annoyed and frustrated with me for not literally fulfilling this assignment. When he chose to suspend his analysis for the time being, for the sake of significant choices he had made in his work, I agreed. I saw his analysis leading into a large reality available to him as his psyche opened up, but I expressed disquiet over the dream he brought to the last session and raised the possibility of his continuing analysis because of it. He chose, however, to follow his plan, guided by something within himself that had replaced me. We parted warmly, open to resuming work at a future time.

Living toward the Self was made possible as his ego enlarged and pressed on him a long hard look at his work life. Unlike the "problem with women," where he "needed help," he said, he felt he could "handle" his job problem. In short, he said, his job "is not my vocation." He had undertaken a business career to make money, had succeeded, had acquired the much-desired house and land. "I gave up a lot for security; even though it seemed too easy at twenty-two to make all that money. Now I want to pursue what matters to me." This meant changing careers.

He stood fast with this decision even though his friends in business thought him demented and it meant a great loss of income. He was turning in a new direction, which required new training. Although unclear as to its outcome in a specific job, he felt certain in choosing this direction. He saw what he called "a void in myself" which the other woman filled up. "Now I must do something about it and that means my work." In reaching toward the Self, he felt a great sea change in priorities and the need to give something of value into the world. It was on this basis that he decided to suspend his analysis. He had had to come a great distance to our sessions, and his new school schedule and rearranged work schedule left him with no time for such long trips.

His last dream moved me very much. He finds himself in an airport, "a no man's land with the potential to go everywhere." There he is to meet a male, a friend, whom he identifies as "sort of promiscuous, that is, sex for sex's sake." Then the dream ends dramatically:

> As soon as I see him, I shoot him. No sooner have I done it than I am aware that while he is hit, I feel the bullet go into my brain and lodge there. There it will stay like a splinter of wood. There is no retrieving it except by time dislodging it. Neither pain nor despair. A natural end. I go on and live.

When he mailed his check for that last month, he wrote a note saying he would be in touch later: "Until then I remain the man with a bullet in his brain."

He had read a piece I had written on transference that included a passage about his father's death and his father's dream about the two women taking aim, each either to shoot the other or his father, and being prevented from doing so (Ulanov 1982). He said, in association to his own dream, "Here was Dad's dream trying to avoid shooting and here I am shooting." He also recalled one of his beloved dogs who had lived for years with a .22 caliber bullet in its head. The bullet was the other woman, he thought, and his disengagement from her sexually. He felt good about the dream: "This part of me causes me pain and I carry it and I accept the wound." I was moved by the image but also disquieted: being shot in the head is terrifying, and his father had died of brain disease. Yet this son had found what seemed to be at first just a sexual adventure and had turned it into a life-changing love. His suffering, his acquiescence, his carrying it and choosing his own path touched me.

Conclusion

Can it be said, in conclusion, that the anima as it came to function as a bridge between ego and Self for each of these men ushered in vital changes in which each man's ego became more masculine, shadow bits became more integrated, and the anima more an articulator for the unconscious? Each of them, one in dying and the other in living, felt himself faced with the awesomeness of life and answered it with a desire to give, to give over to its center in the father's case, to give into the world in the son's. The father finds he is able to offer up his wound in the crisis of his death. The son consciously carries his wound into his life. Could it be that the anima, disguised as a split between two women, as a split between two kinds of mothering, as a wound to the feminine, is really the disguise of the Self putting itself forward to the ego in an irresistible way? This leads to mystic precincts.

Jung was not a mystic and explicitly disavowed "faith," eschewing both compliance and will power as substitutes for immediate experience (Jung 1938, par. 8–11; Jaffé 1989, chapter 1), but does he not bring us finally to a faith, or to multiple faiths in the Self? Is this not the work of all analysts, finally, a leading to the Self? The anima and animus archetypes engender experiences of the Self coming into being, calling the ego to leave its country and journey into strange territories to take up new life, real life. As Jung put it, "One must be able to suffer God. . . . God needs limitation in time and space. Let us therefore be for him limitation in time and space, an earthly tabernacle" (Jung 1975, 65–66).

Notes

1. Examples illustrate this confrontation: a man dreamt of a sick woman trying to run after him in the sand. He was repelled by her. She called after him in protest, saying that the only way she could get any attention from him was to whine and complain to him.

A woman dreamt she was on an important journey. As she drove along in her car, the roads became more primitive, finally going off into a wilderness on a dirt track. There at the end of it stood a stark man, "looking like John the Baptist," as if waiting for her arrival. He had immense authority and spiritual presence and "there was no way I could avoid meeting him."

A woman dreamt of a man she respected who was fishing up out of the watery depths a cure for incurable disease. After speaking about it to everyone, he came over to the dreamer and kissed her, saying he would love her forever (Ulanov 1971, 256–57).

2. When I was lecturing on this subject once in North Carolina, a member of the audience asked what distinguished these Self contents from, for example, shadow materials. I found myself spontaneously answering that Self contents have to do with life and death. I have no quarrel with the bridge analogy being used in relation to the shadow or for other major psychic complexes, like the persona, but there is a different feel to the contents addressing us. Self contents coming across the anima / animus bridge do not face us with the bad in ourselves (or, for some of us, the good, if we think of ourselves as bad). Self contents put questions to our very existence.

3. This is not to say, however, that Jung's theory is problem-free or without the mark of his time in history (see, for example, Ulanov 1971, 335–41; Ellenberger 1970, 293–94, 708–10).

4. Jung himself says, "Take for instance *animus* and *anima*. No philosopher in his senses would invent such irrational and clumsy ideas. When things fit together, it is not always a matter of a philosophical system; sometimes it is the facts that fit together" (Jung 1975, 192).

Animus and anima appear at the threshold to the Self. They usher in Self experiences. They occupy the lowest place on the ladder into the Self. Clumsy as this theory is, it occupies a place on a par with Freud's discovery of the Oedipal complex, Klein's of the depressive position, Winnicott's of the false and true selves, Kohut's of the self that precedes experience of the instinctual drives. Here Jung makes accessible to us, through image, symbol, and theoretical construct, our experience of our own sexuality as it is, not as it should be. Jung shows us that we cannot ask, "What kind of woman (or man) am I?" let alone answer it, if we are not also asking what way an other lives in us from a sexual departure point opposite to our own gender identity. The person reaching toward wholeness is the contrasexual person; we are not either-or, nor neither-nor, but both-and, self and other, same and opposite. We cannot possess the object of the opposite sex except as an image. So there opens between us a space of spirit where imaginatively we experience but do not possess the world of the other. Symbols get born. In the midst of sexuality and body presence, then, Jung gives us a way to talk about the spiritual component of sexuality, not as something tacked on, but as its central motif, opening to us, indeed addressing us, and asking for our response in all the body push-pulls of impulse and need, desire and appetite. Jung penetrates "this difficult field of extremely subtle experience" with these figures of anima and animus which are the "cause of that deep human need to speak of souls or daemons at all" (Jung 1931, pars. 92, 82). Thus he offers a counter argument and a counterpart to Freud's Oedipal complex.

Freud had an experience of anima that seemed to him frightening and dangerous. It threatened to put him into the passive position, and overcome by music, religious illusion, or the "mudtide" of the occult. The anima looked enviously on his chief member, perhaps even plotting to rob him of it. Thus Freud puts her in her place, definitely second in importance. He constructs his Oedipus theory from the male point of view, never inquiring what happens from Jocasta's perspective, let alone the little girl's.

The Oedipal battle between fathers and sons is made too simple because it omits dealing with the incomplete mother, which is less an issue of generations fighting for her favor than it is an issue of a mother who does not present herself and cannot do so *because* of the sins of the fathers. This feminine deficiency passes through male succession, just as the deficiency of animus is passed on through the mothers.

Jung approaches the mystery of the human person including all of our deficiencies and sufficiencies—which engineer as well as express themselves in sexual tangles, including the Oedipal, with as much security as consciousness can provide, without dissipating the mystery. It is not the job of a theory to substitute scientific certainty for mystery. With the symbolic concepts of anima and animus, we have a way to talk about a depth dimension. For the anima and animus do not only pull our egos across their borders toward the otherness of others and through that into the otherness of the Self, but also pull us from consciousness into the unconscious (both personal and objective). They speak not only of the sexual opposites, but also of the opposites of conscious and unconscious (Jung 1944, par. 192; Jung 1955–1956, par. 104; Jung 1912, pars. 306, 335).

5. For a discussion of this rescuing anima, see Ulanov and Ulanov (1987, 250–54).

6. Cited by Karl Haas, Radio Station WMNR CT, December 1989.

7. I have not used the term *mistress* because there was no question of financial support or of providing shelter, clothes, etc. These were deeply emotional relationships.

The split of the anima can present itself in other opposites, too, such as a man feeling that his inner life leads him one way and his outer life another, or his spiritual needs oppose those of the flesh, etc.

8. Jung sees the anima and animus living in a world different from our own, "where the pulse of time beats ever so slowly . . . their aspect is . . . so strange that their intrusion into consciousness often blasts into fragments the all-too-feeble brainpans of unfortunate mortals. Anima and animus contain the greater part of the material which appears in insanity, more especially in schizophrenia." They are "elusive wraiths," "fragmentary personalities," "always strangers to the conscious world"; they "permeate the atmosphere with a feeling of uncanny foreboding, or even a fear of mental derangement" (Jung 1939, 23–25).

9. This kind of transference is one of the main types surrounding the anima, in contrast to another main type where the analyst herself receives the sexual projection. For discussion, see Ulanov (1982).

10. The animus also functions as a bridge, hence the function of anima and animus is the same, but subtle and decisive differences exist, too. When one is in touch with a well-functioning animus, one is in touch with the truth by which one lives; when one is in touch with a well-functioning anima, one is in touch with an animating connection to being (see Jung 1955–1956, pars. 232, 646).

11. Marie-Louise von Franz comments, "the anima behaves very paradoxically, or else she splits into two opposing figures, between which consciousness is torn this way and that, until the ego begins to concern itself with the task of individuation. It is only when a man begins to have an apprehension of the Self behind the anima that he finds the foundation on which he can escape her pulling and tugging in contrary directions" (E. Jung and von Franz 1970, 262).

12. For discussion of the effects of a father's anima on a son's development, see Beebe (1985); see also, Ulanov (1977).

13. By soul I mean both of Jung's meanings—the "partial personality" of the anima and also the Christian meaning of an inner doorway to God, about which Jung says, "it has the dignity of an entity endowed with, and conscious of, a relationship to Deity" (Jung 1944, par. 11; see also, pars. 9, 10).

14. For discussion of controlling instinctual life with the result of loss of vitality, see Winnicott (1988, 85–86).

15. These are examples of what Jung calls the synthetic questions, from the prospective point of view, in contrast to the analytic ones, from the reductive point of view (Jung 1943, par. 121–40).

16. "The Self, the very centre of an individual, is of a conglomerate nature. It is, as it were, a group. It is a collectivity in itself and therefore always, when it works most positively, creates a group" (Jung 1973, 508).

17. In my opening remarks for the discussion of this paper at the Ghost Ranch Conference, on 1 June 1990, I added these comments about the transference-countertransference dimensions of these two cases.

In the work with the father, I found myself arranged and rearranged in different ways. Here he was, a man successful in his profession, a veteran of combat with the rank of sergeant, who stood with courage for unpopular causes in his work, yet who before women was as a boy. Sympathetic to his suffering and worried about his suicidal impulses, I resisted being his mother-approver, feeling myself in an opposite place of stillness, not jumping on cue, not always hospitable to the boy-mother need. Yet he had a sense of humor, and we erupted into laughing more than once. He got his split-anima to a liveable place, where the two women in his dream no longer were going to shoot. But the split was not fully resolved when he stopped treatment. That happened, I believe, in his dying and the short, intense work we had time to do in relation to it.

His sexual transference to women did not shift to me. It was all taken up with the various women in his life. Also, during his treatment I was marrying, and then later pregnant, and still later nursing. I was all taken up. There was a deep abiding connection between us, so he called when he heard he was dying, and we were able to take up and accomplish that last piece of work.

With the son, I was associated nearer to the world of his parents than to his own and the sexual projections were all taken up with women in his life, so they did not fall on me. This is a different experience than I have had in other cases where the work focuses on anima issues. There the erotic tone of the transference is intense and seems to be the necessary heat to match and dislodge the intensity of wherever the man feels stuck as, for example, in one case, in what a man called his lifetime of perversions. With the son, too, a deep sense of and respect for the other's being helped weather periods of negativity because I did not answer everything or speed things up or fix them. I managed to carry periods of worry about his suicidal impulses.

In general, I think with Masud Khan that countertransference works best when it works silently and is used and folded into the patient's life. The patient's life and relation to reality, both societal and psychical, both religious and pragmatic, is what matters. The particular danger of overemphasis on countertransference-transference dynamics, and especially, I would suggest, in anima/animus situations, is that the analysis and the analytical interaction or field can substitute for the analysand's life and then for the analyst's. In analytical jargon, this means that the analytical couple can substitute for the ego-Self couple: the process of analysis can substitute for the process of living toward the Self and thus for the deepest aspects of life.

The issue for me is not in the theory of anima/animus, but in the living of the anima/animus situations which bring us into the center where we feel and know we are in the center of life. We know that this is it. What is here in this moment is what really matters. This is the immediate experience that Jung stressed so much. This theory—for all its clumsy confused nature and awkward language—is the only one I know that approaches this kind of experience on its own level.

References

Bachelard, G. 1969. *The Poetics of Reverie*. Trans. Daniel Russell. New York: Orion.

Beebe, J. 1985. The father's anima. *The Father: Contemporary Jungian Perspectives*. Ed. A. Samuels. London: Free Association Books.

Ellenberger, H. F. 1970. *The Discovery of the Unconscious*. New York: Basic Books.

Goldenberg, N. R. 1976. A feminist critique of Jung. In *Signs: Journal of Women in Culture and Society* 2(2).

Hillman, J. 1972. On psychological femininity. *The Myth of Analysis*. San Francisco: Harpers.

Jaffé, A. 1989. *Was C. G. Jung a Mystic?* Trans. Diana Dackerland and Fiona Cairns. Einsiedeln: Daimon Verlag.

Jung, C. G. 1912. *Symbols of Transformation*. CW 5. Princeton: Princeton University Press, 1952.

———. C. G. 1928. The relations between the ego and the unconscious. In *CW* 7: 123–304. Princeton: Princeton University Press, 1953.

———. 1931. Mind and earth. In *CW* 10: 29–49. Princeton: Princeton University Press, 1964.

———. 1938. Psychology and religion. In *CW* 11: 3–105. Princeton: Princeton University Press, 1958.

————. 1939. *The Integration of the Personality*. Trans. Stanley Dell. New York: Farrar and Rinehart.

————. 1943. On the psychology of the unconscious. In *CW* 7: 3–121. Princeton: Princeton University Press, 1953.

————. 1944. *Psychology and Alchemy*. *CW* 12. Princeton: Princeton University Press, 1953.

————. 1955–1956. *Mysterium Coniunctionis*. *CW* 14. Princeton: Princeton University Press, 1963.

————. 1973. *Letters*. Vol. 1. Ed. G. Adler and A. Jaffé. Princeton: Princeton University Press.

————. 1975. *Letters*. Vol. 2. Ed. G. Adler and A. Jaffé. Princeton: Princeton University Press.

————. 1984. *Dream Analysis*. Ed. W. McGuire. Princeton: Princeton University Press.

Jung, E. and von Franz, M.-L. 1970. *The Grail Legend*. Trans. Andrea Dykes. New York: Putnam.

Kast, V. 1986. *The Nature of Loving: Patterns of Human Relationship*. Trans. Boris Matthews. Wilmette, Ill.: Chiron Publications.

Miller, J. B. 1976. *Toward a New Psychology of Women*. Boston: Beacon.

Neumann, E. 1985. *The Great Mother: An Analysis of an Archetype*. Trans. Ralph Manheim. Princeton: Princeton University Press.

Reuther, R. R. 1983. *Sexism and God-Talk: Toward a Feminist Theology*. Boston: Beacon.

Solovyev, V. 1945. *The Meaning of Love*. Trans. Jane Marshall. London: Geoffrey Bles.

Ulanov, A. B. 1971. *The Feminine in Jungian Psychology and in Christian Theology*. Evanston, Ill.: Northwestern University Press.

————. 1977. The search for paternal roots: Jungian perspectives on fathering. *Fathering: Fact or Fable?* Ed. Edward V. Stein. Nashville, Tenn.: Abingdon Press. Adapted and republished as chap. 5 of this book.

————. 1982. Transference/countertransference: A Jungian perspective. *Jungian Analysis*, 1st ed. Ed. Murray Stein. LaSalle, Ill.: Open Court. Adapted and republished as chap. 7 of this book.

Ulanov, A., and B. Ulanov. 1987. *The Witch and the Clown: Two Archetypes of Human Sexuality*. Wilmette, Ill.: Chiron Publications.

————. 1994. *Transforming Sexuality: The Archetypal World of Anima and Animus*. Boston: Shambhala.

Whitmont, E. C. 1980. Reassessing femininity and masculinity. *Quadrant* 13(2).

Winnicott, D. W. 1965a. The development of the capacity for concern. *The Maturational Processes and the Facilitating Environment*. New York: International Universities Press.

————. 1965b. Communicating and not communicating leading to a study of certain opposites. *The Maturational Processes and the Facilitating Environment*. New York: International Universities Press.

————. 1988. *Human Nature*. London: Free Association.

10

Vicissitudes of Living in the Self

In his article "Vicissitudes of the Instincts," Freud tells us that each instinct has a biological source and a supply of energy derived from the body, an aim which leads to instinctual satisfaction and discharge of the invested energy, and an object in relation to which the aim can be achieved (Freud 1915). Sexual and aggressive instincts may undergo four vicissitudes: reversal into the opposite, such as from active to passive expression; turning against the self to use the self as the instinctual object; repression, which includes all the defenses; and sublimation, in which the instinctual energy is discharged in symbolic expression.

In this article I will concentrate on the vicissitudes of living in the Self. The Self, as Jung defines it, is the center and the circumference of the personality, embracing its conscious and unconscious aspects; it is superordinate to our conscious ego, acting as "our life's goal, for it is the completest expression of that fateful combination we call individuality" (Jung 1963a, 386). The Self originates in the psychosomatic unity we call person, thus possessing instinctive and psychic energy; it aims to express and elaborate itself in increasing complexity, in relation to its object, the ego, both in individuals and in groups. The vicissitudes of the Self are concerned with how it unfolds itself in real living. The Self is evident in the workings of the transcendent function within individual psyches and group processes; it is observable in the Transcendent that comes into focus through our experience of that transcendent function. The Self can be denied, repressed, and detoured into pathological expression; the Self sponsors radical changes in the ego and its own presentation when we engage in ongoing ego-Self conversation.

What has the Self in psychology to do with the spirit in religion? Are we talking about the same things with these two words, or different realities? Is the Self God? No. The Self is not God in us, but is that in us that knows about God and is a principal way through which we know that God knows about us. In psychological literature, Marie-Louise von Franz speaks of living in the Self in terms of alchemical processes of the *coniunctio* and the *circulatio* (von Franz 1980, 162, 166); Aniela Jaffé describes some of Jung's experiences of Self in facing death (Jaffé 1989, 111). In spiritual literature Gregory the Great writes of reaching little chinks of light that reveal God's presence breaking in on us through our darkness, and Bernard of Clairveaux describes the climax of spiritual development as our achieving an illuminating darkness that feels like falling asleep (Butler 1966, 78, 106). We need more descriptions of how we live in the Self and how the Self actually manifests in clinical practice, how people in trouble come upon this life-changing experience, how it affects our work with dreams, and our understanding of transference and countertransference dynamics, and what these clinical facts tell us about the spiritual life.

The main reason, I believe, that we find little written about this living in the Self and its relation to spirit or to God can be traced to a paradox: what we long for and work hard to reach, what we speak about so ardently, when it reaches us, silences us. Words cannot describe it; images falter and break; our senses of hearing, sight, taste, and touch are so far exceeded that they barely can carry the analogy to inform us of what this state is like. Bernard is modern in saying we reach a state of falling asleep, for like the alpha state in meditation and the *samadhi* state in Buddhist practice, we do not even know we have experienced this advanced spiritual state until, with a start, we wake up from it and know we have been somewhere entirely new and different. We are not unconscious, but the transition from sleep to waking comes closest to describing the difference of this new state from our usual waking ego-functioning. Here I am trying to do the paradoxical: to put into words the wordless; to find images for the imageless; to speak the unspeakable which has been addressing us all along.

We need to look at actual clinical work which displays the workings of Self in relation to ego. To grow into ongoing conversation with the Self does not progress in a neat straight line. We go back and forth, and all the perambulations and permutations that get summed up in the word "vicissitudes" describe our path. To Freud's epochal article "Instincts and Their Vicissitudes," we now add "The Vicissitudes of Living in the Self."

What do we mean by living in the Self? What is this goal, which turns out to be a process as much as a content? We know the definitions that Jung gives, the best of which he took from Augustine who was describing God: a circle whose center is everywhere and whose circumference is nowhere. The Self is the archetype of the center operating in the unconscious, a presence or intention that exerts its influence on the ego which is the center of consciousness. The ego responds, hits back, squawks! Out of this interaction, the whole psyche changes, coming gradually to find its orientation not in the unconscious or consciousness, but in conversation with a center that transcends and includes both. This center is also called Self. It makes our ego move over, feel displaced, or feel held in a larger circumference of being. Other schools of depth psychology approach this same conversation in terms of their own vocabularies, but I will use Jung's terms ego and Self to describe the clinical work.

Surprisingly, the crucial thing about clinical work that leads to living in the Self does not concern technique or psychodynamics, but faith. If the Self exists, it will manifest itself. We do not have to do anything to make it happen. Living in the Self is not about doing; it is about being. Do we believe in the reality of the psyche? Do we trust this reality and depend upon it to do its stuff? I am not talking about such dramatic instances in therapy as when, for example, a man in response to what's going on in the session suddenly asks to use the telephone to call his pusher and cancel his drug deal. Nor am I talking about the moment when a woman telling her dream of digging up buried parts of her body suddenly feels a weeping released in her—a weeping that, like the unblocking of an underground river, comes thundering forth because she can at last feel the pain of chopping herself up into dissociated bits in order to survive. Such events are momentous and certainly qualify as spiritual because they bring with them great gusts of healing. What I'm talking about, however, are more ordinary mornings of session after session where we trust in psychic reality, and trust that we do not have to make something happen; it will happen itself. Our job is so to position ourselves and the analysand so that we can "see" psychic reality and respond to it.

Do we trust the psychic process to go where it needs to if we do not interfere? Do we really believe in it? Winnicott recommended to child psychiatrists to ask not how much can be done, but what is the least that we can do, for we can trust the psyche to drive the child to communicate with the doctor in terms of the main problem (Winnicott 1971, 207). The adult analysand will use the analyst and the session to relive the frightening interruptions of being that trauma inflicted in order to rescue them now into the whole personality.

Jung talks about this as the archetype pressing for its own resolution. If it cannot be lived within, it will greet us from without like fate. If we cannot receive the archetype's force into positive living, it will fulfill itself negatively. Many of the mythic punishments in hell can be understood as the negative living out of the urge to individuation. Instead of the stone-hard lapis glowing at the center of us as the result of suffering affliction through to the end of its own transformation, we become petrified in our defenses, rigid in projection, adamantine in arthritis (von Franz 1977, 115). Instead of looking into our envy to see hiding there our hunger for the good, our envy blinds us, like Dante's sinners whose eyes were sewn shut with an iron thread (Ulanov and Ulanov 1983, 117). Sometimes our unlived individuation presses us through our mate. The husband who cannot plumb the depths of childhood trauma, its pain sealed off in him, a dream says, by an ivory door melted over the mouth of the cave to the underworld, finds himself plagued with a drunken wife. She is awash in pain, drowning in it. Individuation extends into family systems, too, and into group life where one person finds himself designated to voice the upset feelings for the others who then treat the situation as only his problem.

The Transcendent Function

The critical questions are: Are we awake to the fact of psyche and to the Transcendent manifesting in the psyche? Are we aware that it is there, coming at us, ready to pour into us, to peal out its presence, to inflame us with its passion, to speak to us in quietness at every moment? What happens if we wake up to this fact? We are led to look into and not just at psychic life in ourselves and our analysands. We are led to see how the psyche builds up this conversation between us and the deeper center. Jung describes the transcendent function as the process of imaginative dialogue, in which we articulate our ego point of view and listen to and challenge a differing point of view, held equally strongly by an unconscious part of us that speaks through a body symptom, a dream person or animal, or a depressive, anxious or enraged mood (Jung 1963b, par. 706; Ulanov and Ulanov 1991, 12–19). We converse back and forth with this other point of view in an imaginative process that proves strenuous and surprising. We do not know in advance what will happen. With luck and hard work, a third perspective will arise from the struggle between the ego and the unconscious figure. It will include and surpass the two former conflicting views.

This is what Jung means by the word transcendent—that third point of view which rises out of, unites, and thus transcends the warring opposites. He takes pains, almost protesting too much, to say he does not mean something metaphysical (Jung 1971, par. 828). I think Jung is avoiding the religious here and suggest that it is precisely through the workings of the transcendent function that we receive evidence of the Transcendent in the metaphysical sense operating within us, much like religious tradition describes the Spirit of God moving us to pray. What comes to us as a successful solution arising out of the transcendent function impresses us as a marvelous, novel, even grace-filled answer to our inner conflict, and convinces us of an abiding presence that knows us in the most intimate battles of our soul. Such an active dialogue in imagination works our ego loose from its rigid position and builds it up to house more of the unconscious. We become more supple, both clearer in our own point of view and more open to its opposite. Our ego gets unshackled in this process and the Self gets constructed. The arrival of this third alternative to the contesting two positions within us seems all but miraculous, not only because it solves our conflict, but also because it includes the precious essence of each competing side.

To arrive at this third position feels like release into a new reality. From this novel beginning point we see that our former suffering was not just random. It was leading us to this third alternative which we could not reach except through the narrow gate of our excruciating conflict. Such a new perspective redeems our suffering from meaningless waste. For example, a woman had a consuming inner hunger that overrode every conscious vow to diet, so that she felt tossed back and forth between starving and stuffing herself. When she entered into imaginative dialogue with this hunger, she was astonished by the solution she reached, or that reached her. She saw that her body weight carried a soul question: Who was in charge of her psyche, the ego or the Self? If she could not enlarge to make room for the Self's dimensions, then her body would carry the extra size and weight of the Self's authority (Ulanov 1979).

The Transcendent and the Clinical

The Self does not arrive ready made, like a prefabricated package waiting to be delivered at a certain stage of individuation. Our relation to it builds over time through important meetings with others and with communal events. Could we say it accumulates as well as breaks through to us in moments of sacred communication? We can take an inner history of our experiences of the Self, stringing them like beads, surprised at how many there are, at how a whole necklace takes shape. If a strand of these priceless pearls encircles us, who then is the Giver?

Such a question must be answered by each of us in order to answer the summary question that is present in any treatment: After analysis, what? Analysis is not, I believe, a way of life, nor its substitute, but is an aid to real living. When its work is done, it flows into a person's life. If real living does not unfold thereafter, the analysis may unravel. The analysand does not live rooted in the Self but falls away after an initial blooming, like a seed falling on shallow ground, quickly thriving, but then, under heat or passage of time, withering and dying. Each analysand must find his or her own way to naming what has claimed them, what face of the Transcendent has touched them through the workings of the transcendent function to which they have learned to pay attention in the course of their analysis. They must name it and go on into real living of that relationship. It is precisely here that living in the Self borders on spiritual life.

For analysts, the crucial questions are Who is the Giver? and How are we engaged in conversation with this center? If our struggle to answer these questions is too long delayed simply because we get immersed in the labors of doing analysis, we can be brought to traumatic events. Our physical or our mental health may break down; our work may be invaded by violations of our ethical code; our work may simply break up, leaving us unable to continue it. Ours is a hazardous profession.

In the following clinical case, I hope to show that the transcendent function really does exist and that through its workings we feel touched by the Transcendent. The conversation between our ego and the Self going on in different parts of us becomes a means through which we engage in conversation with what transcends our psyche—ego, Self, and all. More specifically, we notice that such a conversation has been continuing all the while.

The transcendent function working in the analyst engages the same function in the analysand. The analyst acts like a votary of the Transcendent, not by proselytizing the analysand, but by attending closely to the workings of the transcendent function within himself or herself. This attitude of scrupulous, trustful observation is the essence of the attitude Jung calls "religious" (Jung 1938, pars. 8–9). The transcendent function working in the analyst engages the same function in the analysand. This level of transference and countertransference, often elusive in its articulation but always decisive in its effects, acts as clinical resource for spiritual life. The openness in the analyst to "the Unknown as it immediately affects us," which is Jung's definition of the unconscious, opens the analysand in a similar way (Jung 1957, 68). The field between them grows increasingly hospitable to manifestations of the Transcendent in terms so embodied in the particular life of the analysand that it compels the analysand's attention—indeed, even amazement—not unlike people's reactions to "signs" in Biblical times. The religious instinct in the analysand, which Jung defines as consciousness of our capacity to relate to deity, gets activated (Jung 1953, par. 11).

The Transcendent that comes into view can be described from a clinical perspective as pressing for a wholeness that is not an ideal but a knitting together of all the parts that belong to us, including hopes we despaired of, wounds we could not heal, quests we thought we should have long ago abandoned. The sense of the Transcendent, then, is embodied in the actual facts of our lives and yields to us a sense of purposiveness. We begin to feel that nothing is wasted. Even our worst failures and fumblings, our deepest hurts and the violations dealt us not only by ourselves but also by others and by fate, begin to weave a pattern that brings us again and again into company with transcendence which appears with increasing clarity. We begin to see that being all we can be, fully filling out all dimensions of our humanity, seems to be urged by the Transcendent.

Clinical work thus refutes the traditional religious idea of annihilation of self as the way to God or offers radical reinterpretation of its dread meaning. The advent of transcendence presses us to link up and knit together all the bits and pieces of human life as a means of receiving the Transcendent. Such a numinous encounter can be hard, excruciating, as if we were a piece of hide stretched to bigger size. Such encounter is always momentous, for boundaries between human and divine get crossed and energy so ignites that we feel we will burn up in its blaze. In this way, our ego perspective is indeed offered up, consumed by the "consuming fire" (Hebrews 12: 19), and yet, paradoxically, we need all the ego life we can muster to house this consuming fire and know that it is housing us.

The Self comes into focus, getting gathered and collected, found and created, discovered as already there and yet newly constructed in the conversation with the ego. The Self, I repeat, is not God or the Transcendent in us; it is that in us that knows about the Transcendent, about God, and gives us access to the fact that this Other knows about us. When we know that we are known, we are pushed in two directions simultaneously. We are pushed toward specific ego tasks that confront us and demand our attention; and we are pushed by the energy coming through the Self, pushed on to new ground that demands our contemplation.

The Case

Here I shall give clinical material from a white woman of fifty who illustrates the emergence of the Transcendent through the workings of the transcendent function within her and between us in analytical sessions. She is an unusual example for a number of reasons. Her work in analysis spans almost a quarter of a century, falling into two sections: the first, twenty-four years ago, consisted of three years of individual sessions and six years of group therapy; the second, of ongoing individual sessions which began two years ago. It is rare in my experience to see such a large arc of a person's analytical life. It allows us to see what work got done and stayed done, and what work failed to get done or could only be done now after much living has been accomplished, nearly twenty-five years later.

This woman also illustrates how the Self-ego conversation is embodied in our actual physical life. The psychiatrist who prescribed her medication opined that this woman's depression was biological; that though triggered by psychic events, she could not get out of it without the biological changes drugs induce. This biological propensity to depression might have been caused by after-effects of a severely powerful drug she took in her early twenties to cure a grave heart disease, a drug that some doctors think permanently alters a person's chemical makeup.

She also shows how the perspective of the Self-ego conversation applies to the most serious of cases, for she has tried to kill herself three times. Such a conversation is not an indulgence that a more mildly neurotic person might take up, or that might prove interesting to those drawn to religion. Nor is it an esoteric analytical theory. The Self-ego conversation makes the difference between life or death. This case makes that fact vividly evident. To analyze persons suffering from suicidal compulsion is the hardest work in my experience because there are two deaths to worry about: the physical taking of life and the collapse of the symbolic into the literal. Only within the last year of this case has the promise of a lasting solution emerged with our analysis of the Self hiding in her suicidal complex.

Finally, this analysand is unusual for our purposes of exploring clinical resources for spiritual life because she is violently anti-religious. If something spiritual claims her, it gives hard evidence of the new breaking in, because anything associated with religion is the last thing she wants to hear about. Even me, whom she says she trusts not to manipulate her into any belief system, she watches like a hawk. Every now and then she comments on my religious training, just to let me know she has not forgotten it. She repudiates her Methodist upbringing, objecting that "Jesus is not pink!" Like Jung, she was interested as a child in theological problems and disillusioned by her Sunday school instruction. Her sister, older by twelve years, taught the class and humiliated her when she replied to the question, What is the Trinity? that it was a big river (which existed close by in her southern state). Instead of tackling the intricacies of how we know God, the class focused on the intricacies of matching the shade of one's stockings to the color of one's dress and on how to cross one's ankles when seated.

The Two Analyses

Her first analysis of over two decades ago dealt with the presenting problem of a suicide attempt by gas, precipitated by a young man's rejection. During our work, another suicide was attempted by overdose of pills, in response to rejection by a man, her lover, as they were speaking on the telephone. He immediately called me; I rushed to her apartment, as did he, and the two of us took her to a hospital to get her stomach pumped. Her eventual marriage to this man cost her much suffering and ended in divorce several years later. Her analysis saw her through these traumas, as well as through a serious crisis in her job in the business world, where her beloved boss was indicted and convicted for illegal dealings and she had to testify against him. Though she secured another position, she soon gave up her good salary to pursue a long-held secret ambition which she feared she was not smart enough to do: a Ph.D.

She overcame her inferiority complex, and secured admission to and graduated from a prestigious institution. She married again happily and went on to a new career, bringing her analysis to a close and feeling the hard work had been successful. She sent word that she had landed a job of national importance that combined, to her great pleasure, many parts of herself—her strong commitment to justice issues for women, and especially women of color, her wish to be more than less her own boss, her decision to use her administrative and intellectual skills in public areas in contrast to academic research, and her ambition to make a contribution to the betterment of people's lives.

Her present analysis began suddenly with a phone call as I was leaving for Europe for some lecturing and a brief holiday. Sobbing, she said her husband had fallen into a deep depression and she could not penetrate his withdrawal. Refusing a referral, we arranged to meet immediately upon my return. She began our work again by saying, "I've had a happy, interesting, extraordinary life from age thirty on, and it has a lot to do with you and our work. And," she went on, "what's the matter with me can be summed up by saying I haven't read any fiction in ten years." Her husband had consulted a psychiatrist and felt a little better but she still did not know what had thrown him, and then her, into this crisis. She was worried for him and angry that he so controlled their communication.

Two weeks later he told her he had been having an affair and his lover's departure had precipitated his depression. She was enraged that he endangered their life together and dreamt about his flying both of them in a helicopter straight up through electrical wires. In the dream, she yells, "You could have killed us!" and he replies, "I didn't see them." She felt humiliated that another woman and not herself had occasioned his depression. She felt chagrined to realize her part in his distress: "I've spent twenty years getting life together and becoming independent because I have been so dependent on men, but he felt I didn't need him." He felt he had little impact on her, especially sexually; she had not noticed his unmet desire, but when he tried to speak of it, she dismissed him with sociological data about the sex lives of married couples. Here she felt she had been wrong and had contributed to the problem between them. The first meaning this crisis brought her was the realization she must turn and look into her own sexuality; but she also felt that he overloaded sexuality with all the unexamined problems he suffered—problems having to do with his childhood unhappiness, his dissatisfaction at work, his political disillusionment, and his not making friends but instead piling all his needs for intimacy on his wife.

He was stunned by how upset she was, for all her anger, hurt, humiliation, and chagrin boiled up into a resurgence of depression and suicidal ruminations. Suicidal impulses would come over her in response to feeling that she had no impact on him, that in no other way except through threat of self-harm could she get an emotional response from him. They were joined in their despair of exerting impact on each other—he on her sexually and she on him emotionally. He resisted beginning analytical treatment, seeing the psychiatrist only periodically, but he did agree to see a marriage counselor to improve their ability to talk all this over. That lasted only briefly, however. Her suicidal preoccupations also gave outlet to her sadism toward him, toward life, and occasionally toward me; but the suicidal pull could not be reduced to repressed power urges or even melodrama, though it had plenty of both. It also contained a deep despair about the future of life, about her adequacy as a woman, and about her ability to be a person fully alive and real, connected to a source of and goal in life.

The Shot and the Mute Girl

The pertinent parts of this woman's history were pulled into our analytical focus by the images the transcendent function brought up in her dreams and imaginative work as she struggled with an impulse to suicide. She was struck by how custom-made the images were that touched her and by how much power they had to make the Unknown known. She said these images were real: "They come on their own; they are not imposed by me, or you, or some religion, or some psychology textbook. They bring their own authority." The images brought up specific parts of her history, the geographical and physical roots of her being. I will present her history and the important transference and countertransference dynamics by following the lead of the transcendent function, because that is how we lived it.

A dream of hers helped us to begin linking past with present trauma:

> *There is a bunker and the number seventeen; the bunker guns go off and do their destruction in just one shot. Onlookers in the dream say you cannot do anything in just one shot; you need four to build a house.*

In association to the dream, the woman said that she would have liked to be done with the unhappiness with her husband in one shot, but she knew she would have to build the solution bit by bit. The number four, with its archetypal associations to wholeness, indicated that the solution would involve a lot more than simply the resolution of the marriage problem. It would build the house for her life. Regarding the number seventeen, she said that it was precisely seventeen years ago that she had begun her new career and had met her husband. She said also that when she was sixteen going on seventeen her father had died suddenly. Thus, the dream directed us to the sudden loss of these two pivotal men in her life. She wept and wept. Further, she said that her husband had been shot down as the "good Daddy," just as her father had died of a sudden heart attack immediately after speaking to her firmly about the perils of being wild with boyfriends.

She had never grieved for her father. After his death, her mother went to bed for a year and never remarried; her older sister, married by then, came home, bringing her own young children and managing the house for three months; her older brother stayed all day and all night by their father's casket. She, the youngest child, went right back to school and has no memory of ever crying or talking to anyone about missing her father.

She uncovered, however, a split that had occurred in her identity and that she felt her father, had he lived, might have remedied. "Suzy girl"—a nickname her father gave her—described her identity until puberty. She loved this self because it was authentic, original, and full of aggressive mischief as well as creativity. She had friends and belonged to her beloved Creative School where children painted, put on Shakespeare's plays, and read poetry. This school was for her the creative space of illusion (Winnicott 1953, 10–14), where her imagination was matched by reality, and literature and art fed her imagination. Not until middle age did she again find such food, in the poetry of Rilke and the fiction of Robert Musil, whom she began to read during our analysis at the suggestion of an elderly female friend. At puberty, "Suse"— a nickname friends gave her—took over, an identity she hated and described as fat, with voluptuous breasts and no brain. She hated breasts. Their appearance meant she had to leave the Creative School which limited itself to preadolescent children. Hence for her, getting breasts meant losing her space of creative living and soul nurture. Nothing took its place, though she did opine that had he lived, conversing with her father might have opened the world to her as she got older, because he "was a voice beyond conventions." She refused her husband's gestures to love her breasts, saying, "It made my teeth itch."

The first dream image of the one shot led us to the preadolescent "Suzy-girl," now mute, who was dying of pain from the past loss of her father and the present loss of her husband. In many ways, the latter had become a "good daddy," who did a lot of mothering, too. He supervised her eating, which sometimes included literal baby food, and tucked her into bed each night. She felt that this little-girl part of herself was almost absolutely dependent. She saw that she had simply handed over "Suzy-girl" to her husband's solicitous care, and that it was she he had left in search of an adult sexual companion. I hazarded the notion that her severe disease at nineteen, which had been like a polio of the heart and had kept her strictly confined to bed for a year, unable even to get up for the bathroom, was the mourning she had accomplished through her body—in her paralyzed heart—for her father's death. Her heart had nearly stopped, as his in fact had. Her year of convalescence had imitated her mother's year of collapse after her husband's death, and had reenacted an infant's dependency by forcing her mother to care for her feeding and bathroom functions. Her illness had also changed her body type back to the skinny preadolescent girl which she, and her husband, favored. She said, "I was a boy lover to him as father."

The mute "Suzy-girl" played her role as well in the suicidal complex, for she longed for death simply to stop the pain. I said this mute part of her was trying to communicate her pain through images of cutting her wrist, taking poison, jumping off the balcony. Her task, I suggested, was to imagine holding this little girl on her own lap, instead of passing her off to her husband, and hearing each wave of pain as it washed over her. Her ego had to get into the act and engage this part of her which her psyche was imaginatively giving her. She dreamt that she was in a white elevator, the walls made of modules; that I was trying to get to her by pulling back the modules; and that she was trying to call me, but there was no phone. In response to this dream, she said that it was very important for me to see this mute part of her. During our summer recess, which followed soon after this dream, she did find a phone to call and request to see me, as we had arranged she would do if necessary.

When we resumed our work, she dreamt of "a Yale type of guy" dancing her down the stairs, but she looked "like a stick with a mop on top." Then the scene shifted; she was on a podium and black women were saying she was wonderful. The dream put together her two self-images—the little girl, not yet physically mature but skinny like a mop, and her adult self, who did in fact speak on podiums and was much appreciated by black women. The dream thus encouraged her to connect these two identities. The "guy" was familiar to us from her first analysis. Then, he had appeared in a dream as "a blond sort of jock" standing before her when the door of the elevator was opened. She had never liked him, but he turned up regularly in her dreams and always played a positive role. He was an animus figure trying to help her whom she usually disregarded. In another dream from the first analysis, she had wanted to unhandcuff a criminal from the foot of her bed and the blond man, now an FBI man, had cautioned her against it, as the crook was dangerous. She "pooh-poohed" his advice, saying "Poor Baby" to the criminal, and let him loose, whereupon he attacked her. We knew from this old dream that the blond man wanted to help her harness her lethal aggression. In the present dream, he led her downstairs, to which she associated her first marriage.

Although this first marriage had caused her pain, as she talked now, many years later, about her sexual attraction to her first husband who was smooth, dark and Hispanic in origin, it occurred to me that with him she had made a descent to the underworld to find her lost sexuality. With him she had had a sexual connection but nothing else. In response to my making this observation, she shared a sexual fantasy around the movie *Belle de Jour* which she greatly admired. In the film the heroine takes herself every afternoon to a brothel to work as a whore. What triggered my analysand's fantasy was that this woman prostituted herself out of her own sexual needs to claim a sexuality she could not find in her respectable marriage to a man she loved. Like the movie story, my analysand's attempt with this first husband ended in disaster, and so she had put a lid on her sexuality, settling in her second marriage for a father-daughter intimacy. Her present husband's infidelity now plunged her back into the chthonic world, for she felt rage and lust to regain her sexual power over him.

To the pain of the mute little girl was now added the pain of lost sexuality. The unconscious was gathering all these unpaid bills, presenting them for her attention. A dream signaled precisely this work:

> *I am braiding a wick which is necessary for light. I am flying around a candle which is not yet lit. I think: this is my life getting ready to be illumined.*

No Nipples, the River, and the Poinsettia

The treatment heated up. We had differentiated one piece of my analysand's suicidal complex—the mute girl who just wanted to die to stop the pain—but much more was needed. Power plays to get her husband's attention also compensated for how helpless this girl part of her felt. She suggested to her husband that they separate if that would make it easier for him, because he felt torn between guilt at the pain he caused her and the pull of his other relationship. She hoped he would refuse but he accepted. She staged one suicidal gesture, only to reclaim herself when I suggested a stay in the hospital; but another overdose of pills a month later made it clear, even though this medication could not have killed her, that the hospital was the next step.

She felt the eight days in the hospital benefited her enormously. She could let go to her rage and despair and be protected against harm. She also felt the reality of the hospital incarceration knocked the suicidal temptation out of her. Relating to other inpatients made her see that her suicidal gesture was a spectacular way of commanding the attention she despaired of receiving through lesser routes. Her brother who telephoned during this time confirmed this line of thinking. He said she had always had to work hard, to make herself "exotic," to catch the interest of either parent when she was growing up. She wrote a poem in the hospital about Heraclitus that concluded with saying, "And a river's depth—/even the mighty Jordan's—/Is nothing to be feared."[1]

The psychiatrist assigned to her in the hospital saw her together with her husband, who remained guilty and ambivalent, so she finally told him to go. I kept in daily phone touch with her but decided not to see her at the hospital. I wanted to keep the frame of our sessions intact and hence did not want just to visit her, and I did not want to confuse the sessions she had with the psychiatrist with the ones she had with me. He agreed and therefore did not conduct therapy with her but instead gave her blunt feedback about how he saw her situation. He took over the management of her medication and her subsequent monthly meetings with him proved a good foil to her analysis with me. The fact that he is from South America (recalling her first husband) and clear to the point of being harsh, in contrast to her North American Jewish husband who is so ambivalent and unclear about his course of action, encouraged her to connect with her womanly self and begin to use her aggression to define her situation.

The test of this new strength came shortly thereafter when she was a passenger in a near fatal car accident, and when, a week later, on a train trip for her job, a deranged homeless man tried to strangle her. In both shocking incidents, she held up fine. I noted that she was no longer identified with the lethal aggression; it was now let loose and attacking her from the outside and she could clearly hold her own.

Her psyche responded to this new ego strength with a series of powerful images. She saw that she had relied on suicide as an ever-present bottom line if pain became unbearable. Like a black line, I asked, running beneath everything? Yes, she agreed, and that was why she returned to taking Prozac which she had worked hard to quit. The drug softened this black line, but it never went away. I waded in to analyze the line, emboldened by her transference to me of a security she had found with her father. She said, "I knew I was utterly supported by him, as I am with you." In tackling the black line, we discovered it pictured suicide as a support to her ego. Suicide was something to fall back on, she said, when "my ego gets tired." She explained that she tried hard to keep busy, to see her many good friends, to do her work, to plan against depression, to submit to medication, and that she did well. But she got tired of holding herself up. Only suicide offered a deeper foundation to which to let go. I suddenly saw the suicide as a negative image of the Self—as something that held out arms of relief to her from ego performing, something to depend upon and rest upon, like a mother's breast.

This interpretation quieted my fear of her suicide and stiffened my nerve to pursue the Self hiding in her suicidal complex. Now we looked at her suicide symbolically. At this time she took up Robert Musil and read me a passage about Ulrich, the main character, who wanted to be free from stereotypes, to live in touch with the mysterious indefinable core of his identity. He had just thrown off his mistress and was walking to see his friends. It came to him that at the noon of life we become aware of something or someone present, who has been corresponding with us all these years (Musil 1930, 151). I heard my analysand talking about her own conversation between ego and Self, which had sealed up when she was pushed out of the Creative School, which had tried to come out with her father but was buried when he died, and which was emerging now from hiding in the suicidal complex. We could say that the transcendent function working between me and her material engaged, through my interpretations, the transcendent function working between her and what her suicide symbolized.

Her psyche responded by taking us deeper. She dreamed of a blond hussy with "enormous bosoms and no nipples who gets up and walks off." This image uncovered a deep deprivation of mothering. In her first analysis, we had worked hard to free her from imprisonment in her mother's "maxims for living" that echoed conventional southern stereotypes for women, urged as well by her older sister. We succeeded. She had not only struck out on her own career and style of marriage in another part of the country, but also had formed a loving, funny, free relationship with her mother that both of them enjoyed a lot. However, she said now, "There were and are no nipples for me. We love each other, but there is no holding me, no room for dependence." As a recent example, she said her mother sympathized with her husband, chiding her for not being a better wife. She also confessed a fantasy that had always seemed weird to her of a woman penetrating her anally with her nipple. She saw with new clarity that her hatred of breasts was linked to feeling so unprotected, with no breast to lean upon or back up her striving ego.

The next dream brought her connection to nipples by linking her to the bit of good mothering she had known and that mothering she herself had given generously to others through her job.

> *She is being moved to a new office, and three black women are to have an identical office next door. Subsequently, she and the black women are to be photographed by the press. Looking down, she sees that she wears a baby rainshoe on one foot and a polka-dot sandal with a chichi bow on the other foot. Neither fits her adequately. One of the black women says, "Go get your espadrilles and get in the picture."*

She saw immediately that the dream revealed her standpoint as both too childish and too fey, and that she needed to put on her comfortable adult feminine shoes. The black women in the dream recalled her love for Sadie, the black woman who worked for her parents and who was a good mothering presence. She felt a wordless bond with Sadie, who was so real, practical, and strong. She spoke of her kinship with black persons, feeling she knew something of the hurt that struck at their souls. During her heart disease, her school had become integrated and one of her mother's friends had told her how to make the black children miserable. "Something died in me that day about her and that whole world," she said. Indeed, she now had many close black friends and was appreciated at work by her black colleagues. I thought to myself, "Black women are a Self symbol to her. The black line of suicide has become a black woman's breast to lean upon."

We worked hard with that image for a few months. Then, in another dream, her psyche broke through to the image of the river:

> *She is high up on a diving board getting ready to dive into a huge river, like an ocean, way far down. That same blond guy, here a coach, says he'll dive first to test the water, which is hard and strong, but manageable. She jumps! Getting ashore is awful, but it is a familiar river—the Brazos. Then, she is in the hotel room where she had suggested to her husband that they separate if it would help him.*

She hated diving but felt fine about jumping in. She recognized her dream man: "He is that big, tall, southern type, not Jewish or sensitive or interesting to me sexually at all. He is friend, coach, tutor, brother—the male side of me." That particular river was very important to her; she had lived near it as a child. When her father wanted to emphasize something as really important he would always say, "It's like crossing the Brazos!" Also, he had once taken her and her brother safely "to the high ground" when the river crested in a flood; her mother had been off on a cruise recovering from her sister's wedding at the time. She knew the word *brazos* meant arms, and recalled a Dali painting of Christ with his arms outstretched to embrace the whole world.

The dream-river helped us differentiate the deeper resource that was hiding in suicide and to take the mother's breast one step further. She said, "Suicide is what I have relied upon when all else fails. I feel my husband and life betrayed me and suicide is the closest I've come to betraying myself, but I seem to be licking it. Thank God I got through it with the help of you and my friends and the hospital. I could not have done any better. I'm feeling gentle on myself. Here the river is life; you have to have a river in my part of the country; nothing lives without water. Los Brazos is a God-image to me; it's my poem in the hospital about the river; it's clean and brown, the color of my beloved Sadie." I told her that the unconscious was responding to her efforts.

Then something unexpected happened. She did not come to her next session or call to explain her absence. This was the first time such a thing had happened in all the work we had done. My instinct told me she was all right because of our work on the river image, but I also knew the danger of the thawing-out period from suicide and how easily a sudden impulse can carry any of us away. I created a big commotion, phoning her apartment, her office, and then her husband to get the telephone number of the superintendent of her building so that I could ask him to go into her apartment. I alerted her psychiatrist. I called her friends in the city and in the country, leaving messages everywhere. I did not find her. I was very worried and also not worried, and had a hard time living all day in the tension of these opposite emotions. Finally, that evening she called from Atlantic City, where she had been giving a speech for her job, and had suddenly realized that she had forgotten our early morning session. I was so relieved! I babbled on about how glad I was that she was alive and in Atlantic City, of all places. I also alerted her to the commotion I had caused.

As we analyzed this episode in the next session, she said the work on the river image had gone so deep and given her such peace that she felt she had just been in my office and had had a session, so she did not realize that she had missed the next one. She also said she felt loved by me. And that was true. In my gladness that she was alive, I did feel how much she mattered. I also compared this response to the one I had had to her earlier suicide attempt, while in treatment with me many years ago. Then, I had registered anger, feeling manipulated by her power-play against her lover. When I had put her in the hospital after her last suicidal gesture, I had felt the strain of that necessity.

Now, our transference-countertransference interaction moved in a field of mutual regard that mixed in with the fuss she caused and I created around suicide. This new field between us, plus the new symbol of the river, freed her from the literal threat of suicide by uncovering its symbolic intent. Suicide had represented to her the one resource she could count on when all else had failed, but she acted it out literally, and endangered her life. Now, ironically, as the new symbol of the river replaced suicide, she saw its symbolic value as pointing to a power which the river conveyed more vividly. The river stood for steadfast loving support found in her father, in Sadie, in friends, in the field between us, and in life itself. On the ego level, we could see an end of the treatment coming into view, because she did not need the session she forgot. On the Self level, I realized I could trust that she had forgotten our session because she remembered the work we accomplished, and could trust her not to kill herself out of forgetting what we did.

A month later another pivotal image came from her unconscious. She had the following dream:

She is in an apartment with that same type of "blond waspy guy" and exclaims, "Did you see that!" pointing to a nearly dead Poinsettia plant, the center of which is pouring out "pots of poison," the color a "bright yellow, almost like bile." After the poison is exhausted, the flower emits clear fluid.

She said simply, "This dream is my life and my relation to my husband: the poison is suicide; the bright yellow its spleen; the clear fluid my tears. A poinsettia to me is what God is all about, including the poison; the bad with the good makes more sense to me than the poison communicated to me from the Church, which was full of hypocrisy, teaching charm instead of theology." She felt the Church's God had been usurped by her sister, who had married a clergyman. She felt crippled on the religious front but confided that giving up religion did not mean giving up God. She also said at this moment that she no longer saw me as the mother or sister she never had, but "as part of myself which I trust—intellectual, quiet, interior, with a sense of poetry."

Outwardly, energy flowed into her life. She received excellent evaluations of her work at her job, and she used her aggression to fashion her interactions with her husband in terms of separating all the paraphernalia of their two lives and in terms of expressing her anger at what he had done. She recovered connection to "Suzygirl," including her childish, but not ineffective, displays of angry aggression. She said, "I rely on dreams now, not on suicide. These come to me; they are not 'isms' of movements."

The Black Pot, Endless Tears, and the Unending River

In her subsequent work, my analysand went back and forth, as we all do when struggling with major complexes. She worked on what held her bound to her husband, and on what had initially attracted her to a man who did not react. She also worked on her splitting off the chthonic feminine, represented now by its vaginal fluids and not just by breasts, and on getting herself off Prozac. This period was punctuated by a haunting dream, that continued to be powerful for months. In the dream she makes a pronouncement: "I am a black hole floating in a black pot." When she woke up she reversed it, saying: "No, I am a black pot floating in a black hole." She was struck by the aptness of these two versions to describe her suicidal complex, and by their being "so frighteningly different." She said her version when she awoke, namely, the ego point of view, was exactly what suicide felt like—being out of control, sucked into the void of a black hole in space. The dream's version, namely the Self point of view, was "having a pot to put the suicidal impulse into, a pot to piss in," she said. "It's limited and contains my black hole feelings." What struck me was that the two parts of the conversation—the ego's and the Self's—were in dialogue in the same dream image, and now, having dreamt the dream and remembered it, she held both parts together in her consciousness. She went on about the pot, saying it brought to mind her conviction of the proper care of a special skillet used only to cook her favorite southern breakfast. She took this care as her mother had done and her grandmother before her. I thought, Here is the linking up of the missing feminine matrix.

That interpretation proved correct because the next dream showed her holding a barely pubescent girl, admiring her very soft skin. The dream after that focused on digging up a woman who had been buried alive, and the next showed her with three other women, each of whom had been deeply hurt: "For all of us the only solution was to cry our eyes out." A later dream cinched this theme:

> *Someone takes an impression of me as a newly born baby, and of my little suction-cup, teeny bosoms, saying that from the beginning I'm a little girl with little breasts, and someone cares enough to make a note of it. I am identified.*

We were not out of the woods, however, as the fluctuations in the transference, as well as in her moods, demonstrated. Before one session she knocked on my door, panicked that I was not in my office, and what would she do if I was not there? Coming to another appointment that she had rescheduled at a different time, she walked in on someone else's session. Though she justified her mistake by the time change, I went after the omnipotence and hostility in this intrusion. I was being treated as the mother who belonged to her, regardless of the other client who was in the office. She could just barge in when her panic shook her, and not consider whether it was intrusive to anyone else's session. The fluctuations in her feelings toward her husband revolved on a very deep bond of feeling between them, so that it seemed as impossible to sever ties and go on to a new separate life as it was to return to their former marriage. Hence she was continually feeling shocked that this crisis had happened and feeling the old pull, though fainter, of suicide.

Now she put it differently. She said she claimed her life now and could cope, but for how long? Certainly not for thirty-five years. Her husband's continuing ambivalence did not help, nor did her conviction that she would never find anyone else and that she was not made to live alone. She said it was like living in a cage of brightness, a world without the shadows made by other people living their lives and touching hers. She didn't want a symbiosis; she wanted an adult world with fun, color, hue, and texture, just like the Creative School or the magic moments of *A Midsummer Night's Dream*. She was made for people—for doing good by being with others, feeding, helping, cavorting, creating beauty, "with the wings of other people brushing over you all the time." She said, "My theological vision is Rousseau's painting of animals in the bushes and trees, playing before God." I kept to myself the theological idea of Iraeneus that we show God's glory by being human beings fully alive. Instead, I asked, Did such a life depend on being with her husband? No, not him specifically, she answered, but a man or men in her life.

That opened a new door and I walked right through it, asking, If there was another man or men as a friend or friends, would it be easier to give up her husband? "In a shot," she replied, only to add that, according to statistics, this development was certain not to happen. A dream took us further into this new place:

She finds herself in a little dark house in her hometown, like the house her mother had moved to and lived in as a widow after her father's death.

About this dream, she swore vehemently. "I'll be damned if I'll be stuck in my mother's shoes without my father!" We saw her latent fear suddenly manifest: to be without a man was to be stuck in mother's world, which, though now loving, was originally one without nurture or foundation for her identity as a woman. She said, "My mother and I have a lot of fun together. I don't mother her; we are friends and speak plainly to each other; but she is childish and not a mother to me. If all I have before me is living in this bright cage, I'll be dead in two or three years."

This newly felt link between her present depression at the loss of a man in her life and her original deprivation of maternal support changed the question before her and also necessitated her resuming medication, as the "double whammy" was strong. She noted her mother had been her own present age when she was widowed and had lived the rest of her life alone or with other women. She said, "My impulse to commit suicide would come back if I felt forced to join a society of women as my mother did. Mother's world is a void, with all these fucking rules on how to be a widow!" She said she felt her mother was charming and a survivor, but in some basic ways just not grown up. My analysand, however, wanted to grow up, and this took us back to the river image.

She realized the goal was not to cross the river because the river was life and its end was the sea. She said, "I'm in the river of middle age, but it is a huge way until I die and I can't find a solution that fits me. I'm not a good soldier who will just go on coping, and I cannot stand the common solutions." I saw that she was groping for a way to find and create what she could believe in and to articulate the Transcendent that was coming to her through her engagement with the transcendent function working within her. The fundamental question shifted from "Will I survive or not?" to "How to house the river that houses me?"

Conclusion

In summing up, the issues are these. When we engage the transcendent function working within us, the psyche sets us specific ego tasks at the same time it ushers us into Self territory. For this woman, the ego tasks mean confronting and integrating the lost mute girl and her chthonic sexuality, which together help augment her identity and secure its foundation in a feminine matrix. In addition, she must differentiate her aggression from self-attack to use it to define her relation to her husband and to shape and sustain the creative living of the rest of her life. She also must consider the defensive use of her conviction that to be an adult, one must have men in one's life. On an unconscious level, that conviction had protected her from her terror of being left once again at the mercy of unmet infant dependency on the ungiving maternal.

Evidence of the transcendent function working in this woman comes in the pivotal images she has engaged: the shot, the two identities of "Suzy-girl" and "Suse," the woman with no nipples, the recovery of her black "mother's" breast, the river, the poinsettia, the black pot, and again the river. So much of the aggression that swooped down on her in suicidal attacks she now employs to meet and differentiate her relation to all these parts of her psyche. This conversation between her ego and the psychic reality these images represent makes her ego bigger, tougher, and more supple, and ushers her into the precincts of the Self.

The living in the Self that opened up was her finding what carried the Transcendent for her—the God-images of the river, the

mixture of bad with good in the poinsettia flower, the life of play before God, the interconnection of people pictured as living in a dappled world where the wings of other's lives brush against one's own.
The vicissitudes of Self are the multiple complexities which unfold
in the everyday objects of life and point to the Transcendent as present and trustworthy. Could we say it seems as eager for the conversation as we are?

Such a conversation is aided and abetted in a subtle but decisive
dimension of the transference-countertransference field. It is not so
much what the analyst says that makes a difference here, but more
how we as analysts are conversing with the Transcendent as it appears in our own lives and work.

This leaves us with a final question. This woman ended up asking not, "How shall I survive?" but instead, "How shall I relate to
what is making itself known to me? How shall I house it?" This
leaves us with the question, "After Analysis, then what? How do we
go on nurturing this conversation?" One reason some people stay in
analysis for decades, I believe, has more to do with this question
than with pathology or with the analyst's faulty termination procedures. It is as if the analysand has found only in analysis a place to
conduct this ego-Self conversation. This raises issues for religion in
all its creeds and denominations. The main issue, I believe, is
whether or not religion avails itself of the clinical resources for the
spiritual life.

Postscript

In subsequent work, we continued to focus on the integration of
the lively, original, imaginative "Suzy-girl" who, though preadolescent, was open to future adventures and to the happiness of sexual
life, with the "fat, depressed, invisible" Suze who had voluptuous
breasts but rejected them along with all things sexual.

We discovered that her obdurate wish to resume the marriage
sprang in part from terror in the face of a presumed nothingness if
she were to accept that the marriage was over. She had already
lived that nothingness early in her childhood and at a deep level of
mentation in her suicide ventures. Yet she knew she could not dis-
regard what I called the ruthlessness of sexual choice—that we either feel a sexual *frisson* and connection with another human
being, or we do not. If it is absent, we cannot will it into being. She
never knew the bodily electricity with her second husband that she

had had with her first, and she knew that that lack contributed to the marriage breakup.

When she put these two truths together consciously—instead of wildly swinging between the opposites as before—she saw that her sexuality was a fearsome thing to her. It might bring her to an intimacy where again she might get badly hurt. That her sexuality was quite her own and could be lived at her own disposal, subject to her own choices, whether or not she lived it with another person, was new, even numinous to her.

Following these insights an outer event synchronistically opened a great wash of healing. At a conference that she was running, she suddenly saw her husband's lover in the audience. She discovered, she said, that she "didn't hate her." But the simple fact of her existence—and with her the fact of sexuality—was unavoidable. Right after that she had to meet her husband to settle some business matters. Again they felt the bond between them, but now something new broke in upon her. "He is not interested in me," she said, "nor, really, in going farther with this woman. But I have to give up the illusion of his tender interest in me, in my psyche, in what I have been going through. He is entirely wrapped up in himself. He is a narcissist."

That night, she had a dream that opened the way to healing the wound to her sexuality:

> Someone says to me, "You have to paint your own cubicle. Go do it!" "All right!" I answer. I sneak into someone else's cubicle—maybe it is yours—which is all white and with soft folded mohair blankets, almost like a changing table. I think I will paint mine in mauves, grays, and blues, my colors.

When we spoke about the dream, something new came within reach and covered her over in healing colors. In the dream she saw her own space. Looking at the analyst's space—hence the space of her analysis—she got an idea of what being finished in one's self is like. The dream contained a changing table, an image that at once combines early care for an infant self as well as the grown-up idea that being finished involves much changing. She would bring her own special varied colors to her own cubicle—which is her identity and a womanly sex. Questions formed: Maybe her body had had its own wisdom all along? Maybe her lack of sexual response to her husband in fact had been appropriate because there was no one there to make love to in that he was all taken up with his own drama of self-reflection?

In that session and the following ones, she felt her sexuality all rearranged. She said, "My sexual reluctance was not because I was or am a freak, but rather because too much pain was there, because he was not really interested in me. He was looking at himself sexually through me. His solicitous care of me at meals, at bedtime, when I worked, was all mixed up with this glaring lack of interest in really seeing the other." She summed up: "He is a narcissist in nurse's clothing!" She said, "This relieves me of a lot of guilt." The way now opened for the redeeming of her sexuality as a part of herself she could trust.

I have added this postscript to this chapter and to this book because it suggests the value to all sorts of women of taking seriously their own experiences of identity and of sexuality. They need to be claimed, even in the face of desertion and defection, because the positive outweighs the negative. With that claim comes life.

Note

1. The poem is as follows:

> THINKING OF HERACLITUS
> I ready myself, perforce, to plunge
>   into the river of change
> And swim alone toward whatever life
>   may lie on the other side.
>
> The chance of drowning through fatigue
>   is real:
> My physique is small and untrained,
>   my soul unpredictable.
> And never did I expect to cross at
>   this place in time.
>
> But the currents are not extreme
> And a river's depth—
>   even the mighty Jordan's—
> Is nothing to be feared.

This poem came again into this woman's mind with great force eight months after she wrote it, when she dreamt she was diving into a river. It came to my mind when not long after this dream I saw the Magritte exhibit at the Metropolitan Museum of Art. In his painting, *The Heraclitus Bridge*, I was struck by the fact that while the top half of the painting—the actual bridge—did not link up with the other side of the river but disappeared into the clouds, the image of the bridge was made whole again in its reflection in the water at the bottom of the picture. It struck me that the image in the water precisely depicted this woman's plight, struggle, and task. She felt no conscious linking up of the sides of her life. That had disappeared with her husband's abandonment. Maybe her sense of being a unified self had just seemed to disappear into clouds. It would, however, clear up in time and then she would find that she was, in fact, a firm unity, anchored on both sides of her before-and-after trauma. Then again, perhaps she would never link up again but just be chopped off like the bridge on top and disappear, as her suicide ventures suggested.

Her struggle was to find the bridge in reality, in everyday life; it was to build connection across the gap into which she had plunged with her suicide attempt. Her work was to find this bridge as well as to construct it. In it she could be guided by the wholeness of connection mirrored in the unconscious, which is so clearly depicted in the painting.

The painting gave me hope and the nerve to go on staking my energies in the work with this woman, believing that in the unconscious, as both her poem and the painting portrayed, all she needed was there, present. Our work was to rescue into consciousness the spannings of conscious and unconscious, of river and land, of illusion and reality, that were given her to be.

References

Butler, D. C. 1966. *Western Mystics*. New York: Harper.

Freud, S. 1915. Vicissitudes of the Instincts. *Standard Edition*. Vol. 14. London: Hogarth Press, 1973.

Jaffé, A. 1989. *Was C. G. Jung a Mystic?* Einseideln: Daimon Verlag.

Jung, C. G. 1957. The transcendent function. In *CW* 8: 67–92. New York: Pantheon, 1960.

———. 1938. Psychology and religion. In *CW* 11: 3–107. New York: Pantheon, 1958.

———. 1953. *Psychology and Alchemy*. *CW* 12. New York: Pantheon.

———. 1963a. *Memories, Dreams, Reflections*. New York: Pantheon.

———. 1963b. *Mysterium Coniunctionis*. *CW* 14. New York: Pantheon.

———. 1971. *Psychological Types*. *CW* 6. Princeton: Princeton University Press.

Musil, R. 1930. *The Man Without Qualities*. Vol. 1 of 3. Trans. E. Wilkins and E. Kaiser. London: Picador, 1979.

Ulanov, A. B. 1979. Fatness and the female. *Psychological Perspectives* 10: 18–35. Adapted and republished as chap. 2 of this book.

Ulanov, A. and B. Ulanov. 1983. *Cinderella and Her Sisters: The Envied and the Envying*. Louisville: Westminster.

———. 1991. *The Healing Imagination*. Mahwah, N. J.: Paulist.

von Franz, M. L. 1977. *Individuation in Fairy Tales*. Zurich: Spring Publications.

———. 1980. *Alchemy: An Introduction to the Symbolism and the Psychology*. Toronto: Inner City Books.

Winnicott, D. W. 1953. Transitional objects and transitional phenomena. *Playing and Reality*. London: Tavistock, 1971.

———. 1971. *Therapeutic Consultations in Child Psychiatry*. New York: Basic Books.

Index

A

Abandonment, terror of, 54
Aggression
    acceptance of one's own, 48–50
    need for connecting concern with,
        152–53
    unlived, 47
    wound to, 46
Analysand
    analyst snared into an affair by,
        147
    discovery of religious instinct by,
        6–7
    effects of analyst's pregnancy on, *x,*
        75–96
    follow–up treatment after sexual
        involvement with analyst of,
        113–22. *See also* Patient/
        therapist sex
    individuation of, analyst's
        transformation by, 126
    psyche of, 35, 104, 129–30
    reasons for seeking Jungian
        analysis of, 3
    religious person compared to, 26
    reordering levels of being in, 153
Analysis. *See* Jungian analysis
Analyst
    analysand's individuation as
        transforming, 126
    analysand's psyche embodied by,
        129–30
    analysand's re-collecting as
        impacting, 16–17
    archetypal representation of, 21
    effects on analysand of pregnancy
        of, *x,* 75–96
    noting sexual reactions by, 121
    as one who facilitates connection of
        the ego to resources in the Self,
        134
    opening ego-identity of, 120
    responsibility for preventing sexual
        relationship with analysand as
        lying with, 145
    self service for, *xi,* 143–55

Anger
    as a central unconscious
        motivation, 49
    dream of expressing, 49–50
Anima
    as female analyst for men who had
        lost their fathers, *x,* 97–112
    as bridge between ego and Self,
        173, 183
    as bridge to the Self, 16, 159–63,
        177–78, 184n2
    as bridge to the unconscious, 166
    as changing when it functions as a
        bridge, 175
    as conflict concerning two women,
        163–66
    connecting function of, 135–36
    disguises of, *xi,* 159–89
    ego and archetypal levels of
        reactions to issues of, 148
    extreme transference of, 138
    fear of, 162
    Freud's experience of, 185n4
    gaining consciousness of contents
        of, 134–35
    helped by the ego, 25
    shaping major part of transference,
        151
    at the threshold to the Self, 184n4
    in transference-countertransference
        relationship, 131–32
Animus
    as bridge between the ego and the
        Self, 168
    differences between anima and,
        186n10
    ego and archetypal levels of
        reactions to issues of, 148
    fear of, 162
    individuality of, 160
    shaping major part of transference,
        151
    stepping into the gap in ego of, 48
    at the threshold to the Self, 184n4
    in transference-countertransference
        relationship, 131–32